Subseries of Lecture Notes in Computer Science

476

M. Filgueiras   L. Damas   N. Moreira
A.P. Tomás (Eds.)

Natural Language Processing

EAIA '90, 2nd Advanced School in Artificial Intelligence
Guarda, Portugal, October 1990
Proceedings

Springer-Verlag

T0223712

Lecture Notes in Artificial Intelligence (LNAI)

Lecture Notes in Artificial Intelligence

Subseries of Lecture Notes in Computer Science
Edited by J. Siekmann

Lecture Notes in Computer Science

Edited by G. Goos and J. Hartmanis

Editorial

Artificial Intelligence has become a major discipline under the roof of Computer Science. This is also reflected by a growing number of titles devoted to this fast developing field to be published in our Lecture Notes in Computer Science. To make these volumes immediately visible we have decided to distinguish them by a special cover as Lecture Notes in Artificial Intelligence, constituting a subseries of the Lecture Notes in Computer Science. This subseries is edited by an Editorial Board of experts from all areas of AI, chaired by Jörg Siekmann, who are looking forward to consider further AI monographs and proceedings of high scientific quality for publication.

We hope that the constitution of this subseries will be well accepted by the audience of the Lecture Notes in Computer Science, and we feel confident that the subseries will be recognized as an outstanding opportunity for publication by authors and editors of the AI community.

Editors and publisher

Lecture Notes in Artificial Intelligence

Edited by J. Siekmann

Subseries of Lecture Notes in Computer Science

476

M. Filgueiras   L. Damas   N. Moreira
A.P. Tomás (Eds.)

Natural Language Processing

EAIA '90, 2nd Advanced School in Artificial Intelligence
Guarda, Portugal, October 8–12, 1990
Proceedings

Springer-Verlag

Berlin Heidelberg New York London
Paris Tokyo Hong Kong Barcelona

Editorial Board

D. Barstow W. Brauer P. Brinch Hansen D. Gries D. Luckham
C. Moler A. Pnueli G. Seegmüller J. Stoer N. Wirth

Volume Editors

M. Filgueiras
L. Damas
N. Moreira
A. P. Tomás
Centro de Informática, Universidade do Porto
Rua do Campo Alegre, 823, P-4100 Porto, Portugal

CR Subject Classification (1987): I.2.7

ISBN 3-540-53678-7 Springer-Verlag Berlin Heidelberg New York
ISBN 0-387-53678-7 Springer-Verlag New York Berlin Heidelberg

This work is subject to copyright. All rights are reserved, whether the whole or part of the material
is concerned, specifically the rights of translation, reprinting, re-use of illustrations, recitation,
broadcasting, reproduction on microfilms or in other ways, and storage in data banks. Duplication
of this publication or parts thereof is only permitted under the provisions of the German Copyright
Law of September 9, 1965, in its current version, and a copyright fee must always be paid.
Violations fall under the prosecution act of the German Copyright Law.

© Springer-Verlag Berlin Heidelberg 1991
Printed in Germany

Printing and binding: Druckhaus Beltz, Hemsbach/Bergstr.
2145/3140-543210 – Printed on acid-free paper

Preface

This book contains the lecture notes prepared for the Second Advanced School on Artificial Intelligence (EAIA'90), held in the Hotel de Turismo, Guarda, Portugal, October 8-12,1990. The EAIAs are organized every two years by the Portuguese Artificial Intelligence Association. This year the focus was on Natural Language Processing.

There are some divergences between the present texts and the actual lectures. António Zampolli was most unfortunately unable to come because of health problems. António Porto kindly accepted at very short notice to replace Zampolli's lectures by presenting the last developments of his Intermediate Semantic Representation formalism, for which no text is included here. Luís Damas gave lectures on Constraint Logic Grammars, but did not produce a text for inclusion here.

It is a pleasure to thank all those who helped to make EAIA'90 and this book possible, namely:

- all the lecturers/authors for their successful effort;
- the members of the Programme Committee, António Porto, João Falcão e Cunha, Luís Damas, Luís Moniz Pereira, Luís Monteiro and Miguel Filgueiras, and also José Gabriel Lopes for their comments on drafts of the texts;
- Control Data Portuguesa, Data General Portugal, and Digital Equipment Portugal, for their financial support and provision of equipment for demonstrations;
- Banco Português do Atlântico, for its gift of course material, and
- Centro de Informática da Universidade do Porto, for its secretarial support.

The Organizing Committee
Miguel Filgueiras
Luís Damas
Nelma Moreira
Ana Paula Tomás

Contents

General Introduction

Miguel Filgueiras, Nelma Moreira, Ana Paula Tomás

Centro de Informática, Universidade do Porto

R. do Campo Alegre 823 — Porto 4100 — Portugal

In Portugal, as in most other European countries, the area of Computational Linguistics (CL) is relatively recent, the tradition being that work in Natural Language Processing (NLP) results from research in Artificial Intelligence (AI) and Computer Science by people having no thorough education in Linguistics. This tradition and the arguments about theoretically shaky implementations and about unimplementable theories that went along with it, are gradually vanishing in favour of a situation in which general descriptions of linguistic phenomena, efficient ways of representing them in a computer, and the use of these representations for building practical applications can no longer be separately considered.

These considerations guided our choice of the topics to be presented in this Advanced Course on NLP: our selection went to some of the themes that are now the focus of the research in CL. To an audience largely formed by researchers with a background in Computer Science and AI, the presentation of these themes is likely to be more interesting and useful than addressing AI and programming techniques, case studies and the like, which belong to their day-to-day work. Another difficulty with the latter alternative, and with a small audience, is that an *advanced* lecture in such topics could easily become so specialized as to raise the interest but of those already working on them.

We hope that it will be obvious that the appearance in book form of this compilation of texts is only intended to provide the reader with an overview of some of the ideas that presently seem more promising and appealing in CL — in terms of the usual forest vs. tree dichotomy, the present book tries to give a picture of (a part of) the forest, not of each tree. From the extensive bibibliographic references given, which are listed at the end of the book, the interested reader may be able to get more detailed information.

This book contains 9 contributions whose subject matters we will now briefly introduce.

One of the common criticisms made to NLP systems is that the number of different words that can be accepted is very small (typically, a few hundreds) when compared to the number of different words humans use, even when speaking or writing about a particular matter (typically, several thousands). And the usual answer from the implementors of such a system is that if the system works with a small set of words, it would do the job with a larger one, the problem lying in the lack of manpower to build a huge lexicon. Moreover, it is also usually taken for granted that building a huge lexicon is an easy, although fastidious task. The contribution by Nicoletta Calzolari and António Zampolli describes current research in Lexicography aiming at solving this problem, among others. The key notion is that of *reusability*: reusing the contents of existing sources of lexical information, like the dictionaries used by humans, to different purposes and in different contexts[1].

The strong influence of the ideas due to Noam Chomsky in Linguistics and CL is acknowledged both by his followers and his opponents. In particular, Chomsky's Government and Binding (GB) framework has been a source of inspiration for some aspects of other contemporary theories, namely Generalized Phrase Structure Grammar (GPSG) and Head-driven Phrase Structure Grammar (HPSG). In GB, well-formed syntactic representations are licensed by interacting systems of principles (as opposed to sets of rules). X-Bar Theory is one of those systems and its interaction with the other principles of the GB model is analysed by Inês Duarte.

The notions of head and subcategorization which are central in X-Bar Theory and other contemporary syntax theories, are basic for the definition of HPSG, which is the subject of the contribution by Sergio Balari. The emergence of HPSG, which happened a few years ago, resulted from the concoction of several ingredients from the store-room of attempts to tame NL, among which GPSG, Functional Unification Grammar, Lexical Functional Grammar, Categorial Grammar and GB can be mentioned. But, unlike most of its raw ingredients, HPSG has a distinct information flavouring, and in this is likely to appeal to implementation oriented people — actually, HPSG originates from attempts to implement GPSG. Sergio Balari presents a comprehensive introduction to HPSG and goes well beyond that by proposing his own ideas on how to extend and modify HPSG to deal with the interaction between unbounded dependencies and subject selection. HPSG is not a purely syntactic theory, encompassing a treatment of semantics which builds upon Situation Semantics and Discourse Representation Theory.

Situation Semantics (which is discussed by João Falcão e Cunha in his second text) is the starting point for Situation Theoretic Grammar, a recent framework by Robin Cooper. In it, the description of a language is made by using situation theoretic objects (mathematical objects in a theory of situations), which may convey both syntactic and/or semantic information. In his text, Cooper introduces his framework describing a fragment of English and addressing the interplay of a theory of situations and quantification. The study of quantification is made by adopting and revising notions from the Generalized Quantifier Theory (GQT).

The focus of the text by João Peres is quantification in nominal expressions, one of the theories analysed being the classical GQT, which stems from work by Jon Barwise and Robin Cooper. Other topics are the treatment of determiners taken as relations, and the semantics of plurals.

---

[1] The Authors mention another sense for the word "reusability", but the focus of their contribution is this one.

Another difficult task in NL semantics is the treatment of time and tense. Frank van Eynde puts forward a model intended to be an integrated framework for the analysis of verb tenses and temporal adverbial phrases. His time model, resulting from a contrastive study of European languages, is based on time intervals and temporal relations, and the meanings of tense and aspect are represented as temporal relations between some special time intervals.

As João Peres points out, the modern theories on quantification originated from the ideas used by Montague in his PTQ. It is well-known that Montague Semantics constitutes one of the most important lines of thought in formal semantics for NL. Montague Semantics is the focus of the first text by João Falcão e Cunha. What is shown there is that there exists a simplified version of Montague's Intensional Logic with no intensional operators, but providing an equivalent interpretation of the PTQ's fragment of English. This simplication may happen to lead to the elimination of the meaning postulates.

Situation Semantics is another important line of thought in the formal treatment of NL semantics. Its relations with Montague Semantics in what regards the problem of logical omniscience are discussed in the second text by João Falcão e Cunha. He concludes that logical omniscience may disappear from possible-worlds semantics by imposing restrictions on the use of synonyms and making a careful definition of equivalence. This is in much the same way as the authors of Situation Semantics avoid the problem from the very beginning.

In his last text, João Falcão e Cunha makes a synthesis of the various kinds of logics that have been used in the formalization of the semantics of NL. The interesting conclusion he draws that most of the differences between the more widely accepted formalisms are, in the end, merely syntactic in nature, may contribute to a clarification of what seems, at first sight, a very confusing and formidable scene.

Methods and Tools for Lexical Acquisition*

Nicoletta Calzolari, António Zampolli

Istituto di Linguistica Computazionale del CNR, Pisa

Dipartimento di Linguistica, Universitá di Pisa

Via de la Faggiola, 32 — 56100 Pisa — Italy

1 Introduction

In the very recent years, Computational Linguistics has shown an increasing interest in the development of vast 'reservoirs' of linguistic knowledge, in the form of as complete as possible and reusable linguistic descriptions, structured in various kinds of interconnected linguistic bases.

Several projects are underway or are going to begin, promoted by large international or national organizations, aiming at the creation of large lexical knowledge bases (LKB), grammatical knowledge bases, reference textual corpora.

One of the key-words in the field has recently become the word *reusability*. This word is to be intended in two main senses. The first meaning is that of constructing the linguistic resources in such a way that it is allowed to various users (procedural, e.g. different NLP systems, and possibly human, e.g. lexicographers, translators, normal dictionary users) to extract — with appropriate interfaces — relevant information for their different purposes. The second meaning is that of reusing lexical information implicitly or explicitly present in pre-existing lexical resources.

In this paper we will describe some aspects of our work aiming at reusing (in its second meaning) existing machine readable dictionaries (MRDs) for the construction of LKBs[1].

---

*Part of this article is reprinted, thanks to the permission of the Oxford University Press, from the article: N. Calzolari, A. Zampolli, "Lexical Databases and Textual Corpora: a trend of convergence between Computational Linguistics and Literary and Linguistic Computing", to appear in S. Hockey, N. Ide (eds.), *Literary and Linguistic Computing*, 1989, Oxford University Press, in print.

[1]Our work in this field is now included in the ESPRIT Project "Acquisition of Lexical Knowledge for Natural Language Processing Systems" (AQUILEX) in which groups of researchers in Cambridge, Amsterdam, Dublin, Paris, Barcelona, and Pisa (coordinator) are involved.

2 Reusability of Preexisting Data in the Form of MRDs

A large number of articles and books have already been written on this topic (see e.g. Amsler, Boguraev, Briscoe, Byrd, Calzolari, Nagao, Picchi, Walker, Zampolli, etc). We wish to stress in particular what we consider as the natural evolution of all the work done so far in the field, i.e. the possibility of a procedural exploitation of the "full range" of semantic information implicitly contained in MRDs.

In this framework the dictionary is considered as a primary source of basic general knowledge, and many projects nowadays have as their main objectives word-sense acquisition from MRDs, and knowledge organization in a LKB. The method is inductive and the strategy adopted is heuristic: through progressive generalization from the common elements found in natural language definitions we tend to formalize the basic general knowledge implicitly contained in dictionary definitions, mainly in the attempt to extract the most basic concepts and the semantic relations between them. This means that we are going well beyond the extraction and organization of taxonomies, whose methodology of acquisition is now well established ([Chodorow *et al.*, 1985], [Calzolari, 1982], [Calzolari, 1984]). We simply have to process the first part of the definition, in order to identify the 'genus' term. This can be done by taking into account the fact that the definitions are NPs when the definiendum is a Noun, are VPs for Verbs, and AdjPs for Adjectives. The procedure has thus to look for the head/s of the NP, VP, AdjP, which are respectively a N, V, or Adj. These are the 'genus' terms and are connected by an IS-A link to the definiendum.

When we reorganize a MRD in a taxonomical structure, with only IS-A hierarchies made explicit, we use the MRD as a source of knowledge, but in only one of the possible ways of acquiring from it (in an inductive form) a concept, by linking this concept to all its instances, i.e. all the instances of the same category/class are extracted and connected together pointing to their immediate hypernym.

In the LKB approach the dictionary is seen as a much more powerful "classificatory device", i.e. as an empirical means of instantiating concepts and many types of lexical/semantic relationships among them (see [Calzolari and Picchi, 1988]).

The methodological approach that we follow can be summarized in these points:

a) to start from free-text definitions, in natural language and in linear form, usually formed by a 'genus term' and a 'differentia' part;

b) to analyse their structure and content from a linguistic and a computational point of view;

c) to convert and reorganize them into informationally equivalent structured formats made up by nodes and relations linking them.

Point b) in its turn can be subdivided, for the computational part, into the following steps:

1) to "parse" the dictionary entry, in the sense of "parsing a dictionary tape" which essentially means recognizing the various relevant fields in the lexical entry;

2) to produce a tree-structured lexical entry;

3) to perform a morphological analysis and a homograph disambiguation, i.e. to tag the definitions for parts of speech (POS);

4) after the above preliminary steps, we have adopted the technique of producing a very simple syntactic parse which roughly recognizes NPs and PPs;

5) the most powerful tool is then a "pattern-matching" mechanism, which is fed by:

   i) the results obtained by browsing dictionary data in the LDB (as outlined in the few examples presented below) in view of discovering the most interesting words and word-associations,

   ii) frequency counts on definitions words and syntagms, and obviously

   iii) the linguist's intuition.

Let us illustrate with some examples the process of analysing the definitions. In the figures we try to simulate the process of browsing the Italian LDB and of navigating the dictionary while searching for particular words, structures, patterns, etc.. We can see some of the semantic data it is possible to search for and find in a MRD if appropriately structured. Figure 1 shows part of the taxonomy for the Italian word *libro* (book), i.e. a set of words defined as being "types of" books (we see them together with their definitions).

But there is something more that is said about books in a dictionary. It is also possible to extract the set of the Italian Verbs related to books (see Figure 2), and the set of Adjectives and of other Nouns having to do with books (Figures 3 and 4). In section 2.2 we shall come back to "books", stressing the type of information which, lacking in dictionaries, can instead be found in texts.

Our present work is also devoted to the formalization of the other kind of relations — not as simple as the taxonomical ones — which do hold between words, or between words and concepts, and for whose extraction we must analyse and process the whole definition and not only its 'genus' part.

Let us give some examples of the types of relations that it is possible to extract from MRDs. In Figure 5 we find the first of the about 300 words linked in our LDB by a taxonomical link to the word *strumento* (instrument). The word *attrezzo* (tool) appears in this list. Figure 6 shows the first hyponyms of this second word together with their definitions. From these definitions it is rather simple to extract semantic relations which we could label USED FOR, USED IN, SHAPE, MADE OF, etc.. They are extracted by means of a pattern-matching procedure acting on the 'differentia' part of the definitions, where the different ways in which each relation is actually lexicalized in the definitions is associated with the relation-label. The relation USED FOR, for example,

PASSIONARIO	1SM	ANTICO LIBRO LITURGICO CATTOLICO
OMILIARIO	1SM	ANTICO LIBRO LITURGICO CONTENENTE OMELIE
EPISTOLARIO	1SM	LIBRO CHE CONTENEVA BRANI DI EPISTOLE EVANGELO
ORA	1SF	LIBRO CHE CONTENEVA LE OPERAZIONI PROPRIE DELLE VARIE ORE
SALTERIO	2SM	LIBRO CHE CONTIENE I SALMI
RITUALE	2SM	LIBRO CHE CONTIENE LE NORME CHE REGOLANO UN RITO
UFFICIOLO	1SM	LIBRO CHE CONTIENE LE PREGHIERE IN ONORE DELLA VERGINE
UFIZIOLO	1SM	LIBRO CHE CONTIENE LE PREGHIERE IN ONORE DELLA VERGINE
CANTORINO	1SM	LIBRO CHE CONTIENE LE REGOLE DEL CANTO FERMO
PORTULANO	1SM	1LIBRO CHE DESCRIVE MINUTAMENTE LA COSTA
GUIDA	1SF	LIBRO CHE INSEGNA PRIMI ELEMENTI DI ARTE O TECNICA
GRADUALE	2SM	LIBRO CHE RACCOGLIE I GRADUALI DELL'ANNO LITURGICO
GIORNALMASTRO	1SM	LIBRO CHE RIUNISCE IL GIORNALE E IL MASTRO
ANNUARIO	1SM	LIBRO CHE SI PUBBLICA ANNUALMENTE
...		
EFEMERIDE	1SF	LIBRO IN CUI ERANO ANNOTATI I FATTI CHE ACCADEVANO
EFFEMERIDE	1SF	LIBRO IN CUI ERANO ANNOTATI I FATTI CHE ACCADEVANO
COPIAFATTURE	1SM	LIBRO IN CUI SI COPIANO LE FATTURE
SALDACONTI	1SM	LIBRO IN CUI SONO REGISTRATI I CREDITI E I DEBITI
TASCABILE	2SM	LIBRO IN EDIZIONE ECONOMICA E PICCOLO FORMATO
PERGAMENO	1SM	1LIBRO IN PERGAMENA
BENEDIZIONALE	1SM	LIBRO LITURGICO
MESSALE	1SM	LIBRO LITURGICO CATTOLICO
LEZIONARIO	1SM	LIBRO LITURGICO CON LE#LEZIONI(LEZIONE) DI UFFICI DIVINI
CORALE	2SM	LIBRO LITURGICO CONTENENTE GLI UFFICI DEL#CORO()
EVANGELIARIO	1SM	LIBRO LITURGICO CONTENENTE PASSI DELL' EVANGELO
INNARIO	1SM	LIBRO LITURGICO, NEL CATTOLICESIMO E NELLE CHIESE ORIENTALI
...		
CORANO	1SM	LIBRO SACRO DEI MUSSULMANI
AVESTA	1SM	LIBRO SACRO DELLA RELIGIONE ZOROASTRIANA
GENESI	1SF	PRIMO LIBRO DEL PENTATEUCO NELLA BIBBIA
ALBO	2SM	SPECIE DI LIBRO CONTENENTE FOTOGRAFIE, DISCHI, FRANCOBOLLI
LEVITICO	2SM	TERZO LIBRO BIBLICO DEL PENTATEUCO
SAPIENZA	1SF	UNO DEI LIBRI DELL'ANTICO TESTAMENTO
SAPIENZIA	1SF	1UNO DEI LIBRI DELL'ANTICO TESTAMENTO

Figure 1: Some of the hyponyms of *libro* (book)

ALLIBRARE	1VT	REGISTRARE SU UN LIBRO DI CONTI
CARTOLINARE	1VT	RILEGARE UN LIBRO ALLA RUSTICA
CIRCOLARE	1VIT	PASSARE DALL'UNA ALL'ALTRA PERSONA,DI DANARO,LIBRI
DISTRIBUIRE	1VT	DIFFONDERE TRA TUTTI I RIVENDITORI LIBRI,GIORNALI
DIVOLGARE	1VTP	1RENDERE FINANZIARIAMENTE DISPONIBILI LIBRI,SAGGI
DIVULGARE	1VTP	RENDERE FINANZIARIAMENTE DISPONIBILI LIBRI,SAGGI
INTERFOGLIARE	1VT	INTERPORRE,CUCIRE TRA I FOGLI DI UN LIBRO FOGLI BIANCHI
INTESTARE	1VTP	FORNIRE DI INTESTAZIONE O TITOLO UN LIBRO
RITONDARE	1VT	1PAREGGIARE,TAGLIANDO LE SPORGENZE,DETTO DI LIBRI,TESSUTI
SCARTABELLARE	1VT	SCORRERE IN FRETTA E DISORDINATAMENTE LE PAGINE D'UN LIBRO
SCOMPAGINARE	1VTP	DISFARE,ROVINARE LA LEGATURA DI LIBRI
SCRITTURARE	1VT	ANNOTARE,REGISTRARE SU LIBRI O SCRITTURE CONTABILI
SFASCICOLARE	1VT	SCOMPORRE UN LIBRO,UN QUADERNO NEI FASCICOLI DI CUI E' FATTO
SFOGLIARE	2VTP	SCORRERE UN LIBRO RAPIDAMENTE
SFOGLIARE	2VTP	TAGLIARE LE PAGINE DI UN LIBRO
SQUADERNARE	1VTP	3VOLTARE E RIVOLTARE PAGINE DI LIBRI,QUADERNI
TOSARE	1VT	PAREGGIARE I FOGLI DEI LIBRI NEL RILEGARLI

Figure 2: Verbs related to *libri* (books)

ADESPOTA	1A	3ANONIMO/DETTO DI LIBRO,CODICE,MANOSCRITTO DI AUTORE IGNOTO
ADESPOTO	1A	ANONIMO/DETTO DI LIBRO,CODICE,MANOSCRITTO DI AUTORE IGNOTO
APOCRIFO	1A	DETTO DI LIBRO NON RICONOSCIUTO COME CANONICO
CARTOLIBRARIO	1A	DI COMMERCIO DI LIBRI E OGGETTI DA CANCELLERIA
CIRCOLANTE	1A	CHE DA' LIBRI A PRESTITO AGLI ABBONATI A TURNO
COMMERCIALE	1A	DETTO DI LIBRO,FILM CHE MIRA SOLO A OTTENERE BUONI INCASSI
COPERTINATO	1A	DETTO DI LIBRO O FASCICOLO CON COPERTINA
DEUTEROCANONICO	1A	DEI LIBRI DELL'ANTICO TESTAMENTO RESPINTI COME APOCRIFI
EDITORE	1A	CHI PUBBLICA LIBRI,RIVISTE
ERUDITO	1A	LIBRO ERUDITO
INTESTATO	1A	FORNITO DI TITOLO O INTESTAZIONE,DETTO DI LIBRO,LETTERA
INTONSO	1A	3DI LIBRO CUI NON SONO ANCORA STATE TAGLIATE LE PAGINE
LIBERIANO	3A	CHE RIGUARDA IL LIBRO
LIBRARIO	1A	DI,RELATIVO A LIBRO
LIBRESCO	1A	CHE DERIVA DAI LIBRI E NON DALLA VIVA ESPERIENZA
MASTRO	2A	LIBRO MASTRO
MOSAICO	2A	RELATIVO AI LIBRI BIBLICI
PAGA	4A	LIBRO PAGA
POSTUMO	1A	DI LIBRO PUBBLICATO DOPO LA MORTE DELL'AUTORE
PROTOCANONICO	1A	DETTO DI CIASCUN LIBRO BIBLICO INSERITO PER PRIMO NEL CANONE
SAPIENZIALE	1A	CHE SI RIFERISCE AI LIBRI SAPIENZIALI

Figure 3: Adjectives related to *libri* (books)

RISVOLTO	1SM	ALETTA/ PARTE DELLA SOPRACOPERTA DI LIBRO RIPIEGATA
BIBLIOFILO	1SG	AMATORE,RICERCATORE,COLLEZIONISTA DI LIBRI
BIBLIOFILIA	1SF	AMORE PER I LIBRI
REGGILIBRI	1SM	ARNESE PIEGATO AD ANGOLO RETTO PER REGGERE IN PIEDI LIBRI
BIBLIOIATRICA	1SF	3ARTE DEL RESTAURO DEI LIBRI
ERMENEUTICA	1SF	ARTE DI INTERPRETARE MONUMENTI,LIBRI ANTICHI
SFOGLIATA	2SF	ATTO DELLO SCORRERE UN LIBRO E SIMILI
PUBBLICAZIONE	1SF	ATTO EFFETTO DEL RENDERE PUBBLICO O DEL PUBBLICARE
BANCHEROZZO	1SM	1BANCARELLA DI LIBRI ALL' APERTO
ZAZZERA	1SF	BARBA,RICCIO/ PARTE RUVIDA INTONSA DEI LIBRI
PORTACARTE	1SM	BORSA PER METTERVI CARTE,DOCUMENTI,LIBRI
BOTTELLO	1SM	3CARTELLINO CHE SI METTE SU LIBRI E BOTTIGLIE
CARTOLIBRERIA	1SF	CARTOLERIA AUTORIZZATA ALLA VENDITA DI LIBRI
CANONE	1SM	CATALOGO DEI LIBRI SACRI RICONOSCIUTI AUTENTICI
REDATTORE	1SN	CHI CURA FASI PER PUBBLICAZIONE DI LIBRI IN CASE EDITRICI
CARRETTINISTA	1SM	CHI ESPONE O VENDE LIBRI SU UN CARRETTINO
BIBLIOTECA	1SF	COLLEZIONE DI LIBRI SIMILI PER FORMATO ARGOMENTO EDITORE
LIBRATA	1SF	COLPO DATO CON UN LIBRO
. . .		
BIBLIOTECA	1SF	EDIFICIO CON RACCOLTE DI LIBRI A DISPOSIZIONE DEL PUBBLICO
BIBLIOGRAFIA	1SF	ELENCO DI LIBRI CONSULTATI PER COMPILAZIONE DI OPERE
INDICE	1SM	ELENCO ORDINATO DI CAPITOLI O PARTI DI LIBRO
BIBLIOLATRIA	1SF	FEDE CIECA NEI LIBRI STAMPATI
. . .		
LIBRERIA	1SF	LUOGO O MOBILE IN CUI SONO ACCOLTI E CUSTODITI I LIBRI
BIBLIOTECA	1SF	LUOGO OVE SONO RACCOLTI E CONSERVATI LIBRI
BIBLIOMANIA	1SF	MANIA DI RICERCARE E COLLEZIONARE LIBRI
BIBLIOTECA	1SF	MOBILE A MURO CON SCAFFALI PER LIBRI
CLASSIFICATORE	1SN	MOBILE PER CONTENERE LIBRI DOCUMENTI
LIBRERIA	1SF	NEGOZIO O EMPORIO DI LIBRI
FRONTISPIZIO	1SM	PAGINA ALL' INIZIO DI UN LIBRO CON TITOLO NOTE TIPOGRAFICHE
ANTIPORTA	1SF	PAGINA CON TITOLO PRECEDENTE FRONTESPIZIO DI LIBRO
TAVOLA	1SF	PAGINA FOGLIO DI LIBRO CON ILLUSTRAZIONI
INTERFOGLIO	1SM	PAGINA INTERPOSTA TRA I FOGLI DI UN LIBRO
LIBRERIA	1SF	RACCOLTA DI LIBRI LIBRO
BIBLIOLOGIA	1SF	SCIENZA DEI LIBRI
LIBRAIO	1SN	VENDITORE DI LIBRI
LIBRARO	1SN	1VENDITORE DI LIBRI
VERSO	3SM	VERSETTO/SUDDIVISIONE IN FRASI DELLE PARTI DI LIBRI SACRI

Figure 4: Some of the nouns related to *libri* (books)

comes from lexical patterns like: *per, usato per, atto a, che serve a, utile a* (for, used for, apt to, which serves to, useful to); these lexical patterns acquire this particular relational meaning when found in particular positions in the definition of hyponyms of the word *strumento*. They can also acquire different meanings in other contexts. The result of this analysis of the definitional content will be restructured in a part of a conceptual network which is sketched in Figure 7.

STRUMENTO	→ABBASSALINGUA	1SM	00
	ABERROMETRO	1SM	00
	ACCELEROGRAFO	1SM	00
	ACCELEROMETRO	1SM	00
	ACCHIAPPAMOSCHE	1SN	00
	ACCIAINO	1SM	00
	AEROFONO	1SM	00
	AEROMETRO	1SM	00
	AEROSCOPIO	1SM	00
	AFFILATOIO	1SM	00
	AGGUAGLIATOIO	1SM	00
	AGO	1SM	0A
	ALCOOLIMETRO	1SM	00
	ALGESIMETRO	1SM	00
	AMMOSTATOIO	1SM	00
	AMPEROMETRO	1SM	00
	ANALIZZATORE	1SN	00
	ANCORA	1SF	10
	ANEMOMETRO	1SM	00
	ANEMOSCOPIO	1SM	00
	ANGELICA	1SF	00
	APRIBOCCA	1SM	00
	APRICASSE	1SM	00
	ARCHIPENDOLO	1SM	00
	ARMA	1SF	00
	ARMONICA	1SF	00
	ARMONIO	1SM	00
	ARMONIUM	1SM	00
	ARPA	1SF	10
	ARPEGGIONE	1SM	00
	ARRIDATOIO	1SM	00
	ASPERSORIO	1SM	00
	ASPIRATORE	1SM	00
	ASSIOMETRO	1SM	00
	ASTIGMOMETRO	1SM	00
	ASTROFOTOMETRO	1SM	00
	ASTROGRAFO	1SM	00
	ASTROLABIO	1SM	00
	ATTINOMETRO	1SM	00
	ATTREZZO	1SM	0A
	AUDIOMETRO	1SM	00
	AULOS	1SM	00
	AVENA	1SF	00
	BADILE	1SM	00

Figure 5: The first hyponyms of *strumento* (instrument)

Other types of semantic relations rather easily and straightforwardly extractable from the definitions can be illustrated with some examples.

One is the relation SET OF, which can be further specified as to the type of its members. We have examples of words denoting SET OF *persone* (people), (Figure 8), *oggetti* (objects) (Figure 9), etc..

Other types of useful data concern information on selection restrictions for Verbs or for Adjectives and mainly derives from the lexical pattern *detto di* (said of), after which the type of Nouns is found of which an Adjective or a Verb can be typically predicated (see Figure 10 for Adjectives and Verbs used for nouns denoting *persone* (people), Figure 11

AFFOSSATORE	1SN	ATTREZZO AGRICOLO PER SCAVARE FOSSI
ALLARGATESE	1SM	ATTREZZO USATO PER ALLARGARE LE TESE DEI CAPPELLI
ALLISCIATOIO	1SM	ATTREZZO USATO IN FONDERIA PER PREPARARE LE FORME
ANELLO	1SM	ATTREZZO GEMELLARE IN GINNASTICA
APISCAMPO	1SM	ATTREZZO PER IMPEDIRE L' ASCESA DELLE API AL MELARIO
APPOGGIO	1SM	ATTREZZO GINNICO FORMATO DA BLOCCHETTI RETTANGOLAR DI LEGNO
ARATRO	1SM	ATTREZZO AGRICOLO ATTO A ROMPERE,DISSODARE IL TERRENO
ARNESE	1SM	ATTREZZO DA LAVORO
ASPO	1SM	ASPA,ANNASPO,NASPO/ ATTREZZO CHE SERVE AD ESEGUIRE L'ASPATURA
ASTA	1SF	ATTREZZO DI FORMA TUBOLARE NELL' ATLETICA
BACCHETTA	1SF	ATTREZZO PER ESERCIZI GINNICI COLLETTIVI
BARRAMINA	1SF	ATTREZZO PER LA PERFORAZIONE DELLE ROCCE
BASTONCINO	1SM	ATTREZZO DEGLI SCIATORI CON RACCHETTA CIRCOLARE
BASTONE	1SM	MAZZA/ ATTREZZO SPORTIVO
CACCIAVITE	1SM	ATTREZZO PER STRINGERE O ALLENTARE LE VITI
CAVALLINA	1SF	ATTREZZO PER ESERCIZI DI VOLTEGGIO NELLA GINNASTICA
CAVALLO	1SD	ATTREZZO PER ESERCIZI DI VOLTEGGIO NELLA GINNASTICA
CERCHIO	1SM	ATTREZZO STRUTTURA FIGURA A FORMA DI CERCHIO
CESTA	1SF	CHISTERA/ ATTREZZO DI VIMINI USATO NELLA PELOTA BASCA
CHIAVE	1SF	ATTREZZO METALLICO PER PROVOCARE CONTATTI
CHIAVE	1SF	ATTREZZO METALLICO PER METTERE IN MOTO MECCANISMI
CHIAVE	1SF	ATTREZZO METALLICO PER ALLENTARE E STRINGERE VITI O DADI
CHIODO	1SM	ATTREZZO IN METALLO DEGLI ALPINISTI
CHIOVO	1SM	1ATTREZZO IN METALLO DEGLI ALPINISTI
CILINDRO	1SM	ATTREZZO CILINDRICO NELLA GINNASTICA
CLAVA	1SF	ATTREZZO IN LEGNO USATO PER ESERCIZI GINNICI
COLTIVATORE	2SN	ATTREZZO PER SMUOVERE E SMINUZZARE LA SUPERFICIE DEL TERRENO
CORDA	1SF	ATTREZZO DA ALPINISMO O GINNASTICA
CUCCHIAIA	1SF	ATTREZZO PER ESTRARRE DETRITI DI ROCCIA
CUCITRICE	2SF	ATTREZZO USATO NEGLI UFFICI PER UNIRE FOGLI
DISCO	1SM	ATTREZZO CIRCOLARE CHE SI LANCIA IN GARE SPORTIVE
ERPICE	1SM	ATTREZZO DI FERRO PER LAVORARE IL TERRENO
ESTENSORE	2SI	ATTREZZO GINNICO
ESTIRPATORE	3SM	ATTREZZO PER SMUOVERE O LIBERARE IL TERRENO DA ERBACCE
FALCE	1SF	ATTREZZO PER TAGLIARE A MANO CEREALI ED ERBE
FIOCINA	1SF	ATTREZZO CON TRE O PIU' DENTI FISSI PER CATTURARE PESCI
. . .		
UTENSILE	2SM	OGNI ATTREZZO PER LAVORARE LEGNO,PIETRE,MATERIALI
VANGHETTA	1SF	ATTREZZO LEGGERO DI SOLDATO PER PICCOLI LAVORI DI STERRO
VOGADORE	1SI	1ATTREZZO GINNICO PER MOVIMENTO DA REMATORE
VOGATORE	1SN	ATTREZZO GINNICO PER MOVIMENTO DA REMATORE
VOLTARISO	1SM	ATTREZZO PER RIVOLTARE SULL'AIA MODESTE QUANTITA' DI RISO
ZAPPA	1SF	ATTREZZO MANUALE PER LAVORARE IL TERRENO

Figure 6: Some of the hyponyms of *attrezzo* (tool) with their definitions

INSTRUMENT ← **IS-A** – *attrezo* – **USED FOR** → *tagliare* = *FALCE*
. . . = . . .
– **USED IN** → *ginnastica* = *ANELLO*
. . . = . . .
– **SHAPE** → *tubolare* = *ASTA*
circolare = *DISCO*
– **MADE OF** → *vimini* = *CESTA*
metallo = *CHIODO*

Figure 7: Sketch of a piece of network for *attrezzo* (tool)

FORMICAIO	SM	MOLTITUDINE DI	PERSONE
GREGGE	SN	MOLTITUDINE DI	PERSONE
STORMO	SM	MOLTITUDINE DI	PERSONE
MANO	SF	GRUPPO DI	PERSONE
BRANCO	SM	INSIEME DI	PERSONE
POPOLAZIONE	SF	INSIEME DELLE	PERSONE ABITANTI IN UN LUOCO
ORGANICO	SM	COMPLESSO DI	PERSONE ADDETTE A CERTE ATTIVITA'
SEGRETERIA	SF	INSIEME DELLE	PERSONE ADDETTE A UNA SEGRETTERIA
SQUADRA	SF	COMPLESSO DI	PERSONE ADDETTE A UNO STESSO LAVORO
CIURMA	SF	INSIEME DELLE	PERSONE ADDETTE AI LAVORI DELLA TONNARA
NAZIONE	SF	INSIEME DI	PERSONE APPARTENENTI A STESSA STIRPE
FAMIGLIA	SF	COMPLESSO DI	PERSONE AVENTI UN ASCENDENTE DIRETTO COMUNE
VICINATO	SM	INSIEME DI	PERSONE CHE ABITONO UNA STESSA CASA
LEGA	SF	INSIEME DI	PERSONE CHE AGISCONO PER UTILE PROPRIO
AUDITORIO	SM	UDITORIO/COMPLESSO DI	PERSONE CHE ASCOLTANO
UDIENZA	SF	UDITORIO/INSIEME DI	PERSONE CHE ASCOLTANO
CORO	SM	GRUPPO DI	PERSONE CHE CANTANO INSIEME
MALAVITA	SF	L'INSIEME DELLE	PERSONE CHE CONDUCONO VITA DISSOLUTA
CROCCHIO	SM	GRUPPO DI	PERSONE CHE CONVERSANO
CONCISTORO	SM	GRUPPO DI	PERSONE CHE DISCUTONO
FINANZA	SF	COMPLESSO DI	PERSONE CHE ESPLICANO ATTIVITA' BANCARIA
...			
FRONTE	SN	COMPLESSO DI	PERSONE OMOGENEO PER FINALITA' CONSUETUDINI
CHIESA	SF	INSIEME DI	PERSONE PROFESSANTI LA MEDESIMA DOTTRINA
DRAPPELLO	SM	GRUPPO DI	PERSONE RACCOLTE INSIEME
COMPAGNIA	SF	COMPLESSO DI	PERSONE RIUNITE INSIEME PER ATTIVITA' COMUNI

Figure 8: Some of the nouns denoting SET OF *persone* (people)

ARCIPELAGO	SM	GRUPPO INSIEME DI	OGGETTI
ARGENTERIA	SF	COMPLESSO DI	OGGETTI D'ARGENTO
ORERIA	SF	COMPLESSO DI	OGGETTI D'ORO
COLLEZIONE	SF	RACCOLTA DI	OGGETTI DELLA STESSA SPECIE
CRISTALLERIA	SF	INSIEME DEGLI	OGGETTI DI CRISTALLO DA TAVOLA
ARSENALE	SM	INSIEME DI	OGGETTI DIVERSI
SUPPELLETTILE	SF	OGGETTO O INSIEME DI	OGGETTI IN UNA SCUOLA CHIESA E SIMILI
INTRECCIO	SM	COMPLESSO DI	OGGETTI INTRECCIATI
SUPPELLETTILE	SF	OGGETTO O INSIEME DI	OGGETTI NELL'ARREDAMENTO DELLA CASA
COMPLETO	SM	INSIEME DI	OGGETTI PER UN USO DETERMINATO
BAROCCUME	SM	INSIEME DI	OGGETTI PRETENZIOSI E DI CATTIVO GUSTO
GIOIELLERIA	SF	INSIEME DI	OGGETTI PREZIOSI
SUPPELLETTILE	SF	OGGETTO O INSIEME DI	OGGETTI RINVENUTI IN UNO SCAVO

Figure 9: Nouns denoting SET OF *oggetti* (objects)

for Adjectives which collocate with names of colours, either generic colour names, or specific ones such as *giallo* (yellow), *rosso* (red), etc.).

ASSESTATO	A	ASSENNATO,AVVEDUTO,DETTO DI	PERSONA
BARLACCIO	A	MALATICCIO,DEBOLE,DETTO DI	PERSONA
INSENSATO	A	STUPIDO,DEMENTE,DETTO DI	PERSONA
PRIMITIVO	A	C=INCIVILITO/SEMPLICE,ROZZO,CREDULONE,DETTO DI	PERSONA
PROVETTO	A	MATURO,DETTO DI	PERSONA
RIMESSO	A	LANGUIDO,LENTO,FIACCO,DETTO DI	PERSONA
RINCRESCIOSO	A	CHE SENTE RINCRESCIMENTO,DETTO DI	PERSONA
RIPOSANTE	A	CALMO,TRANQUILLO DETTO DI	PERSONA
RISPETTOSO	A	CHE HA,E' PIENO DI#RISPETTO(),DETTO DI	PERSONA
ROBUSTO	A	FORTE/CHE POSSIEDE FORZA,ENERGIA,DETTO DI	PERSONA
ROCO	A	RAUCO,DETTO DI	PERSONA
ROGNOSO	A	MISERO,MESCHINO,NOIOSO,DETTO DI	PERSONA
RUDE	A	ROZZO,GROSSOLANO,DETTO DI	PERSONA
RUGIADOSO	A	SANO,FLORIDO,DETTO DI	PERSONA
RUSTICO	A	NON MOLTO SOCIEVOLE NE' RAFFINATO,DETTO DI	PERSONA
RUVIDO	A	DI MANIERE ROZZE,DI CARATTERE ASPRO,DETTO DI	PERSONA
...			
ADOMBRARE	VTE	INSOSPETTIRSI,TURBARSI,DETTO DI	PERSONA
ARRABBIARE	VIE	ESSERE PRESO DALL'IRA,DALLA COLLERA DETTO DI	PERSONA
CORVETTARE	VI	SALTARE,BALZARE,DETTO SPEC. DI	PERSONA
CUCCIARE	VET	GIACERSI/STARE A LETTO,DETTO DI	PERSONA
IMBIZZARRIRE	VET	INCOLLERIRE O DIVENTARE IRREQUIETO DETTO DI	PERSONA
IMPROSCIUTTIRE	VI	DIVENTARE ASCIUTTO COME UN PROSCIUTTO,DETTO DI	PERSONA
RABBRUSCARE	VEY	ADOMBRARSI/OFFUSCARSI IN VOLTO,DETTO DI	PERSONA
RICEVERE	VT	AMMETTERE,DETTO DI	PERSONA
RIDURRE	VT P	METTERE IN CONDIZIONI PEGGIORI,DETTO DI	PERSONA
RIMETTERE	VT PI	RISTABILIRSI,DETTO DI	PERSONA
RINFIERIRE	VI	INFIERIRE DI NUOVO O DI PIU',DETTO DI	PERSONA
RINSECCHIRE	VIT	DIVENTARE MAGRO,ASCIUTTO,DETTO DI	PERSONA
RINVENIRE	VI	RIANIMARSI,RIAVERSI/RICUPERARE I SENSI DETTO DI	PERSONA
RISALTARE	VNI	EMERGERE,DISTINGUERSI,DETTO DI	PERSONA
RISORGERE	VI T	SOLLEVARSI,RIAVERSI DETTO DI	PERSONA
RISPUNTARE	VIT	RIAPPARIRE,RICOMPARIRE,DETTO DI	PERSONA
RISURGERE	VI T	SOLLEVARSI,RIAVERSI,DETTO DI	PERSONA
RIUSCIRE	VI	RAGGIUNGERE IL FINE,LO SCOPO,DETTO DI	PERSONA
ROTOLARE	VTIR	GIRARSI SU DI SE',VOLTOLARSI,DETTO DI	PERSONA
ROVINARE	VITR	CADERE IN BASSO,DETTO DI	PERSONA
...			
NAUFRAGARE	VI	ESSERE SUL BASTIMENTO CHE ROMPE IN MARE,DETTO DI	PERSONA
RICONGIUNGERE	VT D	CONGIUNGERSI DI NUOVO,RIUNIRSI,DETTO DI	PERSONA
RIMESCOLARE	VTP	INTROMETTERSI,MISCHIARSI A UN GRUPPO,DETTO DI	PERSONA
ROVESCIARE	VTP	ABBANDONARSI,DETTO DI	PERSONA
SBOCCARE	VIT	ARRIVARE IN UN DATO LUOGO,DETTO DI	PERSONA
SCHIAMAZZARE	VI	VOCIARE,STREPITARE,DETTO DI	PERSONA
SPELLICCIARE	VTB	PICCHIARSI,AZZUFFARSI RABBIOSAMENTE,DETTO DI	PERSONA
ULULARE	VI	EMETTERE PROLUNGATI,CUPI LAMENTI,DETTO DI	PERSONA
...			
CORDIALE	A	DETTO DI	PERSONA AFFABILE,GENTILE,APERTA
PRODIGIO	A	DETTO DI	PERSONA CHE E' ECCEZIONALE
SUPINO	A	C=PRONO/DETTO DI	PERSONA CHE GIACE SUL DORSO
LACERO	A	CENCIOSO/DETTO DI	PERSONA CHE INDOSSA VESTITI LOGORI
SCIVOLOSO	A	DETTO DI	PERSONA CHE NASCONDE LE SUE VERE INTENZIONI
IMPREGIUDICATO	A	DETTO DI	PERSONA CHE NON HA AVUTO CONDANNE PENALI
IMPETTITO	A	DETTO DI	PERSONA CHE STA ERETTA E COL PETTO IN FUORI
ASOCIALE	A	DETTO DI	PERSONA CHIUSA INTROVERSA

Figure 10: Some of the adjectives and verbs which can be predicated of *persone* (people)

An interesting type of relational data which can be extracted for certain types of actions is the information on the words in the lexicon which are lexicalizations of the typical thematic roles of the action itself. Let us clarify what we mean by two examples. In Figure 12 we find the result of querying the Italian LDB for all the entries in whose definitions the word-form *vende* (sells) appears (not in the 'genus' position). The result of the query is the following: we retrieve 242 entries of which well 221 are names of people who "typically sell" something, i.e. of typical AGENTS with respect to the action of selling. These entries represent lexicalized case/role fillers in the case-frame of *vendere*

ACCESO	A	VIVO,INTENSO,DETTO DI		COLORE
CHIARO	A	C=SCURO/PALLIDO,TENUE,POCO INTENSO DETTO DI		COLORE
CUPO	A	DI TONALITA' SCURA DETTO DI		COLORE
SERPATO	A	CHE E' SCREZIATO,COME LA PELLE DEL SERPENTE,DETTO DI		COLORE
SQUILLANTE	A	VIVACE,INTENSO,DETTO DI		COLORE
STABILE	A	CHE NON SBIADISCE,DETTO DI		COLORE
TENUE	A	PALLIDO/NON MOLTO VIVO DETTO DI		COLORE
RISCHIARARE	VTE	FARSI CHIARO,LUMINOSO,DETTO DI		COLORE
SCARICARE	VTRIP	PERDERE VIVACITA',SBIADIRE,DETTO DI		COLORE
SBIADATO	A	SBIADITO,TENUE,PALLIDO,DETTO DI		COLORE
ADDOLCIRE	VTP	AMMORBIDIRE,DETTO DI		COLORE
DISCORDARE	VE	STONARE/NON ARMONIZZARE,DETTO DI		COLORE
SBIADIRE	VET	SCOLORIRE,STINGERE/DIVENTARE PALLIDO,SMORTO,DETTO DI		COLORE
SGARGIARE	VI	ESSERE ECCESSIVAMENTE VIVACE E VISTOSO,DETTO DI		COLORE
SMONTARE	VTIP	SCHIARIRE,SCOLORIRE,STINGERE,DETTO DI		COLORE
TRIONFARE	VIT	RISALTARE/FARE SPICCO,DETTO DI		COLORE
USCIRE	VIT	RISALTARE DETTO DI		COLORE

. . .

BERRETTINO	A	DETTO DI	COLORE AZZURO CINEREO SU VASI DI MAIOLICA
CALCE	A	DETTO DI	COLORE BIANCO INTENSO
GIGLIACEO	A	DETTO DI	COLORE CHE RICORDA QUELLO DEL GIGLIO
SCURO	A	C=CHIARO/DETTO DI	COLORE CHE TENDE AL NERO
BRUNO	A	DETTO DEL	COLORE DEL MANTELLO DEI BOVINI
ALBICOCCA	A	DETTO DI	COLORE GIALLO ARANCIATO
ZAFFERANO	A	DETTO DI	COLORE GIALLO INTENSO
ISABELLA	A	DETTO DI	COLORE GIALLO TIPICO DI MANTELLO EQUINO
PERLA	A	DETTO DI	COLORE LATTIGINOSO E OPALESCENTE
TERRA	A	DETTO DI	COLORE MARRONE CHIARO SFUMATO AL GRIGIO
SUDICIO	A	DETTO DI	COLORE NON BRILLANTE,NON VIVO
DISUGUAGLIATO	A	DETTO DI	COLORE NON UNIFORME DI UNA TINTURA
NEGRO	A	DETTO DEL	COLORE PIU' SCURO
NERO	A	DETTO DEL	COLORE PIU' SCURO
GIACINTINO	A	DETTO DEL	COLORE ROSSASTRO,TIPICO DEL GIACINTO
TANGO	A	DETTO DI	COLORE ROSSO ASSAI BRILLANTE
GRANATA	A	DETTO DI	COLORE ROSSO SCURO
PULCE	A	DETTO DI	COLORE TRA GRIGIO E VERDE
RUGGINE	A	DETTO DI	COLORE TRA IL MARRONE E IL ROSSO SCURO
LILLA'	A	GRIDELLINO/DETTO DI	COLORE TRA ROSA E VIOLA
GIADA	A	DETTO DI	COLORE VERDAZZURO CHIARO

. . .

SMORTO	A	CHE E' PRIVO DI SPLENDORE E VIVACITA' DETTO DI	COLORE E SIM.
ALLEGRO	A	VIVACE,BRIOSO DETTO DI	COLORE SUONI E SIMILI
RISALTARE	VNI	SPICCARE NITIDAMENTE,DETTO DI	COLORE,DISEGNI,PITTURE
TENDERE	VT IP	AVVICINARSI AD UNA GRADAZIONE DETTO DI	COLORE,SAPORI,ODORI

Figure 11: Some of the adjectives and verbs which are typically predicated of *colori* (colours)

(to sell). This is obviously due to the defining pattern used, i.e. *chi vende* (who sells).
Some interesting observations can be made with regard to this example.

VENDE	→AGNELLAIO	1SI	CHI MACELLA O VENDE AGNELLI
	AGORAIO	1SM	CHI FA O VENDE AGHI
	ALABASTRAIO	1SI	CHI VENDE OGGETTI DI ALABASTRO
	ARAZZIERE	1SI	CHI TESSE E VENDE ARAZZI
	ARGENTIERE	1SI	CHI VENDE OGGETTI D'ARGENTO
	ARMAIOLO	1SI	CHI FABBRICA VENDE RIPARA ARMI
	ASTUCCIAIO	1SI	CHI FABBRICA O VENDE ASTUCCI
	BABBUCCIAIO	1SI	CHI FA O VENDE BABBUCCE
	BADILAIO	1SI	CHI FA O VENDE BADILI
	BERRETTAIO	1SN	CHI FABBRICA O VENDE BERRETTI
	BICCHIERAIO	1SI	CHI FABBRICA O VENDE BICCHIERI
	BIGLIETTAIO	1SN	CHI VENDE I BIGLIETTI PER IL VIAGGIO
	BILANCIAIO	1SI	STADERAIO/CHI FABBRICA E VENDE BILANCE
	BILIARDAIO	1SI	CHI FABBRICA O VENDE BILIARDI
	BIRRAIO	1SI	CHI FABBRICA O VENDE BIRRA
	BOCCALAIO	1SI	CHI FABBRICA O VENDE BOCCALI
	BORSAIO	1SG	CHI FABBRICA O VENDE BORSE
	BOTTAIO	1SI	CHI FABBRICA,RIPARA O VENDE BOTTI
	BOTTONAIO	1SN	CHI FABBRICA O VENDE BOTTONI
	BUSTAIA	1SF	DONNA CHE CONFEZIONA O VENDE BUSTI
	CALZETTAIO	1SN	CHI VENDE O FABBRICA CALZE
	CANESTRAIO	1SI	CHI FA O VENDE CANESTRI
	CARBONAIO	1SM	CHI VENDE CARBONE
	...		
	OROLOGIAIO	1SI	CHI FABBRICA,RIPARA O VENDE OROLOGI
	ORTOPEDICO	2SI	CHI FABBRICA O VENDE APPARECCHI ORTOPEDICI
	OTTICO	2SI	CHI CONFEZIONA E VENDE OCCHIALI E LENTI
	PADELLAIO	1SI	CHI FA O VENDE PADELLE
	PANETTIERE	1SN	FORNAIO/CHI FA O VENDE PANE
	PANIERAIO	1SG	CHI FA O VENDE PANIERI
	PANTOFOLAIO	1SN	CHI CONFEZIONA O VENDE PANTOFOLE
	PASTAIO	1SN	CHI FABBRICA O VENDE PASTE ALIMENTARI
	PASTICCERE	1SN	CHI FA O VENDE DOLCIUMI
	PASTICCIERE	1SN	CHI FA O VENDE DOLCIUMI
	PATACCARO	1SI	2CHI VENDE MONETE OD OGGETTI FALSI
	PELLETTIERE	1SG	CHI PRODUCE O VENDE OGGETTI DI PELLETERIA
	PELLICCIAIO	1SN	CHI LAVORA O VENDE PELLICCE
	...		
	VENDITORE	2SI	CHI VENDE
	VETRAIO	1SI	CHI VENDE TAGLIA APPLICA LASTRE DI VETRO
	VINATTIERE	1SM	1CHE VENDE O COMMERCIA VINO
	VIOLINAIO	1SI	LIUTAIO/CHI FABBRICA O VENDE VIOLINI
	ZOCCOLAIO	1SI	CHI FA O VENDE ZOCCOLI

Figure 12: Names of AGENTS for the action of "selling"

The first concerns the fact that the same type of result was obtained by making a
similar search on an English dictionary. After being shown the Italian example, the IBM
Yorktown group repeated the experiment with the same kind of result for the English
data (see [Byrd, 1989]). This shows that there is in fact a correspondence between the
definitional patterns used in lexicographical practice independently from the language.
This similarity in lexicographical conventions appears in many other examples and will
be exploited for the creation of the multilingual LKB which is the ultimate goal of the
above-mentioned ESPRIT project.

Another observation regards the co-occurrence in these definitions of this kind of
verb ("to sell") with another one ("to make", lexicalized in Italian as *fabbricare*, *fare*,
preparare, etc.). Many of these Agent names also apply to the action of "making", and
therefore belong to two portions of the resulting conceptual network.

We can also notice that the Noun Phrase following the verb denotes the type of object
which is typically sold (or also made) by these Agents.

It is obviously possible to obtain the same type of information on Agents' names for the action of selling if we search for all the nouns whose 'genus term' is the word *venditore* (seller): from this query we retrieve other 131 Agent nouns (see some of them in Figure 13). Here again some of the nouns are related also with the action of "making", while the PP introduced by the preposition *di* (of) expresses the object which is sold.

VENDITORE	→ABBACCHIARO	1SI	2VENDITORE DI ABBACCHI
	ACQUAVITAIO	1SI	VENDITORE DI ACQUAVITE
	ARCHIBUGIERE	1SM	FABBRICANTE O VENDITORE DI ARMI
	...		
	BIBITARO	1SI	2VENDITORE DI BIBITE
	BORSETTAIO	1SG	FABBRICANTE O VENDITORE DI BORSE E BORSETTE
	BRONZISTA	1SN	VENDITORE DI OGGETTI ARTISTICI IN BRONZO
	BURATTINAIO	1SI	FABBRICANTE O VENDITORE DI BURATTINI
	CALCOGRAFO	1SI	VENDITORE DI INCISIONI
	CALDARROSTAIO	1SN	VENDITORE DI CALDARROSTE
	CAMICIAIO	1SD	FABBRICANTE O VENDITORE DI CAMICIE
	CAPPELLAIO	1SN	FABBRICANTE O VENDITORE DI CAPPELLI DI UOMO
	CARAMELLAIO	1SN	FABBRICANTE O VENDITORE DI CARAMELLE
	...		
	FRUTTIVENDOLO	1SN	VENDITORE DI FRUTTA E ORTAGGI
	LATTAIO	1SN	VENDITORE DI LATTE
	LIBRAIO	1SN	VENDITORE DI LIBRI
	MACELLAIO	1SN	VENDITORE DI CARNE MACELLATA
	...		
	PROFUMIERE	1SN	FABBRICANTE O VENDITORE DI PROFUMI E COSMETICI
	SALUMIERE	1SN	VENDITORE DI SALUMI
	SPEZIALE	2SI	VENDITORE DI SPEZIE
	STRILLONE	1SN	VENDITORE AMBULANTE DI GIORNALI
	VALIGIAIO	1SN	FABBRICANTE O VENDITORE DI VALIGI BAULI,BORSE
	VINAIO	1SN	VENDITORE FORNITORE DI VINO

Figure 13: Names of AGENTS for the action of "selling"

This example shows the way in which exactly the same information can be retrieved by browsing the dictionary in different ways, by exploiting the knowledge in its structure (in particular the internal structure of the definitions). In the final LKB all this data will be merged in a single piece of network, independently of the different ways of lexicalizing some concepts and relations.

With a slightly different type of query we can very easily retrieve also the names of the LOCATIONS where the action of "selling" is typically performed. Figure 14 shows the result of the search for the entries in whose definitions the word *vendono* (they sell) is present. Again the fact that names of places are found in this way is due to the following "defining formula" used by lexicographers: *dove/in cui si vendono* (where ... are sold). All of the 33 entries retrieved share this definitional pattern: this query is completely without 'noise'.

We can observe that the 'genus' terms are either the generic name *luogo* (place), or those of its hyponyms which are the generic names for the places where something is sold, i.e. *negozio, bottega, bancarella* (shop, store, stall). These are in turn hypernyms of the defined entries. This kind of hierarchical information is already formally coded in the taxonomies stored in the LDB.

What interests us here is the possibility of formalizing and implementing in the LKB the other types of semantic relations, such as LOCATION and THEME with respect to the actions of "selling" and "making". The Theme relation, i.e. the objects which are

VENDONO	→BANCO	1SM	LOCALE DOVE SI VENDONO O SCAMBIANO BENI SERVIZI
	BIGLIETTERIA	1SF	LUOGO IN CUI SI VENDONO BIGLIETTI
	BISCOTTERIA	1SF	NEGOZIO DOVE SI VENDONO I BISCOTTI
	BOTTIGLIERIA	1SF	NEGOZIO DOVE SI VENDONO VINO LIQUORI IN BOTTIGLIA
	BRICABRAC	1	NEGOZIO,BANCARELLA OVE SI VENDONO TALI ANTICAGLIE
	CALZETTERIA	1SF	NEGOZIO IN CUI SI VENDONO CALZE
	CALZOLERIA	1SF	BOTTEGA IN CUI SI FABBRICANO O VENDO SCARPE
	CAMICERIA	1SF	NEGOZIO IN CUI SI VENDONO CAMICIE
	CAPPELLERIA	1SF	NEGOZIO DOVE SI VENDONO CAPPELLI MASCHILI
	CERERIA	1SF	LUOGO DOVE SI FABBRICANO E VENDONO CANDELE
	CREMERIA	1SF	2LATTERIA IN CUI SI VENDONO ANCHE GELATI DOLCI E SIM.
	DIACCIATINO	2SN	2BOTTEGA DOVE SI VENDONO SORBETTI
	DROGHERIA	1SF	BOTTEGA DOVE SI VENDONO DROGHE
	FERRAMENTA	1SF	NEGOZIO IN CUI SI VENDONO OGGETTI DI FERRO
	GELATERIA	1SF	SORBETTERIA/NEGOZIO OVE SI FANNO O VENDONO GELATI
	MAGLIERIA	1SF	BOTTEGA NEGOZIO IN CUI VENDONO INDUMENTI DI MAGLIA
	MESCITA	1SF	BOTTEGA IN CUI SI VENDONO VINO LIQUORI
	MESTICHERIA	1SF	2BOTTEGA IN CUI SI VENDONO COLORI MESTICATI
	NEGOZIO	1SM	BOTTEGA/ LOCALE DOVE SI ESPONGONO E VENDONO MERCI
	NORCINERIA	1SF	2BOTTEGA IN CUI SI VENDONO SOLO CARNI DI MAIALI
	OCCHIALERIA	1SF	NEGOZIO IN CUI SI VENDONO O SI RIPARANO OCCHIALI
	OROLOGERIA	1SF	NEGOZIO DOVE SI VENDONO OROLOGI
	PANTOFOLERIA	1SF	LUOGO IN CUI SI VENDONO PANTOFOLE
	PELLETTERIA	1SF	NEGOZIO IN CUI SI VENDONO OGGETTI DI LAVORATA
	PIATTERIA	1SF	BOTTEGA DOVE SI VENDONO I PIATTI
	ROSTICCERIA	1SF	BOTTEGA DOVE SI PREPARANO O VENDONO ARROSTI
	SALUMERIA	1SF	BOTTEGA,NEGOZIO,IN CUI SI VENDONO I SALUMI
	UTENSILERIA	1SF	BOTTEGA IN CUI SI VENDONO UTENSILI

Figure 14: Some names of PLACES related to the action of "selling"

typically sold in the defined places are again expressed by the NP object of the verb.

Also in this case similar data are retrieved also by querying for the hyponyms of *negozio, bottega*, etc.. Our aim is to formalize all this information in a semantic network, like the piece sketched in Figure 15.

$OROLOGERIA$= ← **LOC** –   *selling*   – **THEME** →   *orologi*   – **IS-A** →   OBJECT
$OROLOGIAIO$= ← **AGENT** –   "   "   "   "   "

Figure 15: Sketch of a piece of network for the action of "selling"

The above examples show that the LDB facilities can be usefully exploited to analyse and extract linguistic data which must then be restructured and represented in the LKB. In the LKB these types of concepts and of relations, and the interdependencies between word-senses will be explicitly spelled out. When we move beyond taxonomies in the LKB, we establish many different types of associations which are usefully represented in a conceptual network, and when we move from a "monolingual" to a "multilingual" environment, we also establish associations among different languages. These associations are obtained (for those parts of the languages which can be reduced to a common set of concepts and relations) through the common conceptual network constructed by working on different languages but within the same "research template", i.e. trying to accomodate in the semantic network:

- the "same" world-knowledge,

- for the "same" purposes (NLP, Text Processing, etc.),

- with the "same" methodology,

- from the "same" type of sources (MRDs),

- into the "same" kind of representation.

The common semantic network will thus become the point of convergence of the results of the knowledge aquisition strategies applied on a number of different but homogeneous sources, and the multilingual environment will constitute a valid testbed to evaluate this strategy of design and implementation of a part of a LKB.

2.1 Reusability of Bilingual Dictionaries

Not only MR monolingual dictionaries, but also bilingual MRDs can be usefully exploited as sources of lexical information for the creation of LDBs and LKBs. These dictionaries can be processed with a twofold purpose, as on the one hand they, too, are a source of interesting 'monolingual' information, on the other hand they may obviously be exploited as a source of links between two monolingual LDBs (see [Calzolari and Picchi, 1986], and [Picchi *et al.*, forthcoming]).

One of the objectives is to integrate the different types of information traditionally contained in monolingual and bilingual dictionaries, so as to expand the informational content of the single components in the new integrated system. Bilingual dictionaries contain more information about examples of usage, fixed expressions or idioms. This kind of information can obviously be well integrated in the monolingual dictionary, and also made easy to access.

We can envisage the original monolingual lexical entries, augmented with the different types of information coming from the corresponding bilingual entry: different sense discriminations, other examples, syntactic information, collocations, idioms, etc.. We can also reverse the perspective, and look at the bilingual entries provided with the information traditionally contained in monolingual entries: mostly definitions. One of the two different viewpoints, both virtually present in the integrated bilingual system, will be simply activated and made available to the user by the first manner of access to the on-line bilingual lexical data base. We would like therefore to maintain in a unique structure both the independent features of the source monolingual and bilingual dictionaries and the integration of the two with different views on the data.

The overall picture of the bilingual LDB system we have in mind is sketched in Figure 16. Also with regard to bilingual dictionaries, the method we are adopting consists of reusing available data in machine-readable form by analysing and transforming the information already contained in common dictionaries. The procedure of processing the bilingual MRD is rather similar to the one outlined above for monolingual dictionaries (i.e. parsing of the lexical entry, design of a new structure, computational reorganization, etc.). After this preliminary part again comes out the utility of browsing the bilingual

LDB, taking advantage of the structural elements already formalized in the LDB, with the purpose of discovering properties and structures not immediately visible in the printed dictionary, but useful for further exploitation in the computational dictionary.

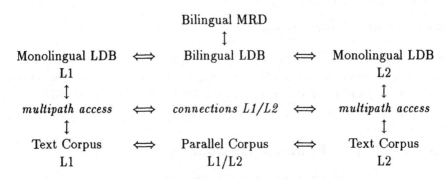

Figure 16: A model of a Bilingual LDB System

After the first processing phases that we have envisaged on the bilingual dictionary data, it will make no difference which of the two languages are taken as a starting point. In a certain sense, we would no longer have a source language and a target language, since the look-up and access procedures are independent and neutral with respect to direction (the object becomes bidirectional). Bidirectional cross-references will also be automatically generated for the information contained at each sense level as semantic indicators, i.e. synonyms/hyperonyms or contextual indicators.

One of the parts of the bilingual dictionary we are processing that can be partially made explicit in all its different meanings, is the field of the so-called *semantic indicators*. These provide the constraints for selecting one translation equivalent or the other. The problem is that these constraints are of a different nature, being either

i) synonyms or hyponyms of the entry, or

ii) contextual indicators such as typical subjects or objects of verbs, typical nouns of which an adjective can be predicated, etc..

It is possible to semi-automatize the process of disambiguation between the different values, after analysing all the different possibilities and designing a typology of what can appear in this field.

Another possibility is the use of the monolingual lexical data base as a tool to expand the information given as a single word to the whole set of words to which it actually refers. For example, the entry *vivido* has different translations according to the contextual indicators referring to the subject (in brackets):

vivido ... **(colori)** bright, vivid

In some cases the generic semantic restrictions on the possible object can be taken as a semantic feature, and can be procedurally expanded by the monolingual thesaurus to all the possible hyponyms (at the query moment) so that the appropriate translation can be chosen in any context where a specific name of *colore* (colour) is found (and this is already possible in our monolingual LDB). The information that can be formalized at the semantic level in a monolingual dictionary — which serves to discriminate among the different word-senses — should be in principle of the same type that is given in bilingual dictionaries in the form of "semantic indicators" or "selective conditions" to constrain the choice of a particular translation.

In the same way we can work on other fields in order to make explicit hidden information or to introduce new information on the basis either of structural or of content clues.

After the re-organization of the bilingual MRD in a well-structured LDB, we face the difficult task of using its data to build links between two monolingual LDBs. The difficulty obviously derives from the ambiguity of the words used both as entries and as translations. We never know which word-sense is meant in a particular situation. We shall try to solve this problem as much as possible in the above-mentioned ESPRIT project, mostly by exploiting the semantic indicators in the bilingual, and the taxonomies and other conceptual information in the monolingual LDBs.

Mapping between word-senses in monolingual dictionaries and different translations in a bilingual dictionary is one of the most interesting of the problems concerning the connection of these different types of dictionaries. As one of the main problems in translation is the correct choice among the various meanings of lexically ambiguous words, we feel that it is absolutely necessary also for a Machine Translation or a Machine Assisted Translation system to be linked to a linguistic data base, i.e. a source of lexical information organized in the form of a thesaurus by multi-dimensional taxonomies, where the possibility of disambiguating lexical items is at least semi-automatized.

One of the main uses of the system should be that of machine-aided translation (MAT), as a powerful aid for translators. The end result may in fact be viewed as a 'translator workstation', where access is provided to many types of dictionaries and other lexical resources, and where the power and the functions of lexical data bases and of textual data bases is exploited at best.

Other purposes of a Bilingual System like the one which appears in Figure 16 are the following:

- a tool for lexicographers;

- a tool for lexicological-contrastive studies;

- a means for improving monolingual LDBs;

- an aid to construct Machine Translation dictionaries;

- a tool for language teaching;

- a computerized dictionary for "normal" users.

In our opinion, one of the main advantages of a bilingual LDB is the completely different type of "navigation" within its data, made possible both by the multiple access to its data and by its links to the monolingual LDB. In particular, it is not only possible to create links between couples of words in the two languages, as in the printed dictionary, but mainly between groups or families of semantically connected words, which we think is an essential property for a true bilingual dictionary and for all the purposes we have listed above.

2.2 Reusability of Textual Corpora and their Integration into LKBs

We have seen that MRDs are very valuable sources of lexical and also of semantic information, but unfortunately not all what is needed to know about the lexicon is there. There are very important pieces of information which in MRDs are completely missing, or incomplete, or simply are not very good or reliable or easily recoverable. For this type of information, we have to resort to different types of sources (see also [Calzolari, 1989b]).

Certain kinds of data can probably be acquired only after theoretical investigation of lexical facts, and their source can be seen in the typical linguists' work, mainly based on introspection and native speaker's intuition. In this paper we do not deal with this data, but we must be aware of its existence.

We want to stress here that there are many types of data which can be usefully extracted, more or less directly, by processing very large corpora of textual data. The results of this processing have also to be analysed and evaluated by the linguist and/or the lexicographer, but it is important to realize that for certain types of linguistic phenomena the study made through corpus analysis is 'favoured' with respect to introspection: typical examples are collocations and fixed phrases. A tentative, but not exhaustive, list of lexical information for which we can find data in textual corpora, with various degrees of difficulty and at various levels of completeness, is the following:

- frequency data (at the level of word, word-form, word-sense, word associations, etc.); .

- subcategorization;

- collocations, fixed phrases, idioms;

- thematic roles, valency;

- semantic constraints on arguments;

- typical Subject, Object, Modifier, etc. (these are different from the types of thematic roles, being in fact their fillers; in a certain sense they are the same information but given "by example");

- aspectual information;

- proper nouns.

Let us take for example the verb *dividere* (to divide), and look at its occurrences and contexts in our Corpus of about 10 million words. From a total of 840 concordances, we obtain the most frequent syntactic patterns which are as follows:

dividere	NP in NP	268
,,	NP	175
,,	NP tra NP, NP, ...	80
,,	NP con NP	78
		601

while the remaining 239 contexts are distributed in about 10 other subcategorization frames. If we analyse the contexts by hand, we see that each subcategorization frame can very often be correlated with one or more word-senses, so that we can think of using these frames as a very useful aid in a meaning disambiguation task. By analyzing concordances we can thus obtain data concerning:

a) syntactic frames;

b) their frequency ordering, and therefore their respective relevance for the user;

c) co-occurrences with other words and word classes (at the syntactic and semantic levels);

d) main word-senses;

e) correlation between word-senses and syntactic frames.

We must notice here that it is essential to pay attention to different types of texts, and therefore it is important a good balancing in a reference corpus, because frequency data (at any level: lexical, syntactical, semantic, collocational, etc.) can be very different for different text types.

Let us now consider again the word *libro* (book) for another example of information obtained from texts. If we look at the verbs related to books in the Italian dictionary we can notice that neither *leggere* (to read) nor *scrivere, pubblicare*, etc. (to write, to publish) are among them. Again, the same observation has been made with regard to English dictionaries (see [Boguraev *et al.*, 1989]), which is not by chance, but is again a clear indication of the similarity even between dictionaries of different languages.

In the definitions of these verbs we usually find more generic words related with printed things, such as *scrittura, parole, segni, lettere, scritto, opera, volume, giornale* (writing, words, signs, letters, script, work, volume, journal). The word "book" appears instead in some examples. The link could only be established indirectly, given that the

word *libro* is defined in terms of words such as *volume, opera, scritti, stampati*, the same
words that appear in the definitions of the above verbs.

These verbs are instead directly associated with *libro* in the corpus of texts. Here, in
fact, out of 3,222 concordances of the lemma *libro*, we find these figures for the above-
mentioned verbs in the same contexts with *libro*:

leggere	187
scrivere	196
pubblicare	107

It is the analysis of large textual corpora that makes it possible to find this type of
collocational information. We are also implementing some statistical/quantitative tools
to allow semi-automatic extraction of this and other types of data from our corpus (see
[Bindi and Calzolari]).

When analysing a large corpus with millions of words in context, we are in a sense
compelled to discover and describe:

- usages which are not described in commercial dictionaries;

- relative frequencies of the different word-senses, and of the different syntactic
  frames/patterns; and, above all,

- the grammatical/syntactic clues by which semantic disambiguation can be at least
  partially achieved, given the fact that

  i) in the presence of different syntactic constituency word-sense usually changes,

  ii) while, vice-versa, we do not necessarily have only one word-sense with the same
      syntactic frame.

When collecting this type of data for a number of words, we often realize that the data
should be reorganized in a different way from how they are presently found in standard
dictionaries, if they are to conform to the actual usage of the language.

In order to automatize the retrieval of this type of information directly from the
corpus we should first be able to tag the corpus for the different POSs. For this task
many systems already exist (see e.g. [Hindle, 1988], [Webster and Marcus, 1989]). It
should then be possible, even without a complete parser, to apply to the text corpus some
pattern-matching procedures (as those we are presently using with dictionary definitions).
These pattern-matching procedures should be explicitly geared to the extraction of the
type of data we are searching (i.e. prepositional phrases, that-clauses, infinitives, etc.).

The same strategy of looking for syntactic (and collocational) clues for semantic
disambiguation (to be used for different translations of the same word) is now evaluated
in a pilot project we are carrying out in a multilingual context.

3 The Lexicographer's Workstation as a Model of Integration of Tools and Data from Different Environments and Expertises

The importance of a collaboration between researchers working in the fields of Computational Linguistics/Natural Language Processing (CL/NLP) and Literary and Linguistic Computing/Text Processing (LLC/TP) is evident when we consider that it is necessary to process large textual corpora in order to achieve better LKBs. The design of these large integrated LKBs can really become the purpose of cooperative projects, where the "typical" data, tools, procedures, knowledge, expertise, results, etc., of the two areas of CL/NLP and LLC/TP "must" work in parallel and cooperate and interact with each other.

In order to achieve at least some of the results outlined so far, we can summarize the needs as follows:

- design and implementation of powerful tools;

- large sets of lexical and textual data;

- very modular systems;

- possibility of sharing resources, data and procedures;

- large cooperation among traditionally different research or industrial communities.

A model of the type of integration we have in mind can be seen in the lexicographer's workstation (LW) we are designing in Pisa (see [Calzolari *et al.*, 1987]). It is conceived as a very modular system, where different types of data and of procedures are integrated. At the level of data the LW contains, or will contain, among other modules:

- a textual data base,

- one or more monolingual lexical databases,

- a thesaurus with taxonomic information,

- bilingual lexical databases,

- a reference corpus

while at the level of procedures, it contains, among others:

- a morphological tool,

- dictionary parsers,

- a hyponym finder,

- an information retrieval system,

- a lemmatization package,

- a pattern-matching procedure for dictionary definitions,

- a redaction tool.

This complex and various set of components reflects our view of the need for an integration and interaction between data and tools traditionally pertinent and pertaining either to CL or to LLC only. It appears therefore important the realization of a factive cooperation among many different groups of researchers (meaning here 'groups' as 'types'), with the aim of linking together worlds which up until now have not been so strongly related to each other, especially perhaps in the American tradition.

X-Bar Theory: Its Role in GB Theory

Inês Duarte

Departamento de Linguística, Universidade de Lisboa

Alameda da Universidade — 1699 Lisboa Codex — Portugal

1 GB Theory: A Principles and Parameters Approach to Grammar

GB is a result of what [Chomsky, 1986b] called the "second conceptual shift" of Generative Grammar — that is, the move from rules to principles associated with parameters. We might say that the main question GB theory is concerned with is the following one:

> "How can a grammatical system be flexible enough to account for language variation while at the same time be, to a large extent, restricted in order to account for the relative ease of language acquisition and the impossibility of certain language types?" [Travis, 1989] p. 263.

This main concern has produced a grammatical model where, in contrast to the long list of phrase structure and transformational rules used to capture syntactic facts in the past, only one rule is used: Affect-α[1]. Affect-α is taken to have three specific realizations: Generate-α[2], the remainder of the base component, responsible for the generation of D-structure representations; Move-α, the remainder of the transformational component, having as output S-structure representations; and Delete-α, which, together with Move-α, yields LF-representations. The form of grammar can be seen in Figure 1, where capital letters are used for the components and bold letters are used for the levels of representation.

In this grammatical model a crucial role is played by interacting systems of principles. Such systems, listed in Figure 2, state general conditions on the well-formedness of syntactic representations (D- and S-structures, LF-representations).

The principles of each of the systems in Figure 2 are taken to be universal, thus accounting for "the relative ease of language acquisition and the impossibility of certain language types". But most of them are associated with parameters that must be fixed by experience "on the basis of quite simple evidence" [Chomsky, 1986b] p. 146; parameter setting is what makes grammar "flexible enough to account for language variation". A

---

[1] See [Lasnik and Saito, 1984].

[2] See [Travis, 1989].

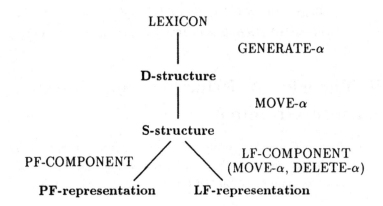

Figure 1: Organization of the GB grammar

X-bar theory
Thematic theory (θ-theory)
Government theory
Case theory
Bounding theory
Binding Theory
Control theory

Figure 2: Systems of principles in GB

particular principle, not included in any of the systems in Figure 2, plays the central role of guiding principle for syntactic representations: the Projection Principle. It guarantees that the properties of lexical items stated in the Lexicon are preserved in the syntactic configurations such items enter in, and may be formulated as in (1):

(1) **Projection Principle**

Lexical properties must be represented by categorial structure at every level of syntactic representation (D- and S-structures, LF-representation)[3].

The Projection Principle has far reaching consequences in what concerns syntactic representations. If we consider a lexical predicate like *ver* (= *to see*), a two-place predicate that takes an object and a subject, the Projection Principle forces the presence of a syntactic position Ω (the position occupied by objects) and of a syntactic position Σ (the position occupied by subjects) in every D-structure, S-structure and LF-representation of the sentences this item enters in. So, the D-structure associated with a sentence like (2a) must contain both a syntactic position Ω and a syntactic position Σ (see (2b)):

(2) a. *O que viram muitas pessoas?*
         What did many people see?
     b. [[$_\Sigma$ muitas pessoas] [viram [$_\Omega$ o que]]]

Although Move-α has applied to the wh-phrase, the S-structure representation of (2a) must, by the Projection Principle, still contain the position Ω (see (2c)):

(2) c. [O que [viram [[$_\Sigma$ muitas pessoas] [[$_\Omega$ -]]]]]

Assuming quantified NPs raise at LF[4], the subject NP has undergone Move-α at LF and is in a pre-sentential position at LF-representation; still, the Projection Principle forces the Σ position to be present at this level of representation (see (2d)):

(2) d. [O que [viram [muitas pessoas [[$_\Sigma$ -] [[$_\Omega$ -]]]]]]

As the representations (2c) and (2d) show, the Projection Principle, together with the idea that θ-assignment is configurational (see Section 3), makes it necessary to assume the so-called Null Hypothesis. The Null Hypothesis embodies the claim that, on a par with full syntactic categories — that is, syntactic categories associated with a phonological matrix —, there exist empty categories — that is, syntactic categories — with no phonetic content.

---

[3] See [Chomsky, 1986b] p. 82; for a somewhat more formal definition of the Projection Principle, see [Chomsky, 1981] p. 38.
[4] See [May, 1977], [May, 1985].

2 X-bar Theory: The Principles and The Headedness Parameter

X-bar theory[5] defines universal conditions on the format of syntactic categories and hence allows the disappearance of phrase structure rules (except for a residue of language-particular phenomena).

This system[6] uses a category neutral vocabulary — the variable X ranges over every syntactic category — and makes the following claims concerning the format of such categories[7]:

(3)

i. Uniqueness of the head: every maximal projection has one and only one head;

ii. Endocentricity: every maximal projection ($= X^{max}$) has the same category as its head ($= X^0$);

iii. Succession: the head term is one bar-level lower ($= X^0$) than the phrasal node immediately dominating it ($= X'$)[8];

iv. Hierarchic difference between specifiers and complements: specifiers appear as sisters of X', whereas complements occur as sisters of X^0;

v. Maximality: only maximal projections appear as nonheads within a phrase;

vi. Boundary adjacency of the head: the head occurs adjacent to one X' boundary;

vii. Structural difference between adjuncts and nonadjuncts: adjuncts occur as sisters to some X^n category and are immediately dominated by the same X bar-level category of X^n.

---

[5]X-bar theory — or, as it was then called, 'X-bar notation' — was proposed in [Chomsky, 1970] as part of an attempt to establish a new division of labour between lexicon and syntax in the model of grammar (see [Chomsky, 1970]; see also a similar proposal in [Harris, 1951], chapter 16, referred to in [Chomsky, 1970] p. 54).

Besides providing a way to express base structures compatible with the lexicalist hypothesis, X-bar theory worked as a powerful constraint on phrase-structure rules: in this respect, it played a role similar to the one the Tensed-S Condition, the Specified Subject Condition and the Subjacency Condition played in constraining transformational rules (see [Chomsky, 1973]).

[6]Throughout, we will use the prime notation instead of the bar notation. As it is well known, the so-called major syntactic categories N(oun), V(erb), A(djective) and P(reposition) are taken to be clusters of +/- values for the features N(ominal) and V(erbal):

N : $[+N, -V]$
A : $[+N, +V]$
V : $[-N, +V]$
P : $[-N, -V]$.

[7]See [Stowell, 1981] p. 70.

[8]For a view where succession only holds of non-lexical, that is functional, projections, see [Fukui and Speas, 1986].

Before we proceed, let us recall what is meant by *complement, specifier* and *adjunct*. If we take any lexical category X^0, the complements of X^0 are its internal arguments — that is, those elements present in the θ-grid of X^0 and both s-selected and c-selected[9] by X^0; its specifier may be either the external argument of X^0 — that is, that element present in the θ-grid of X^0 and s-selected (but not c-selected) by X^0 — or some non-argument constituent (determiners or quantifiers, expletives, degree phrases, ...)[10]. Base-generated adjuncts are modifiers of $X \geq X'$.

Note also that it is generally assumed within GB theory that maximal projections are two bar-level categories[11].

The principles stated in (3) rule out configurations as those represented in Figures (3)-(8). The one in Figure 3 violates the requirement of uniqueness of the head (see (3i)).

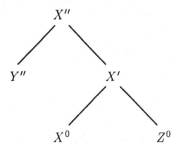

Figure 3: Violation of uniqueness of the head

The configuration in Figure 4 violates the requirement of endocentricity (see (3ii)).

The configuration in Figure 5 violates the requirement of succession, since the node immediately dominating the head is two-bar level higher than the head itself (see (3iii)).

The configuration in Figure 6 is ruled out by (3iv), since there is no structural difference between specifiers and complements.

The configuration in Figure 7 violates the requirement of maximality of the non-heads (see (3v) — the category occuring as complement is a one-bar level projection.

Finally, the configuration in Figure 8 violates the requirement of boundary adjacency of the head (see (3vi)).

The configuration in Figure 9 illustrates a syntactic projection well-formed in respect to the principles stated in (3); in this configuration, there is a left adjunct to X'' and a right adjunct to X' (see (3vii)).

---

[9]*S-selection* stands for semantic selection, that is, the semantic (= thematic) role(s) a lexical item assigns; *c-selection* stands for categorial selection, that is, the syntactic category occupying the position to which that lexical item assigns a specific θ-role. See [Chomsky, 1986b] p. 86.

[10]But see [Abney, 1987] and [Fukui and Speas, 1986] for the view that determiners, quantifiers and degree phrases are functional heads.

[11]That is the reason why the notations X'' and XP are used interchangeably for maximal projections.

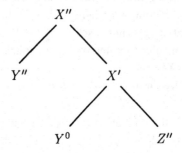

Figure 4: Violation of endocentricity

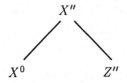

Figure 5: Violation of succession

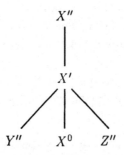

Figure 6: Configuration with no difference between specifiers and complements

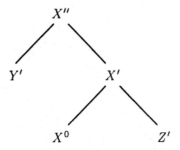

Figure 7: Violation of maximality of non-heads

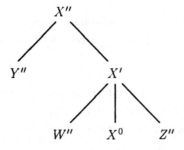

Figure 8: Violation of boundary adjacency of head

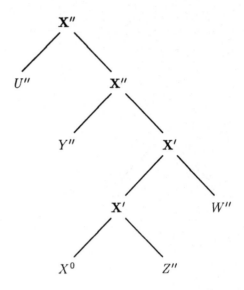

Figure 9: A well-formed syntactic projection

The sentences in (4) illustrate cases of left adjunction to a maximal projection; both in (4a), an instance of Topicalization, and in (4b), an instance of Clitic Left Dislocation, an NP is an adjunct to S[12].

(4) a. **Esse livro**, *ainda não li.*
That book, I haven't read yet.
  b. **Esse livro**, *ainda não o li.*
That book, I haven't read it yet.

The sentences in (5) illustrate cases of adjuncts to the right to one-level bar projections; restrictive relative clauses and most adjectives occur in such a position within NPs — that is, as adjuncts to N'.

(5) a. *Os marinheiros* **que não sabem nadar** *vivem aterrorizados.*
The sailors who can't swim live in fear.
  b. *Os carros* **pequenos** *arrumam-se bem.*
Small cars park well.

None of the principles stated in (3) concern the linear order of heads, complements, specifiers and adjuncts. The essential of the linearization problem is taken to be solved through parameter setting. In particular, the linear order of heads and their complements

---

[12]For the analysis of these constructions in Portuguese see [Duarte, 1987], [Duarte, 1989].

depends crucially on the value each language fixes for the Headedness Parameter, which can be thought of as a parameter associated with principle (3vi) and stated as in (6):

(6)   **Headedness Parameter**

Head is initial/final.

Portuguese, as other Romance languages, is a language which fixes the value `initial` for the Headedness Parameter. Hence, in Portuguese, X' categories are sequences where the head precedes the complement.

(7)   a. $[_{X'} X^0 Y'' \ldots]$

On the contrary a language like Japanese fixes the value `final` for the Headedness Parameter and hence X' categories in this language are sequences where complements precede heads.

(7)   b. $[_{X'} \ldots Y'' X^0]$

The syntactic representations generated by Affect-α and constrained by X-bar theory are a highly restricted case of a language generated by a context-free phrase structure grammar. As expected, the syntactic positions of such representations maintain such relations as **dominate, immediately dominate, be sister of, c-command**.

C-command, a structural relation that plays a crucial role in almost every syntactic process may be defined as in (8):

(8)   **C-command**

α **c-commands** β iff:
i. α does not dominate β; and
ii. the first branching node that dominates α dominates β.

Let us consider a configuration like the one in Figure 10. According to (8), in it X^0 only c-commands Z'', X' ccommands Y'' and Y'' c-commands X', X^0 and Z''; X'' does not c-command anything, since it dominates every other node in the configuration.

A further requirement on syntactic configurations assumed in this framework is binary branching: a mother node cannot have more than two daughters. Binary branching guarantees that paths relating a trace or an anaphor to its antecedent are not ambiguous[13].

So, a configuration like that in Figure 10 is well-formed since it meets the principles of X-bar theory and the binary branching requirement, whereas a configuration like the one on Figure 11 is ruled out because it violates such a requirement.

One construction which argues in favour of the binary branching requirement on syntactic configurations is the double object construction occuring with ditransitive verbs

---

[13]See [Kayne, 1983].

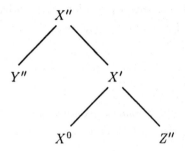

Figure 10: A well-formed configuration

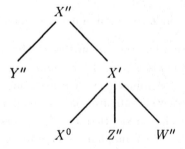

Figure 11: Violation of the binary branching rule

in languages like English. In this construction, the dative argument is the primary object of the verb, displaying all the properties of a regular direct object (e.g., it can be passivized) — see (9a).

(9) a. ... *give Mary a book.*
     b. ... *give a book to Mary.*

Lets us call *Mary* in (9a) NP1 and *a book*, also in (9a), NP2. Several analyses have been proposed for the double object construction. Oehrle, in [Oehrle 1976], proposed a flat structure, not meeting the binary branching requirement and where NP1 and NP2 mutually c-command each other, like the one represented in Figure 12; Chomsky, in [Chomsky, 1981], proposed the structure represented in Figure 13, where NP2 is not a sister of the verb and asymmetrically c-commands NP1; Kayne, in [Kayne, 1983], based on data from Russian, proposes a structure like the one in Figure 14, where the complement of the verb is a predication domain having NP1 as its subject and NP2 as the predicate[14].

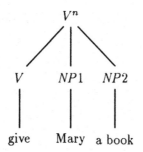

Figure 12: Double object construction according to Oehrle

Note that the three analysis above either predict that no asymmetries will be found in this construction since NP1 and NP2 mutually c-command each other (see Figures 12 and 14) or predict that the asymmetries to be found in this construction will follow from the fact that NP1 is in the c-command domain of NP2 (see Figure 13).

However, as [Barss and Lasnik, 1986] have pointed out, the two predictions made by the analysis above turn out to be wrong. In fact, consider the contrast between the (a) and (b) sentences of (10) to (12) (from [Barss and Lasnik, 1986]):

(10) a. *I showed Mary herself.*
      b. * *I showed herself Mary.*

---

[14] According to [Kayne, 1983], X is S — what would now be considered a small clause, that is, a predication domain distinct from a sentence.

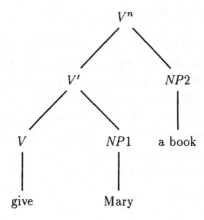

Figure 13: Double object construction according to Chomsky

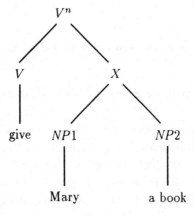

Figure 14: Double object construction according to Kayne

(11)   a.   I gave [every worker]$_i$ his$_i$ paycheck.

          b.   * I gave its$_i$ owner [every paycheck]$_i$.

(12)   a.   *I showed no one anything.*

          b.   * *I showed anyone nothing.*

The sentences in (10) show that NP1 can act as the antecedent of an anaphoric NP2 whereas the reverse is not possible; hence, it provides an argument in favour of an analysis where NP1 asymmetrically c-commands NP2. The sentences in (11) show that there are asymmetries in respect to quantifier-pronoun binding possibilities in the double object construction; assuming that, if a binding relation is to be established between a quantifier phrase and a pronoun, the quantifier phrase must c-command the pronoun at S-structure, the contrast in (11) argues in favour of an analysis where NP1 asymmetrically c-commands NP2. Finally, the sentences (12) illustrate the distribution of negative polarity items in the double object construction; assuming that being in the c-command domain of a negation element is the licensing condition for negative polarity items, the contrast in (12) provides an additional argument in favour of an analysis where NP1 asymmetrically c-commands NP2.

Based on these data, [Larson, 1988] proposes an analysis of the double object construction using strict binary branching and both V-movement and NP-movement where NP1 asymmetrically c-commands NP2 at S-structure (see Figure 15[15]).

3   X-bar Theory and θ-assignment

The claim that lexical items are potential θ-assigner elements — that is, assign thematic (= semantic) roles to their arguments — is common to most contemporary syntactic theories.

But in GB theory θ-role assignment is taken to be configurational: θ-roles are assigned to syntactic positions and not directly to arguments.

So, in a configuration like (13), where $\alpha = X^0$, the head of δ, α θ-marks the position occupied by β, providing it is a property of the θ-grid of α to s-select and c-select β:

(13) $[_\delta \ \tau \ [_{\alpha'} \ \alpha \ \beta]]$

In other words, α θ-marks the position occupied by its complement, a case of θ-role assignment under sisterhood, called direct θ-marking. θ-roles assigned through direct θ-marking are known as internal θ-roles. No X^0 can assign an internal θ-role to a position

---

[15]The D-structure corresponding to Figure 15 is, according to [Larson, 1988],

$[_{VP} \ [_{NP} \ a \ book \ [_{V'} \ [_V \ give \ [_{PP} \ Mary]]]$

Crucially, in his analysis, the double object construction is a result of a process of argument demotion, where NP2 is demoted and hence occurs as a V' adjunct.

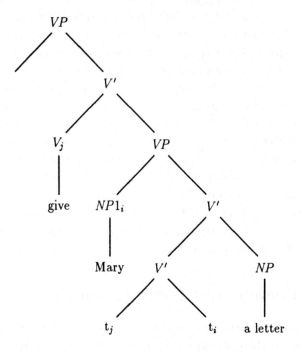

Figure 15: Double object construction according to Larson

outside its one bar-level projection — e.g., in (13), no internal θ-role can be assigned by α to the position occupied by τ.

The interaction of the Projection Principle and X-bar theory guarantees that, if α has an internal θ-role to assign, its one bar-level projection will have a complement position (see (13)); if it is the case that α has no internal θ-role to assign, no complement position of α will be available at any level of syntactic representation.

Most lexical items have also one (and only one) external θ-role to assign — that is the case, for instance of transitive and unergative verbs. External θ-roles are typically assigned by some X^0 to the SPEC position of its maximal projection. So, if in (13) α has an external θ-role, it will be assigned to the position occupied by τ, through a process called indirect θ-marking. Note this kind of θ-marking still operates within the boundaries of a maximal projection.

The idea that there is a distinction between internal and external θ-roles and that this distinction is expressed configurationally gets empirical support from such pairs as those in (14):

(14)   a.   *O menino partiu o vidro.*
              The kid broke the glass.
       b.   *O menino partiu a perna.*
              The kid broke his leg.

Whereas the internal θ-role assigned by the lexical item *partir* (= *break*) is the same in (14a) and (14b), the external θ-role is not: in (14a) *o menino* is understood as an Agent, in (14b) it is understood as a Patient. The claim that the internal θ-role is directly assigned by a lexical head to its complement position, whereas the external θ-role is assigned indirectly, captures the contrast noted above: the last one is assigned compositionally by the one bar-level projection of the head, whereas the first one is assigned directly by the head to its complement position.

This distinction also gets empirical support from well known binding asymmetries (subjects can act as antecedents for complement anaphors, whereas complements can not be chosen as antecedents for subject anaphors) and from long extraction asymmetries. In what concerns long extraction asymmetries, a language like English exhibits the following paradigm ((15) is from [Koopman and Sportiche, 1988]):

(15)   a.   *What do you wonder whether John designed t?*
       b.   * *Who do you wonder whether t designed it?*
       c.   * *Why do you wonder whether John resigned t?*

(16)   a.   *O que é que não sabes quem guardou t?*
              What do you wonder where João kept t?
       b.   *Quem é que não sabes onde t vive?*
              Who do you wonder where t lives?
       c.   * *Onde é que não sabes quem vive t?*

Paradigm (15) shows that in English (and more generally in English-type languages) only complements can be long extracted — that is, only complements in the domain of an embedded clause can come up in a root or higher clause without passing through the intermediate SPEC of CP position (see (15a)). When we try to do the same with external arguments (see (15b)) or with adjuncts (see (15c)), we get ill-formed sentences. As we will see below, this asymmetry can be derived ultimately from the position complements and non-complements occupy in syntactic configurations.

Paradigm (16) shows that long extraction facts are not the same in Portuguese and in English-type languages. In Portuguese (as in other null subject Romance languages) subjects and complements pattern alike in what concerns the possibility of long extraction, whereas adjuncts have the same behaviour in Portuguese and in English-type languages.

Paradigms like (15) and (16) have supported the claim that long extraction is possible only in those cases where the variable left by Wh-Movement is in a θ-position: this condition rules out long extraction of adjuncts both in English- and in Portuguese-type languages. As for the different behaviour displayed by subjects in these two types of languages, it has been argued that it follows from the different properties of I: in English-type languages I is an obligatory raising category, forcing the subject to raise to SPEC of IP, a non-θ-position; in Portuguese-type languages I is not an obligatory raising category, the wh-extraction site for the subject being the θ-position of SPEC of VP[16].

It should also be noted that the claim that indirect θ-marking takes place within the boundaries of a maximal projection has important consequences in what concerns clausal structure (see Section 5).

The central principle ruling the distribution of θ-roles in syntactic configurations is the θ-Criterion, which can be stated as in (17):

(17)   **θ-Criterion**

If α is an argument of β, then the position P occupied by α is assigned one and only one θ-role R; if β has a θ-role R to assign, then this θ-role is assigned to a position P and P is occupied by one and only one argument α.

From the definition given in (17), it gets clear that the θ-Criterion expresses the idea, common to most syntactic theories, that each argument must be assigned one and only one θ-role and each θ-role must be assigned to one and only one argument.

One of the main consequences of the θ-Criterion is that constituents only are allowed to move to non-thematic positions.

---

[16]See [Koopman and Sportiche, 1988] for more details.

4   X-bar Theory and Government: The Structure of The Clause

We have said in Section 3 that θ-role assignment takes place within the boundaries of maximal projections. This requirement follows from the claim that θ-roles are assigned under government. The intuitive idea behind the concept of government is that a head governs the syntactic positions occupied by its thematic dependents, provided a specific structural relationship exists between that head and such positions. If we bear in mind that indirect θ-marking takes place under government (see Section 3), the structural relationship mentioned above cannot be c-command: in fact, heads do not c-command the SPEC position. A considerable amount of evidence has been presented supporting the claim that the relationship involved in government is a variant of c-command, m-command[17]:

(18)   **M-command**

> α **m-commands** β iff:
> **i.** α does not dominate β; and
> **ii.** every δ, δ a maximal projection, that dominates α dominates β[18].

Note that, according to definition (18), in a configuration like the one in Figure 10, repeated below, although X^0 does not c-command Y'', it m-commands Y''.

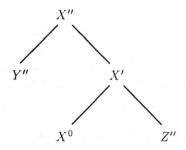

Figure 16: A well-formed configuration

We can now define government as in (19):

(19)   **Government**

> α **governs** β iff:
> **i.** $\alpha = X^0$; and

---

[17]See, for instance, [Aoun and Sportiche, 1982].
[18]See [Chomsky, 1986a] p. 8.

ii. α **m-commands** β; and

iii. there is no δ, $\delta = Y''$, such that δ intervenes between α and β[19].

The definition of *intervene* is given in (20).

(20) **Intervene**

δ intervenes between α and β if δ dominates β and does not dominate α.

As definitions (18) to (20) show, the crucial idea behind government is that: (i) a head has access to every syntactic position inside its maximal projection; (ii) maximal projections are barriers, thus preventing any head X^0 to have access to positions internal to a maximal projection Y''.

The statement made in (ii) above must be slightly revised. In fact, considerable empirical evidence supports the claim that, if a head X^0 governs a maximal projection Y'', it also governs its head Y^0, an expected consequence due to X-bar theory[20]. Hence, (ii) above may be restated as: maximal projections are barriers, thus preventing any head X^0 governing a maximal projection Y'' to have access to all the non-head positions internal to Y''.

As we have said in Section 3, indirect θ-marking takes place under government. If this is the case, how is assigned the external θ-role of clausal main predicates?

Let us consider a sentence like (14a), repeated below:

(14)   a.   *O menino partiu o vidro.*
               The kid broke the glass.

It is clear that the main predicate of (14a) is an inflected form of the transitive verb *partir* (= *to break*). According to our definition of indirect θ-marking, the verbal head must assign the external θ-role to the SPEC position of its maximal projection; that is, at D-structure, the SPEC position of V'' must be available and must be occupied by the external argument *o menino* (= *the kid*) – see (21).

(21)   ... $[_{V''}[_{N''}$ o menino$]$ $[_{V'}$ $[_V$ [parti-$]$ $[_{N''}$ o vidro$]]]$ ...

We must now decide whether representation (21), a consequence of the Projection Principle, X-bar theory, the θ-Criterion and the requirement that θ-marking takes place under government, is the D-structure representation of clause (14a) or only part of that representation.

Since [Chomsky, 1981], it has been widely assumed that the head of a clausal domain (= S) is I(nflection), a non-lexical (or functional) head — that is, a head with no associated θ-grid — which is the locus of T(ense) and AGR(eement) information. In

---

[19]See [Chomsky, 1986a] p. 8.
[20]See [Belletti and Rizzi, 1981]. An interesting piece of evidence supporting this claim is provided by the distribution of the inflected infinitive in European Portuguese — see [Raposo, 1987].

[Chomsky, 1986b], a proposal was made to extend X-bar theory to the non-lexical head I. As a consequence of this proposal, the D-structure representation of clause (14a), irrelevant details omitted, is the one given in (22).

(22) $[_{I''}[_{N''} -] [_{I'}[_I \text{ T AGR}] [_{V''}[_{N''} \text{ o menino}] [_{V'} [_V [\text{parti-}] [_{N''} \text{ o vidro}]]]]]$

Some questions arise, when we compare sentence (14a) with its D-structure configuration (22): (i) does the external argument remain *in situ* at S-structure? (ii) when and how do the affixes in I combine with the verb root?

We will try to answer question (i) in Section 5 and question (ii) in Section 6.

5 X-bar Theory and Case Theory

It has been argued since [Chomsky and Lasnik, 1977] that NPs are categories which must be marked with a special syntactic relationship in order to be visible to PF-rules. This idea has been elaborated upon the notion of morphological case: as it is well known, many natural languages use (or used at some stage of its evolution) morphological case as a device to mark grammatical functions — Greek and Latin used morphological case, so does contemporary German, and residues of case distinctions still survive in the personal pronoun paradigm of English and, more extensively, of Romance languages.

In GB theory, it is assumed that, even in languages lacking case morphology, abstract (or syntactic) Case plays a role. The system of principles responsible for Case assignment and for licensing conditions related to Case matters is Case theory. The crucial principle of Case theory is the Case Filter — which is believed to have two "sides", a phonological "side" (see (23i)) and a semantic "side" (see (23ii)).

(23) **Case Filter**

    i. Every NP with phonetic content must be Case marked;

    ii. Every argument NP (distinct from PRO) must be Case marked[21].

(23i) is supposed to be relevant for PF, whereas (23ii) is supposed to be relevant for LF.

Another assumption embodied in Case theory is that Case is assigned under government by certain X^0 categories: specifically, [-N] lexical categories — that is, V and P — and I (provided I is positively specified for AGR). I assigns nominative Case, V assigns accusative Case and, in Romance languages, P assigns oblique Case[22].

Note that (23i) and (23ii) are not redundant: (23i) applies to NPs not covered by (23ii) and vice-versa. Let us consider expletive NPs like weather *it* (in sentences like

---

[21]This does not apply to PRO, the empty category occurring in subject position in untensed clauses, due to the fact that its conflicting properties with respect to Binding theory restrict its distribution to ungoverned contexts, and that is, to contexts where it cannot be assigned Case.

[22]On the contrary, it has been claimed that, in English, prepositions are accusative Case assigners. See [Kayne, 1981].

it rains, it will snow tomorrow) or the *it* associated with extraposed clausal subjects (in sentences like *it surprised me that he insulted you*)[23]. In neither of the cases above mentioned is *it* an argument of the verb predicates *rain, snow, surprise*. Hence, by (23ii), it should not be submitted to the Case Filter; however, by (23i), it must.

It happens to be the case that expletives have the distribution predicted by (23i). In fact, in contexts where there is no source for nominative Case — e.g., in untensed clauses where I is [- AGR][24] — , weather *it* is excluded — see the contrast between (24a) and (24b).

(24) a.   I think [$_{IP}$ it will rain tomorrow]
      b.   * I think [$_{IP}$ it to rain tomorrow]

On the other hand, (23ii) makes the right prediction in what concerns the distribution of empty arguments. So, for instance, in Portuguese, the empty subject of both tensed embedded clauses and inflected infinitives is allowed to be disjoint in reference from the subject of the root-sentence (see (25)).

(25) a.   [O professor]$_i$ lamenta [que [-]$_j$ o$_{i/k}$ tenham enganado]
           [The teacher]$_i$ regrets [that they$_j$ have cheated him$_{i/k}$]
      b.   [O professor]$_i$ lamenta [[-]$_j$ terem-no$_{i/k}$ enganado]
           [The teacher]$_i$ regrets [[-]$_j$ to have+3+plu him$_{i/k}$ cheated]
           [The teacher]$_i$ regrets [that they$_j$ have cheated him$_{i/k}$]

On the contrary, the empty subject of untensed embedded clauses where the inflected infinitive is not allowed — e.g., the case of volitional predicates clausal complements[25] — cannot be disjoint in reference from the subject of the root-clause (see (26)).

(26) a.   [O professor]$_i$ não quer [que [[-]$_j$ o$_{i/k}$ enganem]
           [The teacher]$_i$ doesn't want [that they$_j$ cheat him$_{i/k}$]
           [The teacher]$_i$ doesn't want [them$_j$ to cheat him$_{i/k}$]
      b.   * [O professor]$_i$ não quer [[-]$_j$ enganarem-no$_{i/k}$]
           [The teacher]$_i$ doesn't want [[-]$_j$ to cheat+3+plu him$_{i/k}$]
           [The teacher]$_i$ doesn't want [them$_j$ to cheat him$_{i/k}$]
      c.   [O professor]$_i$ não quer [[-]$_i$ enganá-lo$_j$]
           [The teacher]$_i$ doesn't want [[-]$_i$ to cheat him$_j$]

---

[23]Even in a Null Subject language like Portuguese, expletives parallel to English *it* may occur marginally: e.g. *ele há cada uma!* (literally, *it exists each one!*, meaning roughly *what an amazing/unexpected thing!*) is a marginal way to say *há cada uma!*.

[24]In languages where I is specified for Tense and Agreement, the unmarked option seems to be the following one: if I is [- T], then it is [- AGR]; in this respect, Portuguese represents the marked option, since in [- T] contexts, I may be [+ AGR] — that is what happens in inflected infinitive contexts. See [Raposo, 1987].

[25]See [Raposo, 1987].

The contrast between (25b) and (26b) is captured if we assume that the base-generated empty category pro — the null counterpart of pronouns — is able to be disjoint in reference, whereas PRO, a pronominal anaphor, is not. And we get a plausible explanation for paradigms (25) and (26) if we follow claim in [Rizzi, 1986] that pro needs Case to be licensed. In fact, the empty embedded subject of (25) and (26) is allowed to have disjoint reference in precisely those contexts where it is assigned Case (by [+ AGR] I) — that is, where it is pro.

Let us now consider again sentence (14a) and its D-structure representation (22):

(14) a. *O menino partiu o vidro.*
          The kid broke the glass.

(22) $[_{I''}[_{N''} -] [_{I'}[_{I} \text{ T AGR}] [_{V''}[_{N''} \text{ o menino}] [_{V'} [_{V} \text{ [parti-]}] [_{N''} \text{ o vidro}]]]]]$

Let us recall what we have said before; when we compare sentence (14a) with its D-structure configuration (22), the first question one may ask is whether the external argument remains *in situ* at S-structure.

The answer to this question is given by Case theory. Both "sides" of the Case Filter require the external argument *o menino* to be Case-marked. As Case is assigned under government, I cannot assign nominative Case to the D-structure position occupied by the external argument — the SPEC position of the maximal projection V'' — (see the definitions of *government* and *intervene* above). Hence, in order to satisfy the Case Filter, the external argument is forced to move to a non θ-marked Case-marked position, the only one available in (22) being the SPEC position of I'', as shown in (27):

(27) $[_{I''}[_{N''} \text{ o menino}]_i [_{I'}[_{I} \text{ T AGR}] [_{V''}[_{N''} \text{ t}]_i [_{V'} [_{V} \text{ [parti-]}] [_{N''} \text{ o vidro}]]]]]$

(27) is obtained through the application of Move-α to (22): it satisfies the Projection Principle — the trace of the moved NP occupies the D-structure position to which the external θ-role of the verb is assigned —, the θ-Criterion and the Case Filter. Let us now see if this representation obeys other well-formedness conditions constraining Move-α and the distribution of the traces left by this rule.

6 X-bar Theory and Movement: Lexical vs. Functional Heads

The constraints on Move-α (or its output, depending on whether we adopt a derivational or a representational approach) may be considered as specific answers to the following questions: (i) what can be moved? (ii) where to? (iii) how? (iv) how far apart can a moved constituent and its trace be?

The answer to the first question is given in X-bar terms: Move-α applies to heads and to maximal projections.

The second question concerns the landing site problem. A partial answer to this question is given by the θ-Criterion: the target of any movement must be a non-thematic position. It is X-bar theory that provides the other part of the answer: a head can only move to another head position; a maximal projection can only move to another maximal projection position[26].

In what concerns the third question, it has been assumed that constituents may be moved either by substitution or by adjunction. Move-α by substitution operates when the target position is an empty SPEC or head position; otherwise, it operates by adjunction. Both substitution and adjunction must meet the requirement referred to in the last paragraph.

What was said in the last paragraphs may be summarized in (28):

(28) **Conditions on Movement**

    i. Move-α operates either by substitution or by adjunction;

    ii. Only heads and maximal projections are visible for Move-α;

    iii. Only X^0 can move to head position;

    iv. Only X'' can move to maximal projection position;

    v. A maximal projection can adjoin only to non-argument X''.

Sentences (29a) and (29b) illustrate movement by substitution of a maximal projection ($= N''$) to SPEC of *IP* position — these are standard cases of what was first called NP-Movement; (29c) illustrates a similar case under a recent analysis of quantifier floating[27]:

(29)   a.   *A manteiga derreteu t.*
            The butter melted.

      b.   *A decisão foi aprovada t pela direcção.*
            The decision was approved t by the board.

      c.   *Os candidatos foram todos t rejeitados.*
            The candidates were all t rejected.

Sentences (30) illustrate a case of movement by adjunction in topicalization constructions. The contrast between (30a) and (30b) might suggest that in Portuguese topicalized constituents can left-adjoin only to *IP*, along the lines proposed for English by [Baltin, 1982]:

(30)   a.   O João jurou [$_{CP}$ que [$_{IP}$ à Maria, [$_{IP}$ não volta a telefonar t]]]
            João swore that, to Maria, he won't phone again.

      b.   * O João jurou [$_{CP}$ Maria, [$_{CP}$ que [$_{IP}$ não volta a telefonar t]]]
            João swore, to Maria, that he won't phone again.

---

[26]See [Chomsky, 1986a] p. 4. This requirement calls to mind Emonds's Structure Preserving Condition.

[27]See [Sportiche, 1988].

However, this first conclusion turns out to be wrong. In fact, the well-formedness of sentences like (31a) below shows that adjunction to CP is a legitimate landing site for topicalized constituents in Portuguese; besides, the ill-formedness of sentences like (31b) shows that not every IP node is a legitimate landing site for such constituents:

(31) a. [$_{CP}$ À Maria, [$_{CP}$ quando é que telefonaste t?]]
          To Mary, when did you phone?
      b. * O João quer [$_{IP}$ esse livro, [$_{IP}$ ler t]]

Paradigms (30) and (31) get a straightforward explanation if we assume the condition on adjunction stated in (28v) above holds: in the well-formed (a) sentences of both (30) and (31) a constituent is adjoined to a nonargument maximal projection, whereas in the ill-formed (b) sentences the topicalized constituent is adjoined to an argument maximal projection.

Finally, the locality problem (see question (iv) above) concerns several systems of principles.

In the first place, it concerns Bounding theory, the main principle of this system being Subjacency:

(32) **Subjacency**

No instance of Move-α can cross more than one barrier.

We will adopt the following definition of barrier:

(33) **Barrier**

Every non-θ-marked fully specified maximal projection of a functional head is a barrier[28].

According to the definition in (33), only maximal projections of functional heads having the SPEC position filled[29] can be barriers for a potential governor. These include C'' (= CP), the maximal projection of COMP (= C^0)[30], I'' (= IP), D'' (= DP) — the maximal projection of a determiner[31] — and Q'' (= QP) — the maximal projection of a quantifier). Throughout, the only functional X'' that will concern us will be I'' (= IP).

We can now re-define government in terms of the concept of *barrier*:

---

[28] See [Fukui and Speas, 1986].

[29] See [Fukui and Speas, 1986] p. 154-55.

[30] [Chomsky, 1986a] has proposed to generalize X-bar theory to the COMP system. See [Chomsky, 1986a] p. 3.

[31] See [Abney, 1987].

(34) **Government**

α **governs** β iff:

i. $\alpha = X^0$ [32]; and

ii. α **m-commands** β; and

iii. there is no barrier that dominates β and does not dominate α[33].

In the second place, the locality problem concerns Government theory — in particular, it is assumed that, in order to be licensed, traces must be in a specific relationship of government, called *proper government*. The principle that expresses this claim is the E(mpty) C(ategory) P(rinciple):

(35) **ECP**

α **properly governs** β if α **governs** β and:

a. α is a lexical head — lexical government

or:

b. α is co-indexed with β — antecedent government[34].

It should be noted that lexical government — the specific variety of proper government defined in the ECP — is supposed to be directional — contrary to government "tout court". It is assumed that the directionality of lexical government is a consequence of parameter setting — specifically, a consequence on the value fixed for the Headedness Parameter. If a language fixes the value `initial` for the Headedness Parameter, lexical government operates from left to right — that is the case of Portuguese; if a language fixes the value `final` for the Headedness Parameter, lexical government operates from right to left — that is the case of Japanese. Note also that it follows from the definitions of government and of proper government that antecedent government is subject to severe locality constraints: no barrier can intervene between the governor and the governee.

In the third place, the locality problem concerns Binding Theory, since it is assumed that every instance of Move-α creates a configuration where the moved category serves as an antecedent for its trace.

Bearing in mind the conditions and principles introduced in this section, let us consider again representation (22):

(22) $[_{I''}[_{N''} -] [_{I'}[_{I} \text{ T AGR}] [_{V''}[_{N''} \text{ o menino}] [_{V'} [_{V} \text{ [parti-]}] [_{N''} \text{ o vidro}]]]]]$

---

[32]When the kind of government involved is antecedent-government maximal projections also qualify as governors.

[33]See [Chomsky, 1986a] p. 8.

[34]See [Lasnik and Saito, 1984] p. 240. Some authors have claimed that the ECP should have a conjunctive and not a disjunctive formulation — that is, that both lexical and antecedent government should be needed for the trace licensing. We will adopt here the disjunctive version along the lines of [Lasnik and Saito, 1984].

Move-α has applied to a maximal projection, the target position is also a maximal projection and, as required by the θ-Criterion, a non-thematic one. It correctly operated by substitution. Subjacency is respected, since the moved NP does not cross any barrier. The trace $[t]_i$ satisfies the ECP: although it is not lexically governed by V^0, it is antecedent-governed by $[o\ menino]_i$: they are co-indexed, the moved NP governs the trace and no barrier intervenes between the two. Hence, (22) is a well-formed syntactic representation.

We can now try to answer the last question formulated in Section 4: when and how do the affixes in I combine with the verb root?

[Emonds, 1978] and, more recently, [Pollock, 1989] have proposed that differences exhibited by French and English concerning, e.g., the distribution of adverbs, negation and quantifier floating are derivable from one single difference between the two languages: whereas French allows generalized Verb movement, English only allows Auxiliary verb movement[35]. Let us consider the following paradigms in English and in Portuguese, a language that allows generalized Verb movement even more extensively than French:

(36)   a.   *That girl often writes poems.*
       b.   * *That girl writes often poems.*

(37)   a.   ??/? *Essa rapariga frequentemente escreve poemas*[36].
       b.   *Essa rapariga escreve frequentemente poemas.*

(36) and (37) show a slight contrast in what concerns (a), and a sharp one in what concerns (b). The two paradigms get a straightforward explanation under the assumptions that: (i) VP-oriented adverbs are base-generated as left- (or right-) adjuncts to *VP*; (ii) Verb movement is restricted in English to Auxiliary verbs, whereas it applies to every verb class in Portuguese.

Given the two assumptions above, it follows that: (i) in every sentence of (23) the main verb must remain in its D-structure position — hence, VP-oriented adverbs may occur at its left (see the well-formedness of (36a)), but not in between the verb and its complements (see the ill-formed (36b)). In what concerns (37), the inflected verb of every sentence has moved to I; hence, (i) the order inflected verb-adverb is always possible (see (37b)); (ii) the order VP-oriented adverb-inflected verb is slightly marginal (see (37a)).

Note that *V-to-I* movement is a syntactic strategy producing a result similar to Affix-Hopping — an instance of Move-α applying at PF: they both take separate syntactic constituents — T and AGR features; verb roots — and combine them into a single constituent. A language like English must use both strategies; a language like Portuguese uses mainly (or perhaps exclusively) the syntactic one.

---

[35] [Pollock, 1989] derives this difference from the status of AGR in French (more generally, in Romance languages) and in English.

[36] The '??/?' signs refer to the interpretation of (24a) where no intonational breaks separate the adverb from the rest of the sentence.

Let us now consider again sentence (14a) and its syntactic representation (27):

(27) $[_{I''}[_{N''}$ o menino$]_i$ $[_{I'}[_I$ T AGR$]$ $[_{V''}[_{N''}$ t$]_i$ $[_{V'}$ $[_V$ [parti-$]$ $[_{N''}$ o vidro$]]]]]$

It follows from what we have said in the preceding paragraphs that V-to-I is the responsible for the combination of the affixes in I with the verb root; so, the S-structure representation of (14a), irrelevant details omitted, is the one given in (38):

(38) $[_{I''}[_{N''}$ o menino$]_i$ $[_{I'}[_{IV}$ [parti-$]_j$ $[_I$ T AGR$]]$ $[_{V''}[_{N''}$ t$]_i$ $[_{V'}$ $[_V$ $[v]_j$ $[_{N''}$ o vidro$]]]]]$

Note that the instance of Move-α that yields (38) correctly left-adjoins a head V to another head I, and both Subjacency and the ECP are satisfied: (i) the moved head does not cross more that one barrier (in fact, it crosses none); (ii) its trace is antecedent-governed.

7   X-bar Theory and Binding

Binding theory is the system of principles ruling the distribution of (full and empty) NPs.

Such paradigms as the ones in (39)-(41) show that not every kind of NP is free to be either referentially independent or referentially dependent in every syntactic context:

(39)   a.   Ele apresentou [a Maria e a Paula]$_i$ **[uma à outra]**$_i$.
             He introduced [Maria and Paula]$_i$ to [each other]$_i$.
       b.   * [A Maria e a Paula]$_i$ disseram que o João apresentou
             [os amigos]$_j$ **[uma à outra]**$_i$.
             * [Maria and Paula]$_i$ said that João introduced
             [his friends]$_j$ to [each other]$_i$.

(40)   a.   * [A testemunha]$_i$ viu-[a]$_i$ na estação de comboio.
             * [The witness]$_i$ saw [her]$_i$ at the railway station.
       b.   [A testemunha]$_i$ disse que o assassino [a]$_i$ viu na estação
             de comboio.
             [The witness]$_i$ said that the murderer saw [her]$_i$ at the
             railway station.

(41)   a.   * [Ela]$_i$ ouviu [a Maria]$_i$ na rádio.
             * [She]$_i$ heard [Maria]$_i$ on the radio.
       b.   * [Ela]$_i$ disse que o João ouviu [a Maria]$_i$ na rádio.
             * [She]$_i$ said João heard [Maria]$_i$ on the radio.

The sentences in (39) show that NPs like the ones in bold need to have a "close enough" antecedent — that is, are intrinsic referentially dependent expressions (we will precise below what "close enough"means). (40a) shows that NPs like the one in bold cannot have a "close enough" antecedent; (40b) shows that such NPs accept a "distant" antecedent, although they do not need it: (40b) is perfectly OK under the interpretation where the person the witness said that the murderer had seen at the railway station was not the witness herself). Finally, (41) shows that NPs like the bold ones cannot have (either a "close enough" or a "distant") antecedent.

Binding theory elaborates on the behaviour exhibited by NPs in such paradigms as the one in (39) to (41) and proposes the following typology for nominal expressions: NPs (more precisely, their heads) are categories marked for the features [-anaphoric, pronominal]. As usual, such features of supposed to be binary; hence, it is predicted that four different subtypes of nominal expressions are to be found in natural languages:

(42) i.   [+ anaphoric, + pronominal]
      ii.   [+ anaphoric, - pronominal]
      iii. [- anaphoric, + pronominal]
      iv.   [- anaphoric, - pronominal]

Type (42i) is restricted to the empty category PRO, and will not be our concern here; type (42ii) covers anaphors (both lexical anaphors and (NP-)traces); type (42iii) covers pronominals (that is, pronouns and the empty category pro); finally, type (42iv) covers R(eferential-)expressions: names and variables. Given this typology , our comments on the paradigm above might be restated as: anaphors need a "close enough" antecedent; pronominals must not have a "close enough" antecedent, although they accept a "distant" one; R-expressions do not accept antecedents at all.

The claims made above may be considered too strong and falsified by empirical facts, unless we precise what is meant by antecedent in this context. In the first place, recall that Binding theory, as the other systems of Grammar, does not work extra-sententially, that is, it works within the boundaries of (complex) sentences. So, it is not concerned with discourse anaphora since in this case the antecedent and the anaphoric term occur in different complex sentences. In the second place, for something to be considered an antecedent by Binding theory it is supposed to be related in a specific formal way to the anaphoric term. The claim is that this formal relation is binding, which may be defined as in (43):

(43) **Binding**

α **binds** β iff:
i. α **c-commands** β; and
ii. α and β are co-indexed[37].

The idea that c-command is necessary for binding is supported by such contrasts such as those existing between the ill-formed cases (40a)-(41) and well-formed sentences like (44):

---

[37]See [Chomsky, 1982] p. 20.

(44)   Quando conhecem [a **Maria**]$_i$, todos acham que [**ela**]$_i$ é simpática.
       When they meet [Maria]$_i$, they all think [she]$_i$ is nice.

In (44), the bold NPs are interpreted as co-referential; however, neither binds the other one. In fact, the R-expression *a Maria* is inside the V' of an adjunct clause: so, its c-command domain only includes the V node of that clause; as for the pronominal *ela*, it is in the SPEC of I'' position of an embedded complement clause: so, its c-command domain only includes its sister node I'.

It should also be added that binding is sensitive to the "type" of position occupied by the potential antecedents: only antecedents occupying certain types of syntactic positions are visible for Binding theory. Such positions are the so-called Apositions, that is, complement positions and SPEC positions of every category but C''.

We can now define more accurately the binding conditions on anaphors, pronominals and R-expresssions:

(45)   **Binding Principles**

Principle A: An anaphor must be bound in a local domain α.

Principle B: A pronominal must be free in a local domain α.

Principle C: An R-expression must be free everywhere[38].

(Where "free" means "not bound")

Let us precise what is meant by "local domain α" in (45). It is the syntactic domain containing the relevant NP, its governor and a SUBJECT — in the sense of the most prominent nominal element of that syntactic domain. This domain is called governing category (GC) and may be defined as in (46):

(46)   **Governing category**

α is the governing category for β if α is the minimal maximal projection containing β, the governor of β and a SUBJECT[39]. (Where SUBJECT may be: AGR, with respect to I''; a subject NP, with respect to NPs and small clauses)

Let us consider again the paradigm in (39)-(41), repeated below:

---

[38] In fact, if we want Principle C to apply to variables we have to formulate it along the following lines: an R-expression is free in the domain of the operator that locally A'-binds it.

It should also be noted that in equative sentences (e.g., *eu sou a Maria* (= *I am Maria*)) Principle C is cancelled — cf. [Evans, 1980]. The same is true of sentences with predicates like Portuguese *chamar-se* or French *s'appeler* (e.g., *chamo-me Maria*, *je m'appelle Maria* — literally *I call myself Maria*).

[39] See [Chomsky, 1981] p. 211.

(39) a.   Ele apresentou [a Maria e a Paula]$_i$ [**uma à outra**]$_i$.
        He introduced [Maria and Paula]$_i$ to [each other]$_i$.

     b.   * [A Maria e a Paula]$_i$ disseram que o João apresentou
        [os amigos]$_j$ [**uma à outra**]$_i$.
        * [Maria and Paula]$_i$ said that João introduced
        [his friends]$_j$ to [each other]$_i$.

(40) a.   * [A testemunha]$_i$ viu-[a]$_i$ na estação de comboio.
        * [The witness]$_i$ saw [her]$_i$ at the railway station.

     b.   [A testemunha]$_i$ disse que o assassino [a]$_i$ viu na estação
        de comboio.
        [The witness]$_i$ said that the murderer saw [her]$_i$ at the
        railway station.

(41) a.   * [Ela]$_i$ ouviu [a **Maria**]$_i$ na rádio.
        * [She]$_i$ heard [Maria]$_i$ on the radio.

     b.   * [Ela]$_i$ disse que o João ouviu [a **Maria**]$_i$ na rádio.
        * [She]$_i$ said João heard [Maria]$_i$ on the radio.

We see that in (39a) the GC for the anaphor is the root sentence: in its GC, the anaphor is bound by the NP with the grammatical function of direct object and, thus, Principle A of Binding Theory is satisfied. But in (39b) the GC for the anaphor is the embedded I'': but this time, the anaphor is not bound in its GC, Principle A is not satisfied, and the sentence is ruled out. In (40a), the GC for the pronominal is the root clause: in its GC the pronominal is bound by the subject NP, thus violating Principle B and hence, the sentence is ruled out under the bound interpretation of the pronoun; on the contrary, in (40b) the GC for the pronoun is the embedded I'': in its GC it is free, satisfying Principle B. In (41), the concept of GC plays no role, due to the formulation of Principle C; according to this principle, the relevant R-expression must be free everywhere: this is not the case in both (41a) and (41b).

8 Conclusion

We have shown that in GB theory X-bar theory plays a crucial role.

In the first place, it constrains the format of syntactic representations in a radical way, thus allowing Grammar to do without specific phrase structure rules (except for a residue of language particular phenomena), and contributing "to account for the relative ease of language acquisition and the impossibility of certain language types". At the same time, since some of its principles are associated with parameters, X-bar theory is a flexible enough tool to account for language variation.

In the second place, X-bar theory makes it possible to "translate" into configurational terms lexical properties on which are based distinctions between arguments and adjuncts;

moreover, the translation of such properties into configurational terms makes it possible to distinguish structurally between external and internal arguments — a distinction that is well supported by empirical facts.

Finally, X-bar theory (together with c-command or some of its variants) provides the referential frame for the formulation of local relations (e.g., government, proper government, Case-assignment, θ-assignment) and of local domains (e.g., for movement and binding). In particular, the distinction between lexical and functional heads plays a crucial role in the definition of barriers for government and movement.

Information-Based Linguistics and Head-Driven Phrase Structure

Sergio Balari Ravera

EUROTRA-España

Avda. Vallvidrera 25–27 — Barcelona — Spain

1 Introduction

In the last few years, those branches of linguistic theory that have kept a closer look to the new developments within such neighboring disciplines as computer science, philosophy, logic and psycholinguistics have been moving toward an approach to the study of natural languages in which the notion of *information* plays a central role. Consequently, linguistic objects are considered as bearers of information. This slight methodological shift (I do not think one can claim it is a new linguistic paradigm) has the advantage of providing new intellectual and formal tools for the study of language, which may prove very useful in the attainment of the ultimate goals of linguistic theory. Thus, along with the traditional questions faced by linguistics (see e.g. [Chomsky, 1986b], [Chomsky, 1988]):

i. What constitutes knowledge of language?

ii. How is knowledge of language acquired?

iii. How is knowledge of language put to use?

iv. What are the physical mechanisms that serve as the material basis for this system of knowledge and for the use of this knowledge?

we may assume that by taking the information-based view to linguistics one will find useful to try to answer the following instrumental questions:

a. What kind of information is represented in linguistic objects?

b. How do the different kinds of information interact with each other?

c. How is information represented and structured in linguistic objects?

That there is in fact some connection between the answers we may find to the questions in (a–b) with the ultimate answers to (i–iv) may become clearer if we consider some quick examples. If we hypothesize that phonological, syntactic and semantic information (whatever it may be)[1] is simultaneously present in linguistic representations versus an hypothesis in which each type of information is found in different representations, we are making a strong claim about the nature of the interface of the different components, which may form the basis for an answer to question (iii); on this matter see for example [Altmann, 1987]. Similarly, by making hypothesis about how is information structured in lexical entries and how it is further structured when lexical entries are combined to form phrases, we will have a clue of how the rules and principles of grammar should work and, consequently, a first answer to question (i); moreover, if we are able to draw a principled distinction between those rules and principles that are necessary to account for language particular issues and those that seem to have a universal basis, we will be opening a path to a solution to the logical problem of language acquisition, i.e. an answer to question (ii); see [Grimshaw, 1981] for some observations about the implications for acquisition of this and the previous hypotheses.

In this paper I would like to introduce Head-driven Phrase Structure Grammar (henceforth HPSG), one of the major representatives of information-based linguistics, as it is developed in Carl Pollard and Ivan Sag's book *Information-Based Syntax and Semantics* ([Pollard and Sag, 1987]; henceforth IBSS) and further work. HPSG has its roots in several contemporary approaches to the study of natural languages like GPSG ([Gazdar *et al.*, 1985]), LFG ([Bresnan, 1982]), GB ([Chomsky, 1981]), FUG ([Kay, 1985]), Categorial Grammar, etc., from which it borrows many interesting ideas.

One of the features of HPSG I take to be the most appealing to those who are interested in any area of research related to natural languages is that it provides a very rich formal basis to model linguistic knowledge. More interestingly, HPSG has not committed itself to very strong programmatic issues apart from those expressed by questions (a–c) above. This makes HPSG a rather eclectic and open-minded theory which, as we mentioned, leaves the linguist considerable freedom to borrow, synthesize and reelaborate insights coming from other linguistic theories. From this facts, one should not consider HPSG as a kind of anti-theory or as a grammatical formalism good for natural language processing but unable to build interesting empirical hypotheses about the nature of language; rather, this just means that HPSG is not constrained by substantive claims like, for instance, the idea that grammatical relations should be considered as primitives of the theory. On the contrary, HPSG looks at this claims as more or less

---

[1]Question (a) is intimately related to the much more difficult to answer question (a'):

a'. What is and what is not linguistic information?

In fact, between the information that the word *green* is an adjective and the information that my grandmother likes green because it reminds her of the fields of the Basque Country where she was born (as the two extremes of what is linguistic and what is not), mediates a large gray area of types of information whose classification is surely controversial.

good working hypotheses that the linguist should be ready to abandon or to accept on the light of new evidence (this position is particularly clear in the introduction to IBSS and in [Pollock, 1989]). It is obvious, however, that HPSG is not totally unconstrained, but, while it lacks global constraints of the kind we mentioned above almost completely, its restrictiveness comes from its formal architecture, a methodological strategy already advocated within GPSG.

As the authors point out in IBSS "The fundamental nature of linguistic information remains a mystery" (IBSS, p. 27). But this is not, of course, a motivation for considering the enterprise of information-based linguistics impossible. They go on saying: "[s]till, although we are not sure what linguistic information is, we can still theorize about it trying to say what it is like. To be more precise, we can try to construct formal *models* that reflect certain interesting aspects of the things we are studying" (IBSS, p. 27). In fact, we can follow the practice of most natural sciences in constructing mathematical models of what we are studying, but to do that we need a formalism. A formalism which shows accurate enough to make predictions about the nature of language and linguistic information, and which is able to accommodate our own observations. It is clear, then, that the choice of a formalism is a crucial issue one cannot neglect. Thus, I will spend some time, before I start with other aspects of the HPSG theory, examining its formal foundations. This will be the topic of the following subsection. Next, I will focus on linguistic issues; there I will consider some of the main aspects of the HPSG theory of linguistic information as set forth in IBSS as well as some improvements and extensions. Finally, I leave the final section of this paper to some concluding remarks.

2 Head-Driven Phrase Structure Grammar

2.1 The Formal Architecture

2.1.1 Feature Structures

The formal foundations of HPSG come at least from two different sources: one is the GPSG framework developed by [Gazdar *et al.*, 1985] and the Head Grammars (HG) developed by Carl Pollard in his thesis ([Pollard, 1984]);[2] the other is the LFG theory (cf. [Kaplan and Bresnan, 1982] for the more formal aspects) and the FUG formalism ([Kay, 1985]). All these theories and formalisms, though different in many respects, share some particular design choices of how a grammar formalism should look like. Following Shieber ([Shieber, 1986]) we can summarize these requirements as follows:

- *surface-based*: providing a direct characterization of the actual surface order of string elements in a sentence;

---

[2]In fact, HPSG was born at the Hewlett Packard laboratories as a result of research into implementation of GPSG. See, for some details, [Flickinger *et al.*, 1985]; and [Proudian and Pollard, 1985].

- *informational*: associating with the strings information from some informational domain;

- *inductive*: defining the association of strings and informational elements recursively, with new pairings being derived by merging substrings according to prescribed string combining operations, and merging the associated informational elements according to prescribed information-combining operations; and

- *declarative*: defining the association between strings and informational elements in terms of what associations are permissible, not how they are computed.

More specifically, we can say that these formalisms have all in common the answer they provide to question (c) above, namely, that information is represented and structured in linguistic objects in the form of *features*. A feature is an attribute-value pair like the following:

(1) $$number = singular$$

Where the value which is assigned to the attribute *number* is chosen from some arbitrary set of values, for example $\{singular, plural\}$.

To a certain extent, this is not a particularly innovative answer if we consider that the notion of feature can be traced back, in linguistic theory, at least as far as the work of Chomsky and Halle ([Chomsky and Halle, 1968]) on phonological representations. In fact, the notion of feature has played a very important role in phonological theory and — only recently — in syntactic theory. However, unlike phonology (see for example [Clements, 1985]; [van der Hulst and Smith, 1982]; [van der Hulst and Smith, 1985]) there are very few works in syntactic theory which have shown real interest in the theory of features, a notorious exception being the abovementioned theories. Particularly GPSG deserves the credit of trying to develop an articulated theory of syntactic categories by pursuing the idea, originally due to Chomsky ([Chomsky, 1970]), that they are not atomic entities, but, rather, *feature bundles*. Feature bundles are collections of features, which we usually represent as *feature matrices*:

(2)
$$\begin{bmatrix} category = noun \\ number = singular \\ person = 3 \\ gender = masculine \end{bmatrix}$$

The matrix (2) could be a partial representation of a lexical entry for the Spanish word *gato* (cat), among many others satisfying the same description. But we can do much more interesting things with features and feature matrices. Suppose we want to encode that the verb *comer* (eat), in its third person, singular form *come* requires a subject and an object to form a sentence like *el gato come sardinas* (the cat eats sardinas). In fact, we can represent subcategorization frames by allowing features to take complex values like the feature matrix in (2). Thus, we can have feature structures like the following:

$$
(3) \quad \left[\begin{array}{l} \text{category} = \text{verb} \\ \\ \text{frame} = \left[\begin{array}{l} \text{subject} = \left[\begin{array}{l} \text{category} = \text{noun} \\ \text{case} = \text{nominative} \\ \text{number} = \text{singular} \\ \text{person} = 3 \end{array} \right] \\ \\ \text{object} = \left[\begin{array}{l} \text{category} = \text{noun} \\ \text{case} = \text{accusative} \end{array} \right] \end{array} \right] \end{array} \right]
$$

In (3) we have the information that a verb like *come* has a frame which consists of two elements, a subject and an object; moreover, we have already the information of how the verb requires its subject and object to be. Note that we have added three new features — *frame, subject,* and *object* — with an obvious interpretation, but which, unlike the features we have been using so far, do not take atomic values, but arbitrary feature structures instead. This is, in fact, a fifth requirement shared by the formalisms above we may add to the previous ones, i.e. that the informational elements used to describe linguistic objects be complex-feature-based.

Given this potential for embedding features structures within features structures, it is useful to have the notion of a *path of attributes.* A path is just a finite sequence of attributes, so that we can generalize the notion of value of an attribute to the notion of value of a path. For example, in (3) we have the path *frame|subject|case* whose value is the path *nominative,* and the path *frame|object|case* whose value is the path *accusative.*[3] The notion of path is better understood if we look at feature structures as graph-theoretical objects; more specifically, as rooted, directed, acyclic graphs (*dags,* for short) where non-value features are represented by directed arcs labelled with features, feature structures are represented by (sub)graphs, and atomic feature values are graph nodes labelled with the values which have no outgoing arcs. Thus, the dag representation of (3) is that of Figure 1.

We can learn some more things about feature structures from our example in (3). If we compare the feature structures which are values of the path *frame|subject* and the path *frame|object* we see that the former contains more information than the latter; in fact, it contains the same kind of information (i.e. about category and case) plus some additional agreement information (about number and person), but still both feature structures are partial in the sense that both may be descriptions of many more nominal elements that could function as subject and object of *come.* A natural way to look at feature structures is as *partial information structures,* that is as structures which encode partial information about linguistic objects. By looking at them this way, we can define relations and operations between feature structures depending on their informational content. On the basis of the degree of informativeness of feature structures we can look at the whole set of feature structures as partially ordered according to the *subsumption*

---

[3]It is useful to regard atomic values such as *accusative* or *nominative* as being themselves feature structures of a very simple kind in which the only path is the empty path (i.e. the sequence of attributes of length zero).

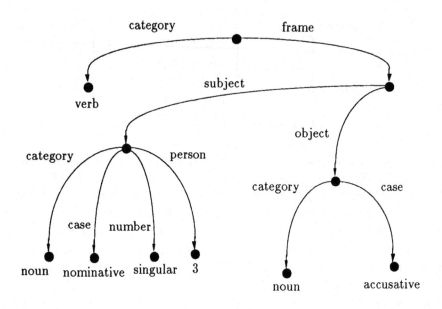

Figure 1: Dag representation for feature structure (3)

relation. In general, two feature structures A and B stand in the subsumption relation if A is equally informative or more informative than B, in which case we say that B subsumes A, written $A \leq B$.[4] Informally, we can think of subsumption as making a statement about the ability of feature structures to describe linguistic objects, such that if A appropriately describes a certain object, so does B. An immediate consequence of this ordering based on the amount of information contained by feature structures is the existence of a feature structure which contains no information at all and, consequently, subsumes all other feature structures. This feature structure is usually represented as in (4):

(4)   [ ]

Note that the subsumption relation $\leq$ defines an algebraic structure over the domain of feature structures, namely a *reflexive partial ordering* with the following properties:

(5)

i. reflexive: for every A, $A \leq A$

---

[4]Some authors use the term *extension* as the inverse of subsumption. That is, everything being equal in the example above, we can say that A *extends* (or is an *extension* of) B, and still write $A \leq B$.

ii. transitive: if $A \leq B$ and $B \leq C$, then $A \leq C$

iii. antisymmetric: if $A \leq B$ and $B \leq A$, then $A = B$

The ordering has a maximum element, that is the totally uninformative feature structure (4) which is often known as the *top*, written $\top$.

The previous discussion, in which we have examined some algebraic properties of feature structures, leads us to a crucial issue in the formal basis of information-based linguistics. So far we have been looking at feature structures as mere information carriers, but feature structures, as descriptions of linguistic objects, have a potential ability to combine with other feature structures to produce larger ones. Thus, pursuing our algebraic interpretation, we can define an operation which allows us to combine feature structures in such a way that all the information contained in both operands is also contained in the result. This operation is called *unification* and it is central to the formalisms used in information-based linguistics, which are also known as *unification-based formalisms*.[5]

We can define unification in terms of subsumption as follows: the unification of feature structures A and B (written $A \wedge B$) is that feature structure C, such that $C \leq A$ and $C \leq B$. Thus, C is the greatest lower bound of A and B with respect to the subsumption ordering. Let us see an example:

$$(6) \quad \begin{bmatrix} \text{category} = \text{noun} \\ \text{agreement} = [\ \text{number} = \text{singular}\ ] \end{bmatrix}$$

$$(7) \quad \begin{bmatrix} \text{category} = \text{noun} \\ \text{agreement} = \begin{bmatrix} \text{person} = \text{third} \\ \text{gender} = \text{masculine} \end{bmatrix} \end{bmatrix}$$

Just as our previous example (2), both (6) and (7) could be partial descriptions of a lexical entry for *gato*. We have only introduced the refinement of gathering all agreement information in a single feature structure, which will be useful later. However, (6) and (7) by themselves do not provide the same information as (2), but their unification (8) does:

$$(8) \quad \begin{bmatrix} \text{category} = \text{noun} \\ \text{agreement} = \begin{bmatrix} \text{person} = \text{third} \\ \text{number} = \text{singular} \\ \text{gender} = \text{masculine} \end{bmatrix} \end{bmatrix}$$

---

[5] At this point it may be fair to clarify a few points as to what the terms information-based, feature-based, unification-based refer to. Following Shieber ([Shieber, 1987]), we can conceive of the structure of a linguistic theory as a series of relations. First we have a *theory* (say, $HPSG$) which somehow restricts the *formalism* (say, $HPSG_F$) in which an *analysis* (say, a grammar of Portuguese) is expressed, which, in turn, predicts the *analyses* of the constructions of the Portuguese language. Thus, the term information-based is to be related to the theory (i.e., $HPSG$ is an information-based linguistic theory), while the terms (complex) feature-based and unification-based should be related to the formalism (i.e., $HPSG_F$ is a complex-feature- and unification-based formalism). Thus, in principle, an information-based theory need not necessarily be complex-feature-based nor unification-based, and vice versa.

Observe that unification has quite interesting properties, particularly as far as identical information is concerned. In fact, in our example the unification of the substructure [*category = noun*], which is present in both operands, is the very same substructure; that is, unification behaves very much like set union with type-identical information. Similarly, the *agreement* path is kept as a single path, but in this case, being different the values in both operands, each piece of information is merged into a single value containing all the information found in the corresponding feature structures. In this case, dag notation also serves to clarify the issue, since unification can be seen as the result of superimposing two dags.

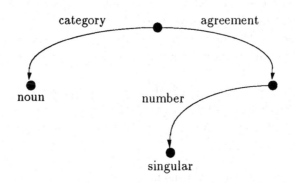

Figure 2: Dag representation for feature structure (6)

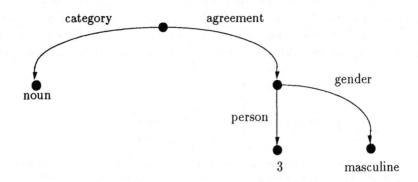

Figure 3: Dag representation for feature structure (7)

In Figure 2 and Figure 3 we have the dags corresponding to the feature structures in (6) and (7), and in Figure 4 we have their unification.

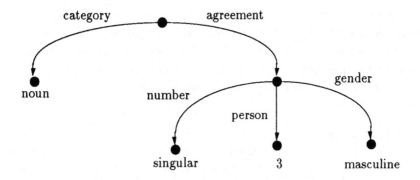

Figure 4: The unification of dags in Figure 2 and Figure 3

So far however we have been looking at well behaved examples of unification where the information contained in both operands is always consistent, but what would happen if we tried to unify two feature structures with inconsistent information, as for example in the case where the value of the *category* path in (6) were *verb* instead of *noun*? It is obvious that we have to disallow such unifications or, at least, we will have to give them a special status, on the contrary we would have descriptions of non-existent linguistic objects. Formally, we have two solutions: one is just assume that in these cases unification is not defined, it fails; another solution is assume that unification is defined just as in any other case, but that the result is a feature structure of a special type, one which contains too much information, which is overspecified to the point of being inconsistent and, consequently, which cannot be an appropriate description of any object. This feature structure would be the opposite of $\top$ (the top); it would be, in fact, the minimum element, the bottom (written $\bot$), in the $\leq$ ordering.

This last solution is the most attractive from the mathematical point of view, since we can have a more complete interpretation of the algebraic properties of subsumption and unification. In fact, we can establish the following axioms:

(9)

i. idempotency: $A \wedge A = A$

ii. commutativity: $A \wedge B = B \wedge A$

iii. associativity: $(A \wedge B) \wedge C = A \wedge (B \wedge C)$

iv. identity: $A \wedge \top = A$

v. zero: $A \wedge \bot = \bot$

Up to this point we have reviewed almost all basic properties of feature structures, but there is still one left. It is often the case that we want that two or more paths in a feature structure have the same value, i.e. that they *share* the same value. Feature structures have this property which we call *structure sharing*. Recall our example (3) that we repeat here as (10) with the new agreement path:

$$
(10) \quad
\begin{bmatrix}
\text{category} = \text{verb} \\[2pt]
\text{frame} =
\begin{bmatrix}
\text{subject} =
\begin{bmatrix}
\text{category} = \text{noun} \\
\text{case} = \text{nominative} \\
\text{agreement} =
\begin{bmatrix}
\text{number} = \text{singular} \\
\text{person} = 3
\end{bmatrix}
\end{bmatrix} \\[2pt]
\text{object} =
\begin{bmatrix}
\text{category} = \text{noun} \\
\text{case} = \text{accusative}
\end{bmatrix}
\end{bmatrix}
\end{bmatrix}
$$

Now suppose that we want to represent the fact that the verb agrees with its subject. We can do that just by introducing an *agreement* path for the verb and make it share its value with the *agreement* path of the subject as in (11), where boxed integers represent shared values:[6]

$$
(11) \quad
\begin{bmatrix}
\text{category} = \text{verb} \\[2pt]
\text{agreement} =
\begin{bmatrix}
\text{number} = \text{singular} \\
\text{person} = 3
\end{bmatrix}
\boxed{1} \\[2pt]
\text{frame} =
\begin{bmatrix}
\text{subject} =
\begin{bmatrix}
\text{category} = \text{noun} \\
\text{case} = \text{nominative} \\
\text{agreement} = \boxed{1}
\end{bmatrix} \\[2pt]
\text{object} =
\begin{bmatrix}
\text{category} = \text{noun} \\
\text{case} = \text{accusative}
\end{bmatrix}
\end{bmatrix}
\end{bmatrix}
$$

We say that the paths *agreement* and *frame|subject|agreement* are *reentrant*. As for their values, we say that they are *token-identical*. As before, the dag representation helps to understand the notions of reentrancy and token-identity. The relevant parts of feature structure (11) are represented in the dag in Figure 5.

It is interesting to see how reentrancy behaves with respect to unification. Consider the following semi-formal examples:

$$
(12) \quad a. \quad
\begin{bmatrix}
a = [c = d] \ \boxed{1} \\
b = [c = d] \ \boxed{1}
\end{bmatrix}
$$

$$
b. \quad
\begin{bmatrix}
a = [c = d] \\
b = [c = d]
\end{bmatrix}
$$

---

[6]Boxed integers is the standard convention for this.

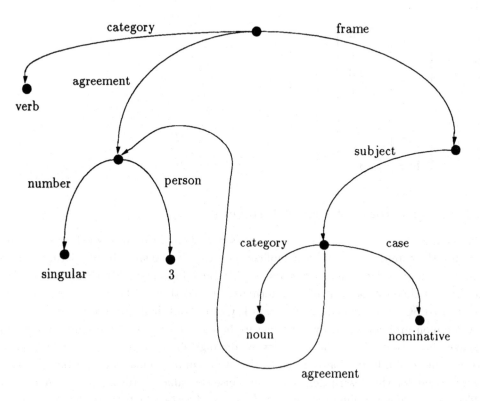

Figure 5: Partial dag representation of feature structure (11)

In (12a) a and b are reentrant, although we have represented two values for exemplification purposes, the boxed tags indicate that they are the same feature structure; the two occurrences of the feature structure $[c = d]$ are token-identical. On the other hand, in (12b) there is no reentrancy, the values of a and b are said to be *type-identical*. Suppose now that we unify $[a = [e = f]]$ to both (12a) and (12b). The result is that of (13a–b):

$$(13) \quad a. \quad \begin{bmatrix} a = \begin{bmatrix} c = d \\ e = f \end{bmatrix} \boxed{1} \\ b = \begin{bmatrix} c = d \\ e = f \end{bmatrix} \boxed{1} \end{bmatrix}$$

$$b. \quad \begin{bmatrix} a = \begin{bmatrix} c = d \\ e = f \end{bmatrix} \\ b = [c = d] \end{bmatrix}$$

2.1.2 Augmentations of Feature Structures

So far we have been reviewing those properties of feature structures which more or less constitute the common core of most unification-based formalisms. In the paragraphs to follow we will consider some extensions to this *basic* formalism, which have been felt necessary for the development of an information-based theory. They have in fact been central to HPSG in its modelling of certain key aspects of linguistic information.

A common problem faced by most feature-based approaches to the study of natural languages has always been the necessity to distinguish between cases in which some feature or piece of information is actually absent or, simply, remains unspecified because it is irrelevant for the description or just because its value is still unknown. A related problem is that of controlling the presence/absence of certain features in the appropriate places. For example, if we want to provide a description of some nominal element, we may want to have features representing its agreement properties like number, person, gender, but at the same time we do not want to have features that we would typically find in other categories (e.g. tense is usually found in verbs, but not in nouns).

It is obvious then that not all features are appropriate for all objects, but it is also obvious that the formalism we have reviewed so far does not provide any tool to account for this fact. Recall however that in our discussion about reentrancy we were using some implicit classification of feature structures when we distinguished between token- and type-identical values. Our first augmentation of the formalism will in fact consist in making explicit this classification by adding the notion of *type* of feature structure. That is, feature structures are classified in different types and each type is appropriate to describe different kinds of objects in virtue of the fact that different sets of attributes are appropriate for each type of feature structure. Types are usually expressed as subscripts to the left of the feature structure:

(14) $_{type}[\ ]$

Note that there is a crucial difference between (14) and [ ], because (14) being explicitly classified as belonging to a certain type is much more informative than [ ], since, even though no informational content is expressed, all linguistic information associated with that specific type is *already there*. For instance, if (14) were of type *agreement-value* it would contain *person*, *number* and *gender* features.

There is a clear connection between typing of feature structures and the subsumption ordering, since it seems natural to assume that the subsumption relation also holds between types, such that we can talk about *subtypes* and *supertypes* of some type t. This assumption has two immediate consequences: (i) any attribute which is appropriate for a given type is also appropriate for any subtype of that type; and (ii) if a given type requires that one of its attributes takes values of a certain type, then the same is true for any subtype of the given type. That is, feature structures of a certain type *inherit* all the attributes and corresponding type restrictions on their values from all of its supertypes. In addition to all the information inherited from its supertypes, a specific type may introduce new attributes of its own which distinguish it from other types at the same level in the ordering. We will illustrate this idea of inheritance with an example.

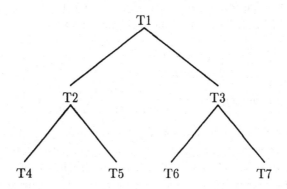

Figure 6: An example of type hierarchy

In Figure 6 we have a small type hierarchy with types $T1$ to $T7$. $T1$ is the top of the hierarchy and is characterized by containing attributes A, B and C. In virtue of the inheritance of information, attributes A, B and C will also be appropriate attributes for all subtypes of $T1$, i.e. from $T2$ to $T7$. So we already know part of the content of types $T2$ and $T3$, the immediate subtypes of $T1$; $T2$ is distinguished from $T3$ and $T1$ because it introduces attribute D, which is inherited by its subtypes $T4$ and $T5$. $T3$, in turn, introduces attribute E which distinguishes it from $T2$ and $T1$ and it is inherited by subtypes $T6$ and $T7$. Similarly with the rest of types, $T4$ is distinguished from $T5$

and $T2$ by introducing attribute F, $T5$ introduces attribute G, $T6$ attribute H and $T7$ attribute I.

Typing and inheritance are very powerful tools which, as we will see later, will prove very useful in developing a theory and a taxonomy of linguistic information.

Continuing with our task of enlarging the power of the formalism, let us return for a while to unification. Recall that we defined unification as an information-merging operation with striking similarities with set union, but also very similar to logical conjunction. It seems natural then to define new operations related to the logical notions of disjunction, negation and implication. The motivations for doing this are mainly linguistic, since there is plenty of situations in which it seems more natural to describe certain objects in a disjunctive or negative way. There are many of these cases, one is the German article *die* which is used in the nominative and accusative cases of singular feminine nouns and all plural nouns. This can be easily expressed using disjunction:

$$
(15) \quad \begin{bmatrix} \text{phonology} = \text{die} \\ \text{case} = \text{nominative} \vee \text{accusative} \\ \text{agreement} = \begin{bmatrix} \text{gender} = \text{feminine} \\ \text{number} = \text{singular} \end{bmatrix} \vee [\text{number} = \text{plural}] \end{bmatrix}
$$

Another example is that of English regular verbs in the present tense; as it is well known all forms in the paradigm are equal (e.g. *love*) with the exception of the third person singular form (e.g. *loves*). An economical way to express this is using negation:

$$
(16) \quad \begin{bmatrix} \text{phonology} = \text{love} \\ \text{tense} = \text{present} \\ \text{agreement} = \neg \begin{bmatrix} \text{person} = 3 \\ \text{number} = \text{singular} \end{bmatrix} \end{bmatrix}
$$

As for implication it is useful to express rules and principles of grammar, since it is often the case that we want to state that *if* some object satisfies description A *then* it must also satisfy description B. I will stop here my discussion of logical extensions to the formalism till the next section, since some formal problems arise with them as they are presented in IBSS. I will turn then to other extensions of feature structures.

So far, we have only seen attributes whose values were either atoms or feature structures, but it is possible to have other types of complex-valued features, namely list-valued and set-valued features; we will also consider the possibility that certain values be functionally dependent.

List-valued features take an ordered sequence of feature structures enclosed in angle brackets. An example of list-valued feature could be the *frame* attribute in example (11):

$$
(17) \quad \begin{bmatrix} \text{category} = \text{verb} \\ \text{frame} = \langle \text{OBJ}, \text{SUBJ} \rangle \end{bmatrix}
$$

Here, SUBJ and OBJ are abbreviations for features structures describing the corresponding objects.

It may be the case however that we want an attribute to take an unordered sequence of feature structures; in that case we can resort to set-valued features which we will represent as taking sequences of feature structures enclosed in curly brackets. As in the case of disjunction, negation and implication I will not pursue the matter here, since the functioning of list- and set-valued features will be more clearly understood when we discuss the linguistic aspects of HPSG.

Finally, we may want that the value of some attribute be functionally dependent on the values of other attributes. This is a particularly reasonable assumption taking into account that we will be working with lists and sets, so that in some cases we may need to express the fact that the value of some attribute is the result of appending (i.e. joining) two or more lists, or of taking the union of two or more sets. For example:

$$(18) \quad \left[\begin{array}{l} \text{a} = \boxed{1} \\ \text{b} = \left[\begin{array}{l} \text{c} = \text{append}(\, \boxed{1}\, ,\, \boxed{2}\,) \\ \text{d} = \boxed{2} \end{array} \right] \end{array} \right]$$

Where a, c and d are list-valued features, and the value of c is the result of appending the values of a and d.

2.1.3 Background and Further Issues

As we said before there are many linguistic theories apart from HPSG which employ some variant of the formalism we have discussed here. We already mentioned some of them like GPSG ([Gazdar et al., 1985]), and LFG ([Kaplan and Bresnan, 1982]), to which we could add CUG ([Karttunen, 1989]; [Uszkoreit, 1986]) and UCG ([Zeevat et al., 1987]). All have been influenced in some way or another by the work in FUG by Kay ([Kay, 1985]) and in the PATR II formalism ([Shieber, 1984]; [Shieber, 1986]; [Shieber et al., 1983], the second one being a very good introduction to unification-based grammatical formalisms).

Here we have not given a precise mathematical definition of the notion of feature and feature structure. Features are usually thought as partial functions from a set A of attributes to a set V of values. This idea was originally formalized within the GPSG framework and extended by Gazdar and others in their work on a logical language for category definition ([Gazdar and Pullum, 1987]; [Gazdar et al., 1986]). Reape ([Reape, 1989]) and Johnson ([Johnson, 1988]) make precise this interpretation for feature structures.

The first to note that negation and disjunction could be useful for unification-based formalisms was Karttunen ([Karttunen, 1984]). Since then many problems have been noted in connection with the exact interpretation of this (and other) operations within these formalisms, most of them related to the dichotomy feature structure vs. description of a feature structure. The main problem is what it means for an object to be a negated or disjunctive (or, for that matter, implicative) object. Karttunen's original interpretation was that negative and disjunctive feature specifications were *constraints* which were part of the feature structure itself about what kind of feature structures could be unified with them. So that, in Karttunen's view, there are no actual negative or disjunctive values, just constraints, but these constraints are part of the feature structure. Unfortunately Karttunen's paper was not able to settle down the issue and the confusion between objects and their description remains. Kaplan and Bresnan ([Kaplan and Bresnan, 1982]) made a clear distinction between linguistic objects and their description, but this distinction disappears in further work in unification grammars, particularly in HPSG when we read in IBSS that "linguistic information can be of a disjunctive, implicative (i.e. conditional), or negative nature" (p. 40). However, this idea leads to serious technical and philosophical problems concerning the semantics of unification formalisms and the nature of linguistic information. With the aim of solving this problem there has been considerable research on the semantics of grammar formalisms, which started with a seminal paper by Pereira and Shieber ([Pereira and Shieber, 1984]) and continued with the work by Kasper, Moshier, Rounds, Johnson and Pereira in feature logics ([Johnson, 1988]; [Kasper and Rounds, 1986]; [Kasper and Rounds, 1990]; [Moshier and Rounds, 1986]; [Pereira, 1987]; [Rounds and Kasper, 1986]). Now it seems that the question has been settled and that no identification is possible between an object and its description, rather it is necessary to keep the distinction because it seems to correspond to the distinction between the syntax of a logic and its semantics. Thus, negation, disjunction, implication may appear in the logical formulae of the language (the descriptions) but not in their denotations (the objects). This better understanding of the semantics of such grammar formalisms has facilitated the design of new and richer formalisms like CLG ([Balari *et al.*, 1990]; [Damas and Varile, 1989]) which in addition to all logical predicates incorporates quantification.

2.2 HPSG: A Sign-Based Theory

Now that we have characterized HPSG's formalism as complex-feature and unification-based, and we have given formal content to these notions, let us further characterize the information-based aspect of HPSG as a linguistic theory. Recall that the linguistic objects that make up a natural language are considered as bearers of information. We already know how we are going to model such linguistic objects, i.e. as feature structures, but we do not know what information we are going to find in them. More concretely, we have not yet provided an answer to the question of what sort of thing is a natural language object. According to HPSG a linguistic object is the combination of three types of information: phonological, syntactic and semantic. Following an already old idea, originally due to the Swiss philologist Ferdinand de Saussure, Pollard and Sag call these groupings of information *signs*.[7] Signs are the basis of HPSG linguistics, all

---

[7]Following the position taken in IBSS by Pollard and Sag I will be rather neutral as to what is the exact nature of signs, whether they are mental objects or real objects. The position of HPSG with respect to such issues as the conceptualism vs. realism debate is to remain silent. They acknowledge that there are good arguments for both positions, but they do not consider any of them to be conclusive. The aim of HPSG is then to work out a theory of linguistic information and of signs as information bearers independently of what is the exact nature of such entities. As Pollard and Sag put it: "we believe it

linguistic objects are some type of sign. *Sign* is the main type of feature structure:

(19)
$$\begin{bmatrix} \text{PHON} \\ \text{SYN} \\ \text{SEM} \end{bmatrix}_{sign}$$

The feature structure (19) is of type *sign*, which is specified for values of the attributes PHONOLOGY, SYNTAX, and SEMANTICS. Here I already follow the HPSG practice of writing types in italics and attribute-names in capitals; I also use the usual abbreviations for attribute-names.

Being *sign* the top in the hierarchy of types, we know that all its subtypes will also be specified for the attributes PHON, SYN and SEM, plus those attributes specific of each type. We also know that any restriction imposed on their values by PHON, SYN and SEM will be inherited by all subtypes of *sign* as well. Although our sign in (19) is still incomplete, there is more information about signs to be added. The PHONOLOGY of signs is not at all developed in HPSG, so that the value for PHON is not a true phonological representation but just a string of characters. The SYNTAX attribute is much more well developed; SYN takes feature structures of type *syntactic-category*. Syntactic categories, or simply categories, are feature structures specified for two attributes: LOCAL and BIND. Feature structures of type *local* carry that information which is related to the inherent syntactic properties of the sign such as part of speech, morphosyntactic information like case, verbal form, etc., subcategorization information, and lexicality information. These feature structures specify values for three attributes in which all these information is gathered. These attributes are HEAD, SUBCAT and LEX. HEAD takes feature structures of different types, which, in turn, contain different types of information depending on their type; HEAD features are those features shared between a lexical head and its projections, i.e. those features shared between a noun and a noun phrase, between a verb and a verb phrase, etc.. Thus, within HEAD we will find things like part of speech information and other morphosyntactic information. Later on we will give a closer look to HEAD features, but now let us turn to SUBCAT. SUBCAT is also a very important feature, it gives information about the valence of a sign, that is about how many and what kind of signs it combines with (or subcategorizes for); SUBCAT, unlike the other features we have discussed so far, does not take a feature structure as its value, rather, it takes a list of feature structures of type sign. Then we have LEX which takes values of type *boolean*, that is + or −, and encodes the distinction between lexical and non-lexical signs; this distinction is reminiscent of the X^0 vs. $X^n (n > 0)$ categories in X-bar theory ([Chomsky, 1986a]; [Duarte, this volume]). Finally, feature structures

---

would be premature to make particular claims about the relationship between the information structures that we posit and the structures of those mental objects that actually encode linguistic knowledge inside human brains. If indeed the hypotheses that we set forth about the nature of universal grammar can be correctly construed as being about mental phenomena, then they should be subjected to empirical verification on the basis of psycholinguistic experimentation" (IBSS, p. 6).

of type *bind* carry information about those syntactic dependencies which are non-local such as topicalizations, relative clauses and interrogative clauses. Within *bind* feature structures we find three attributes: SLASH, REL and QUE, all of them set-valued, i.e. taking a set of feature structures (later we will see of which type). Without entering in too much details, we will just note that SLASH carries the information about unbound gaps (or traces), while REL and QUE carry information about unbound relative and interrogative pronouns respectively.

Given what we have said so far, a sign looks like (20):

$$(20) \quad \begin{bmatrix} \text{PHON} & string \\ \\ \text{SYN} & \begin{bmatrix} \text{LOC} & \begin{bmatrix} \text{HEAD} \\ \text{SUBCAT} \\ \text{LEX} \end{bmatrix} \\ \\ \text{BIND} & \begin{bmatrix} \text{SLASH} \\ \text{REL} \\ \text{QUE} \end{bmatrix} \end{bmatrix} \\ \\ \text{SEM} \end{bmatrix}$$

The reader familiar with GPSG theory will find a striking parallelism between the content of LOCAL and BIND features and GPSG HEAD and FOOT features. In fact, the former are just a refinement of the latter. The major differences are found in LOCAL features, where SUBCAT and LEX (the HPSG correlate of GPSG's BAR feature) are taken out of the original set of GPSG HEAD features to work independently. In addition, SUBCAT is much more complex than it was in GPSG where it ranged over the set of positive integers acting as a pointer to those phrase structure rules in which a lexical head could be inserted; on the other hand LEX is an impoverished version of BAR which ranged over the set $\{0, 1, 2\}$ to encode the different levels of projection of a head. As for BIND features, these are exactly the same as the GPSG FOOT features, the only difference being that HPSG BIND features can encode more that one dependency at the time (recall that they are set valued), while in GPSG these features could take just one category as their value.[8]

We have only SEM left. This is a bit more complex, just as complex as it is the task of dealing with semantic information. So far there is a relatively fixed set of ideas of how may SEM look like, but many open questions remain which will surely call for a refinement of the structure of semantic information. The work in semantics carried out within HPSG has been strongly influenced by Barwise and Perry's ([Barwise and Perry, 1983]) Situation Semantics (SS) and, particularly, by the the work of Fenstad, Halvorsen, Langholm and van Benthem ([Fenstad *et al.*, 1987]) in developing a complex-feature-based representation for situation-theoretic objects, which they called *situation schemata*. The value of SEM in HPSG is in fact an extension of these situation schemata. It is a feature structure specifying values for two attributes: CONTENT and INDICES[9], where CONTENT

---

[8] Another difference is that in GPSG SLASH was also a HEAD feature, which is not in HPSG.

[9] In later work the name INDICES is sometimes changed to CONTEXT.

has roughly the same structure as Fenstad, Halvorsen, Langholm and van Benthem ([Fenstad *et al.*, 1987]) situation schemata and INDICES is a set-valued feature where semantic indices are collected, playing a role similar to Discourse Representation Theory (DRT; [Kamp, 1981]) reference markers. In addition, the internal structure of CONTENT varies depending on the type of semantic category we are dealing with; these are mainly three, corresponding to SS schemes of individuation, namely *individuals*, *properties* and *relations*; in addition to these, we also have *circumstances* (in SS *states-of-affairs*, or simply *soas*) which are made up of a relation, an assignment of objects to each role in that relation, and a polarity. Circumstances may in turn be *basic* (i.e simple declarative sentences), *quantified* (e.g. declarative sentences with quantified NPs) or *compound* (e.g. coordinate clauses). Thus, there is a certain parallelism between syntax and semantics in that CONTENT encodes local semantic information (basically, argument structure), while INDICES encodes semantic information that may not be local (e.g. reference of pronouns). I will not pursue the matter here, which will become clearer when we look at some analyses, but to do that we need some more linguistic tools. For the moment it is enough to know that a sign contains the following information:

$$
(21) \quad
\begin{bmatrix}
\text{PHON} & \textit{string} \\
\text{SYN} &
\begin{bmatrix}
\text{LOC} & \begin{bmatrix} \text{HEAD} \\ \text{SUBCAT} \\ \text{LEX} \end{bmatrix} \\
\text{BIND} & \begin{bmatrix} \text{SLASH} \\ \text{REL} \\ \text{QUE} \end{bmatrix}
\end{bmatrix} \\
\text{SEM} & \begin{bmatrix} \text{CONT} \\ \text{INDS} \end{bmatrix}
\end{bmatrix}
$$

2.2.1 Heads and Head-Driven Phrase Structure

The notion of *head* has a long tradition in linguistic theory and plays a central role in most frameworks. However, there is still considerable disagreement as to what properties a linguistic object must have to count as a head. For example, recent work in X-bar theory within GB seems to assume that only lexical items (i.e. X^0 categories) may be heads,while in GPSG heads may be phrasal; thus in an X-bar configuration like that in Figure 7, which is the basic structure for NPs assumed by both GB and GPSG, N^0 is the only head, both of N^1 (or N') and N^2 (or N'', or NP) under GB assumptions, while in GPSG N^0 is the (lexical) head of both N^1 and N^2, but N^1 is also the (non-lexical) head of N^2.

These discrepancies arise because of the lack of a clear definition of head. Headedness is in general related to the capability of certain distinguished elements to transmit morphosyntactic properties, to the capability of acting as a semantic functor, to the capability of being a subcategorizand, to the capability of being distributionally equiv-

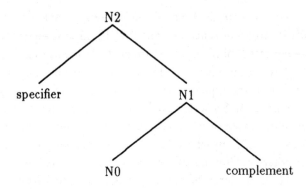

Figure 7: The structure of the NP according to most X-bar systems

alent to its phrase as a whole, and other minor criteria; on heads and headedness see [Hudson, 1987] and [Zwicky, 1985]. The problem is that these criteria very rarely lead to a definitive conclusion, such that some authors have argued for multiple heads in phrases (e.g. [Warner, 1989]). Current HPSG, however, still relies in the intuition "that each phrase contains a certain word which is centrally important in the sense that it determines many of the syntactic properties of the phrase as a whole" (IBSS, p. 53). This distinguished element is called *lexical head* of the phrase. The notion of head is then generalized to phrasal elements: "the *head* of a phrase is that daughter (immediate constituent) of the phrase which either is or contains the phrase's lexical head" (IBSS, p. 53). Therefore, head is defined structurally on the basis of the presence of a lexical head. Lexical signs are classified as lexical heads or not in virtue of their capability of being subcategorizands: "major lexical signs are the substantive words that can serve as heads of phrases and for which the notion of subcategorization makes sense; minor lexical signs are little words such as determiners, complementizers, and conjunctions, about which we will have no more to say" (IBSS, p. 197). This is a questionable move that has been challenged many times, particularly within the GB framework (e.g. [Bowers, 1987]; [Chomsky, 1986a]; [Fukui and Speas, 1986]; [Stowell, 1989]), to which we will return later.

Subcategorization is the key notion then. But before adressing it, let us give a quick look at HEAD features which, with minor changes, are the same as those of Gazdar, Klein, Pullum and Sag ([Gazdar *et al.*, 1985]):

	Attributes	Values
	MAJ	N, V, A, P, D, ADV,
	CASE	NOM, ACC,
	VFORM	FIN, BSE, PSP, PRP, PAS, INF, GER
(22)	NFORM	NORM, IT, THERE
	PFORM	OF, ON, TO, FROM,
	AUX	+, −
	INV	+, −
	PRD	+, −

MAJ (for major) is the attribute carrying the information about part of speech. Note that the traditional $[\pm N, \pm V]$ features defining the four major lexical categories have disappeared, MAJ takes atomic values corresponding to each category; thus, we have N for nouns and nominals in general, V for verbs and sentences (V in HPSG is, as in GPSG, the lexical head of S), A for adjectives, P for prepositions/postpositions, D for determiners, and ADV for adverbs.[10] As for the other features it is obvious that not all of them are appropriate to describe all categories; some are good for Ns, some are good for Vs, etc. Here is where typing of the feature structures that can be values of HEAD lets us define the cooccurrence restrictions for each lexical category (for English). We have, at least, four types: *nhead*, *vhead*, *ahead*, and *phead*:

(23) a.
$$nhead \begin{bmatrix} \text{MAJ} & \text{N} \\ \text{NFORM} & \\ \text{CASE} & \end{bmatrix}$$

b.
$$vhead \begin{bmatrix} \text{MAJ} & \text{V} \\ \text{VFORM} & \\ \text{AUX} & \\ \text{INV} & \end{bmatrix}$$

c.
$$ahead \begin{bmatrix} \text{MAJ} & \text{A} \end{bmatrix}$$

d.
$$phead \begin{bmatrix} \text{MAJ} & \text{P} \\ \text{PFORM} & \end{bmatrix}$$

---

[10]In my opinion there is an inconsistency here. When Pollard and Sag discuss HEAD features at the beginning of the book they classify D as a value for MAJ, but later in the book, as the quote above shows, they consider determiners to be minor lexical-signs, which do not seem to have HEAD features. For the moment we will just discuss Pollard and Sag's presentation, later we will suggest some modifications to it. As for adverbs, they are only mentioned again later in the book with respect to word order, but no detailed analysis is provided.

But, as we have said, subcategorization is the key notion. The subcategorization of a sign (phrasal or lexical) is a specification of the number and kind of other signs that the sign in question characteristically combines with in order to form a full phrase or, in other words, to become *saturated*. For example, we know that in all languages we find intransitive verbs like *morir* (die) or *estornudar* (sneeze) which require a single NP (the subject) to form full sentences like *Juan estornudó* (Juan sneezed); we also find transitive verbs like *comer* (eat) and *besar* (kiss) which require two NPs (the subject and the object), as in *el gato come pescado* (the cat eats fish); and verbs which require more signs to become saturated like *dar* (give) in *Juan dio un libro a María* (Juan gave a book to María), which requires two NPs and a PP (the subject, the object, and the indirect object). This information — which is not present in verbs only, but also in all other lexical heads — is encoded in HPSG in the SUBCAT feature. SUBCAT is a list-valued feature, taking as values lists of (partially specified) signs, the length of which is equal to the number of signs that the sign in question subcategorizes for. Thus, the SUBCAT list of an intransitive verb will contain just one sign corresponding to its subject; a transitive verb will have two signs in its SUBCAT list corresponding to its subject and object, and so forth. A special type of signs is that of *saturated* signs, their SUBCAT list being empty. Some lexical heads are already saturated like, for example, proper nouns, but the typical case of a saturated sign is that of certain phrasal signs like clauses and NPs.

Now we can provide a feature structure representation for some of the lexical items above:

$$(24) \quad a. \quad \begin{bmatrix} \text{PHON} & \textit{Juan} \\ \text{SYN | LOC} & \begin{bmatrix} \text{HEAD} & \begin{bmatrix} \text{MAJ} & \text{N} \\ \text{NFORM} & \text{NORM} \end{bmatrix} \\ \text{SUBCAT} & \langle\rangle \\ \text{LEX} & + \end{bmatrix} \end{bmatrix}$$

$$b. \quad \begin{bmatrix} \text{PHON} & \textit{dio} \\ \text{SYN | LOC} & \begin{bmatrix} \text{HEAD} & \begin{bmatrix} \text{MAJ} & \text{V} \\ \text{VFORM} & \text{FIN} \\ \text{AUX} & - \end{bmatrix} \\ \text{SUBCAT} & \langle \text{NP, NP, PP} \rangle \\ \text{LEX} & + \end{bmatrix} \end{bmatrix}$$

Note that in SUBCAT lists we use the traditional symbols NP, PP, etc. These are abbreviations for actual signs, which we will use throughout in this paper. Each symbol corresponds to a sign of a particular type; for instance NP corresponds to a saturated nominal, and PP to a saturated preposition. Similarly, we will use S for a saturated verb (i.e. a sentence), AP for a saturated adjective, and VP for a verb which still is has an NP in its SUBCAT list (i.e. which is still looking for its subject). Moreover, if a lexical head imposes further restrictions on the signs it subcategorizes for we will add the necessary features next to the symbol enclosed in square brackets; for example, if a verb subcategorizes for a nominative NP, and accusative NP and an infinitive VP, its SUBCAT list will be as in (25):

(25)   SUBCAT ⟨NP[NOM], NP[ACC], VP[INF]⟩

We can model lexical items, but what about phrases? How is phrase structure represented in HPSG? As it is well known traditional phrase structure frameworks represent constituency and other information concerning structural relations as trees like that in Figure 7, where each node in the tree is labelled with a symbol corresponding to a category. This is not the case in HPSG, where phrase structure is represented just as another feature, the attribute DAUGHTERS (DTRS, for short) which is characteristic of signs of type *phrasal-sign*:

$$(26) \qquad \begin{bmatrix} \text{PHON} \\ \text{SYN} \\ \text{SEM} \\ \text{DTRS} \end{bmatrix}_{phrasal-sign}$$

DTRS takes feature structures of different types as values. This is because there are many different types of daughters like *heads, complements, fillers* (i.e. *moved* phrases in long-distance dependencies), etc. Thus, the values of DTRS are of type *constituent-structure*, which in turn has such subtypes as *head-complement-structure, head-filler-structure*, etc., in which we find such attributes as HEAD-DTR, COMP-DTRS, FILLER-DTR, etc. Thus, the phrase structure representation for the sentence *el gato come pescado* is that of (27):

$$(27) \quad \begin{bmatrix} \text{DTRS} \begin{bmatrix} \text{COMP-DTRS} \ \langle [\text{PHON } el\ gato] \rangle \\ \text{HEAD-DTR} \begin{bmatrix} \text{DTRS} \begin{bmatrix} \text{HEAD-DTR } [\text{PHON } come] \\ \text{COMP-DTRS} \ \langle [\text{PHON } pescado] \rangle \end{bmatrix} \end{bmatrix} \end{bmatrix} \end{bmatrix}$$

This representation is equivalent to the tree representation in Figure 8, where, following the HPSG practice, we have labelled the branches with the symbols H and C to denote the corresponding attributes in the feature structure representation.

Sometimes, when in exemplification we are mainly concerned with phrase structure, we will use these tree representations, since the more information feature structures contain, the more unwieldy they become.

Now we have a more or less clear idea of the kind of representation that we want, but we have only hinted at some other, perhaps more interesting aspects, of these representations. For example, we have mentioned the role of HEAD features as those which are shared between a mother category and its head daughter. Similarly, in our discussion about the SUBCAT feature we distinguished between saturated and non-saturated signs, and when we defined category labels we saw that saturated signs have their SUBCAT

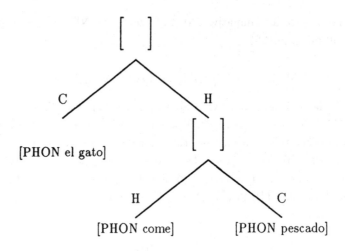

Figure 8: Simplified tree representation for the structural relations among signs

lists empty, while the length of SUBCAT in non-saturated signs may vary depending their degree of saturation (e.g. the SUBCAT list of an S is empty, the SUBCAT list of a VP contains just one element, and the SUBCAT list of a V lexical head still contains all its elements). Thus, what we really want for our example is something like the representation in Figure 9.

How is the grammar going to ensure that the desired sharings obtain, and, moreover, how is it going to licence the adequate phrase structure configuration? The answer to the first question is that the grammar contains two universal *principles* which control the *flow* of HEAD and SUBCAT information in feature structures; as for the second question, the grammar of each particular languages contains rules to licence those phrase structure configurations that we find in the language in question.

The principles of grammar in HPSG are stated in implicative-feature-structure form, and those which concern us here are the Head Feature Principle (HFP)[11] and the Subcategorization Principle (SP):

(28) Head Feature Principle

$$\left[\text{DTRS}\ _{headed-structure}\ [\ ]\right] \Rightarrow$$
$$\left[\begin{array}{ll}\text{SYN} \mid \text{LOC} \mid \text{HEAD} & \boxed{1} \\ \text{DTRS} \mid \text{HEAD-DTR} \mid \text{SYN} \mid \text{LOC} \mid \text{HEAD} & \boxed{1}\end{array}\right]$$

---

[11] The HFP is a close relative of the GPSG Head Feature Convention (HFC), the main difference between them being that the HFC works as a default inheritance mechanism; see [Gazdar, 1987].

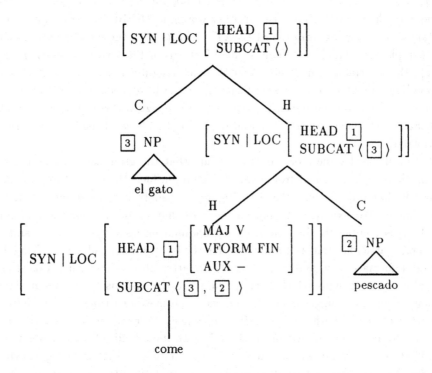

Figure 9: The sharing of subcategorization and head information in a sign

(29) Subcategorization Principle

$$\left[\text{DTRS} \quad {}_{headed-structure} \quad [\,] \right] \Rightarrow$$

$$\left[\begin{array}{l} \text{SYN} \mid \text{LOC} \mid \text{SUBCAT} \quad \boxed{2} \\ \text{DTRS} \quad \left[\begin{array}{ll} \text{HEAD-DTR} \mid \text{SYN} \mid \text{LOC} \mid \text{SUBCAT} & \text{append(} \boxed{1}, \boxed{2}) \\ \text{COMP-DTRS} \quad \boxed{1} \end{array} \right] \end{array} \right]$$

Informally, what the HFP says is that if a phrase (this is specified by the DTRS attribute in the left-hand side feature structure) has a head-daughter, then they must share the same HEAD features. Similarly, the SP says that in a phrase the SUBCAT list of its head-daughter is the result of appending the SUBCAT list of the phrase in question with the COMP-DTRS list; in other words, the SUBCAT list of a phrase is the list obtained by removing from the SUBCAT list of its head those specifications satisfied by the complement-daughters. This means that, given the structure sharing tags $\boxed{1}$ and $\boxed{2}$, the information from each complement daughter is actually unified with the corresponding subcategorization specification on the head; thus the subcategorization requirements of a head can only be satisfied by some sign if this sign is consistent with the subcategorization specifications found in the SUBCAT list of the head, otherwise the SP is violated.

But we still need some more tools to ensure that the grammar licences the correct representations and prevent it from overgenerating; in fact, there is nothing in the HFP and the SP that tells us that the S in Figure 9 actually has the phrase structure we depicted there. For example, it may be the case that we do not want a configuration where the S is completely flat, immediately dominating its subject, object and verbal head. This particular role is fulfilled in HPSG by grammar rules specifying how is structural information organized in the DTRS attribute. These rules take the form of partially specified signs which specify what are the options for a specific language to combine signs into bigger ones. In our case, we need two rules, one to licence the combination of the V with its first NP complement to form the VP constituent, and another to licence the combination of the VP with its second NP complement to form the S. That is, the latter will account for the structure of saturated signs, while the former for the structure of partially saturated signs; these rules are, respectively, those in (30) and (31):

(30) Rule 1
$$\left[\begin{array}{l} \text{SYN} \mid \text{LOC} \mid \text{SUBCAT} \quad \langle \rangle \\ \text{DTRS} \quad \left[\begin{array}{ll} \text{HEAD-DTR} \mid \text{SYN} \mid \text{LOC} \mid \text{LEX} & - \\ \text{COMP-DTRS} \quad \langle [\,] \rangle \end{array} \right] \end{array} \right]$$

(31) Rule 2
$$\left[\begin{array}{l} \text{SYN} \mid \text{LOC} \mid \text{SUBCAT} \quad \langle [\,] \rangle \\ \text{DTRS} \mid \text{HEAD-DTR} \mid \text{SYN} \mid \text{LOC} \quad \left[\begin{array}{ll} \text{HEAD} \mid \text{INV} & - \\ \text{LEX} & + \end{array} \right] \end{array} \right]$$

The feature structure for Rule 1 subsumes all those signs which are saturated (note the empty SUBCAT list), which have a non-lexical (LEX −) head daughter and a single complement daughter (note the COMP-DTRS list with just one element). On the other hand, feature structure (31) subsumes all those signs which are close to saturation (i.e. their SUBCAT list contains just one element), and whose head daughter is an uninverted (INV −) lexical sign.[12] There is something very important about these rules, they are category-neutral, i.e. they do not specify values for the MAJ attribute of the described sign — in fact, they do not specify values for *any* HEAD feature, since this is accounted for independently by the HFP — which makes them very close to the phrase structure schemata of GB's X-bar theory. Thus, Rule 1, for instance, describes saturated signs of any category (i.e. S, NP, AP, etc.).

Another important thing worth to point our about these rules is that they say nothing about the linear order of the constituents, they only specify the immediate dominance (ID) relations that hold among a phrase and its immediate constituents, just as GPSG ID rules do. We can use the more familiar rewrite notation for ID rules to express the same rules:

(32)   *a.*   R1:   [SUBCAT ⟨⟩] → H[LEX −], C

      b.   R2:   [SUBCAT ⟨[ ]⟩] → H[INV −, LEX +], C*

Metaphorically speaking, then, we can say that head and subcategorization information *flow* from the head daughter to the mother, as phrase structure is built around heads, producing the *head-driven* effect which gives its name to the theory.[13]

Now we have already looked at the three main linguistic tools of HPSG: principles, grammar rules, and lexical entries. Most principles are part of Universal Grammar (UG), i.e. part of the shared knowledge that human beings have of language, while rules and lexical entries are part of the knowledge that speakers of a particular language have of that language.[14] The combination of these three types of linguistic information tells us what counts as a well-formed sign of a particular language. Thus, we have an idea of how grammar is organized, of what is the structure of the theory. All signs must conform to all principles of grammar, such that we can conceive of UG as the conjunction of all universal principles:

(33) $$UG = P_1 \wedge \ldots \wedge P_n$$

In fact, we can unify the two principles we have seen so far to produce a single feature structure:

---

[12]Rules 1 and 2 are in principle designed to account for English signs, but they would work for many other languages as well.

[13]Let me insist on the fact that *head-drivenness* as movement of information from the lexical head to its phrasal projections is just a metaphor of what really is sharing of information.

[14]It is also recognized the existence of language particular principles.

(34)

$$
\left[\text{DTRS} \quad {}_{headed-structure}{}^{[\,]} \right] \Rightarrow
$$

$$
\left[
\begin{array}{l}
\text{SYN} \mid \text{LOC} \left[\begin{array}{ll} \text{HEAD} & \boxed{1} \\ \text{SUBCAT} & \boxed{2} \end{array} \right] \\[2mm]
\text{DTRS} \left[\begin{array}{l} \text{HEAD-DTR} \left[\text{SYN} \mid \text{LOC} \left[\begin{array}{ll} \text{HEAD} & \boxed{1} \\ \text{SUBCAT} & \text{append(}\,\boxed{3}\,,\,\boxed{2}\,\text{)} \end{array} \right] \right] \\ \text{COMP-DTRS} \ \boxed{3} \end{array} \right]
\end{array}
\right]
$$

Thus, we have a universal definition of well-formed sign, namely, a well-formed sign in any language is that object which is subsumed by the feature structure in (34). But in addition, for a sign of a particular language like English or Spanish to be well-formed, it must instantiate some lexical sign or some grammar rule of that language. Consequently, the structure of the theory of a particular language grammar G_L can be understood as the conjunction of all principles in turn conjoined with the disjunction of all lexical signs and rules of G_L:

$$
(35) \qquad G_L = P_1 \wedge \ldots \wedge P_n \wedge (L_1 \vee \ldots \vee L_m \vee R_1 \vee \ldots \vee R_p)
$$

Now that we have discussed the essentials of the theory, we can proceed to a deeper examination of what is the nature of linguistic information and how this information interacts according to HPSG to explain the facts about natural language.

2.2.2 Subcategorization and the Grammatical Hierarchy

In the previous section we could see that subcategorization plays a crucial role in this head-driven conception of phrase structure, so it will be useful to give a more detailed look to the HPSG theory of subcategorization, which will help us understand the treatment of more complex linguistic phenomena that we will discuss in the sections to come.

So far we have just given a very sketchy presentation of HPSG's theory of subcategorization, leaving aside three very important issues: (i) what is the status of grammatical relations in the theory; (ii) what is the relevant information for subcategorization or, in other words, which properties of subcategorized for signs can be specified in the elements of a SUBCAT list; and (iii) what is the relation between subcategorization and semantics.

As for grammatical relations like subject, direct object, indirect object, etc., two main positions among theorists can be identified. Some linguists believe that grammatical relations have to be defined in terms of other concepts of syntactic theory; this is the approach taken within transformational grammar in its different versions (e.g. [Chomsky, 1965]; [Chomsky, 1981]), where such notions as subject and object are defined configurationally, i.e. in terms of structural relations in syntactic representations, such that, for example, *subject* is defined as [NP, S], the NP immediately dominated by S. By contrast, other linguists assume that grammatical relations cannot be defined, i.e. they are primitives of syntactic theory; this position has been defended within Relational Grammar (RG; see the papers in [Perlmutter, 1983]) and Lexical-Functional Grammar (LFG; see the papers in [Bresnan, 1982]). HPSG lies somewhere in between these two positions, since without being a theory like GB where grammatical relations are purely derivative notions which almost play no role in syntactic processes, we cannot really say that grammatical relations are primitives in HPSG. What is really primitive in HPSG is the idea that grammatical relations are *hierarchically* encoded. That is, notions such as subject and direct object are defined in terms of the order of the corresponding saturated elements in the head's SUBCAT list, such that *subject* is defined as the last element in the SUBCAT list, *object* is the second from last, *indirect object* (or *second object*) is the third from last, etc., as long as no unsaturated complement (e.g. an infinitival VP) intervenes.[15] This conception of grammatical relations is reminiscent of the position taken in Montague Grammar by Dowty ([Dowty, 1982]) and in GPSG, where grammatical relations are defined according to the order in which arguments are combined with functions in semantic translations. Thus, by adopting a hierarchical encoding of grammatical relations instead of a keyword direct encoding as in LFG, HPSG predicts that subcategorization is sensitive to other information in addition to simple grammatical relations.[16]

This yields us to the next question, i.e. that of the information to which subcategorization is sensitive. Pollard and Sag overtly challenge in IBSS (see [Sag and Pollard, 1989]) those views in which it is assumed that subcategorization can be reduced to just selection of semantic properties of complements or stated in terms of grammatical relations only. Their argument is based on the fact that lexical heads select for many different properties of signs, which makes rather unplausible the assumption that such properties can be reduced to a small set of semantic or relational properties. For example, two Spanish verbs with very close meanings like *pensar* (think) and *reflexionar* (reflect) show rather different selection patterns of syntactic category:

(36)

a. Gabriel piensa el problema (G thinks the problem)

b. Gabriel piensa en el problema (G thinks about the problem)

c. Gabriel piensa que el problema es difícil (G thinks that the problem is difficult)

d. Gabriel piensa resolver el problema (G thinks of solving the problem)

---

[15]Note that subjects appear in the SUBCAT list of lexical heads and, consequently, are treated as subcategorized for, just like in LFG (but unlike GB and GPSG). We will return to subject selection in the last section.

[16]The advantages of a hierarchical encoding of grammatical relations are discussed in [Johnson, 1987], [Johnson, 1988]. For a different approach in which no hierarchical encoding is used and grammatical relations are assumed to be primitives, see [Gunji, 1987], where SUBCAT sets are used instead of SUBCAT lists.

(37)

a. *Gabriel reflexiona el problema (G reflects on the problem)

b. Gabriel reflexiona sobre el problema (G reflects upon the problem)

c. *Gabriel reflexiona que el problema es difícil (G reflects that the problem is difficult)

d. *Gabriel reflexiona resolver el problema (G reflects solving the problem)

Thus while *pensar* shows a quite varied subcategorization pattern (i.e. NP, PP, S, VP), *reflexionar* just subcategorizes for PP complement with a determined preposition (just as *pensar*), since no other preposition would work. The PP examples show that selection may be sensitive to finer distinction than just syntactic category; other examples of this kind are the selection of the inflectional form and the mood of the embedded head verb:

(38)

a. Gabriel piensa resolver el problema (G thinks of solving the problem)

b. Gabriel piensa que resolverá el problema (G thinks that he will solve the problem)

c. Gabriel quiere resolver el problema (G wants to solve the problem)

d. Gabriel quiere que resuelva el problema (G wants somebody to solve the problem)

In (38) we see that both *pensar* and *querer* select finite or infinitival forms of the embedded head verb, with the difference that the former selects finite indicative forms and the latter finite subjunctive forms, while the reverse is impossible.[17]

Similar patterns can be found in different languages in which other properties are selected like case forms of nominal complements in German, Latin, etc. (see IBSS, pp. 124–125). This leads to the conclusion that both syntactic and semantic information may be present in the signs of a SUBCAT list. But we said very little about semantics, we just mentioned the case of mood which is probably semantic in nature; however, there must be a closer relation between SUBCAT and the semantics of the lexical head, on the contrary we would not have a means to ensure that the signs that in virtue of the SP syntactically combine with a lexical head are actually interpreted as the arguments of that lexical head. What we need then is a role assignment mechanism to ensure that complements get assigned a role in the CONTENT attribute of the lexical head. This is done by means of specifying in the lexicon that the semantics of complements is shared by the role attributes of the lexical head. Thus, in an intransitive verb like *caminar* (walk) the single element in its SUBCAT list (i.e. the subject) is assigned the WALKER

---

[17]Here we have the additional difference that while the missing subject of the finite complement of *pensar* may be either bound by the matrix subject or free, the missing subject of the finite complement of *querer* must be free.

role, in a transitive verb like *comer* (eat) the subject is assigned the EATER role and the object the EATEN role (as a notational convention I use subscript tags to indicate that only the SEM attribute of the sign is shared):[18]

$$
(39) \quad a. \quad
\begin{bmatrix}
\text{PHON} & caminar \\
\text{SYN} & \begin{bmatrix} \text{HEAD} & [\text{MAJ} \ \text{V}] \\ \text{SUBCAT} & \langle \text{NP}_{\boxed{1}} \rangle \end{bmatrix} \\
\text{SEM} \mid \text{CONT} & \begin{bmatrix} \text{RELN} & \text{WALK} \\ \text{WALKER} & \boxed{1} \end{bmatrix}
\end{bmatrix}
$$

$$
b. \quad
\begin{bmatrix}
\text{PHON} & comer \\
\text{SYN} & \begin{bmatrix} \text{HEAD} & [\text{MAJ} \ \text{V}] \\ \text{SUBCAT} & \langle \text{NP}_{\boxed{1}}, \text{NP}_{\boxed{2}} \rangle \end{bmatrix} \\
\text{SEM} \mid \text{CONT} & \begin{bmatrix} \text{RELN} & \text{EAT} \\ \text{EATER} & \boxed{1} \\ \text{EATEN} & \boxed{2} \end{bmatrix}
\end{bmatrix}
$$

As we have seen, the SUBCAT feature is the basis for the treatment of lexical dependencies in HPSG: complement subcategorization, grammatical relations, semantic role assignment and specific selectional properties of lexical heads are all accounted for by just one single complex feature. Note that however varied is the information to which subcategorization is sensitive, there is one unifying property: it is strictly *local*. No element in a SUBCAT list makes reference to internal properties of complements like, for example, the case of some properly contained NP or the arity of some embedded verb (i.e. whether it is transitive, intransitive, etc.). All these restrictions follow from what is called the *Locality Principle* according to which the SUBCAT element of lexical signs specifies values for SYN and SEM, but never for DTRS. The locality principle is assumed to be a universal constraint on lexical signs.[19]

2.2.3 Extending the Coverage of the Grammar: Long-Distance Dependencies

So far all the mechanisms we have examined take into account extremely local relations like subcategorization, sharing of head features, immediate dominance among categories, that take place in the domain defined by a mother category and its daughters — i.e. what is known as a local tree (when tree representations are used). We know however that there

---

[18] Here I follow IBSS in keeping role labels distinct for each verb. This situation seems to have changed recently and traditional role-names like agent, patient, goal, etc. have been introduced in the CONTENT attribute, as for example in [Pollard, 1990].

[19] Observe that in fact this principle has the status of a global (or substantive) constraint within the grammar, since it is not a consequence of the formalism. It is one of the very few global constraints that we find in HPSG.

are certain dependencies that appear to occur in larger domains; these dependencies, which include relative clauses, interrogative clauses, topicalizations, among others, are traditionally known as *unbounded* or *long-distance dependencies* and have always been assumed to pose a serious problem to such monostratal theories which do not rely on movement transformations. This was long hold to be true until Gazdar ([Gazdar, 1981]) showed how a simple and elegant analysis of unbounded dependencies can be provided without having resort to transformational operations. The core of Gazdar's analysis — which was later refined by Gazdar, Klein, Pullum and Sag ([Gazdar *et al.*, 1985]) — is the category-valued feature SLASH which links the *moved* element with its *canonical* position in the tree. So, for example, a topicalization structure like *John Mary loves* would be represented as in Figure 10.

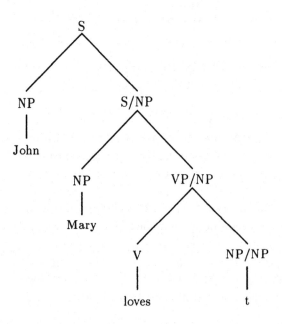

Figure 10: Schematic GPSG representation for a topicalization structure

I used the traditional convention of representing SLASH as /, such that the category symbol on the right encodes the category of the displaced element and the category symbol on the left represents the label of the node in the tree. Observe how SLASH links the topicalized position and the *gap* in the complement position (here represented as t, for *trace*). A very important and attractive feature of this analysis is that it factors an unbounded dependency into a series of extremely local dependency between a mother node and some of its daughters. This is accomplished by having resort to two principles of grammar: the Foot Feature Principle (FFP) and the Control Agreement Principle (CAP). Roughly, by the FFP it is guaranteed that a path of SLASHes exists between the two positions, since it forces the presence of a FOOT feature on the mother node if it is present on some daughter, while the CAP ensures that there is agreement among the SLASH values of each node as well as between the category of the topic and the SLASH value of its sibling category.

I made this short excursion into the GPSG analysis of unbounded dependencies because it is the basis, with minor modifications, of the HPSG analysis. As the reader will remember from our discussion of BIND features, in HPSG there is also a SLASH feature, the sole difference being that in HPSG is set-valued rather than just category-valued. This is motivated by the fact that, unlike English, many languages such as Romance, Scandinavian or Slavonic ([Maling and Zaenen, 1982]; [Rizzi, 1982]; [Rudin, 1988]) allow for multiple unbounded dependencies.[20]

The mechanisms to handle unbounded dependencies in HPSG are very similar to those of GPSG. Going back to GPSG again then, recall that there unbounded dependencies are described as having three parts: the top, the middle, and the bottom. The top is the substructure which introduces the dependency, the middle is the domain of structure that the dependency spans (which can be arbitrarily long), and the bottom is the substructure in which the dependency ends. Thus, in our example in Figure 10, the top is the local tree having its root at the node labelled S, the middle is the local tree having its root at the node labelled S/NP, and the bottom is the local tree having its root at the node labelled VP/NP. In GPSG, the well-formedness of each part is accounted for by different principles: the top is admitted by a special ID rule which directly specifies SLASH in one of its right-hand side categories and which moreover requires that the value of SLASH be equal to the sister category:

$$(40) \qquad\qquad S \rightarrow X^2, H/X^2$$

Similarly, the bottom is also admitted by an ID rule, with the particularity that this ID rule is related to a kernel lexical ID rule by a metarule, which implies that a possibility for a complement is that it be null. Finally, the FFP and the HFC (recall that SLASH in GPSG is both a FOOT and a HEAD feature) ensure that SLASH be instantiated in all intervening nodes between that introducing the dependency and that in which the dependency terminates.

In HPSG the same strategy is followed. Thus, we have a rule for the top, where SLASH is bound:

---

[20]There is also a motivation for it being a set rather than a list. In case SLASH were list-valued, unbounded dependencies should be computed on a last-in/first-out basis, which would allow for nested dependencies only. This is linguistically unmotivated since it is a well known fact that unbounded dependencies can be nested, but they can also be crossed or even a mixture of the two when more than two dependencies occur. This is however a place for language particular variation, since it may well be the case that certain languages require their SLASH features to be list-valued or, even, just sign-valued, depending on the type of dependencies that they allow.

(41) Rule 3

a. $\left[\ \text{DTRS}\ \left[\begin{array}{l}\text{HEAD-DTR} \mid \text{SYN} \mid \text{LOC} \mid \text{BIND} \mid \text{SLASH}\quad \{\boxed{1}\} \\ \text{FILLER-DTR}\quad \{\boxed{1}\}\end{array}\right]\ \right]$

b. M → H[SLASH {$\boxed{1}$}], $\boxed{1}$ F

As for the bottom, we need a different mechanism, since we cannot resort to metarules in HPSG. The solution, however, must be somehow related to subcategorization, as the bottom of unbounded dependencies is a violation of the SP, because some of the elements specified in the SUBCAT list of the lexical head do not appear in the COMP-DTRS list. It seems reasonable to suppose then that the SP must be further qualified so as to be able to handle these exceptions. This is in fact the approach taken by Pollard in two papers ([Pollard, 1985]; [Pollard, 1988]), where the SP contains two clauses, the SP per se and a Gap Introduction Principle (GIP):

(42) *Remove symbols from the front of the SUBCAT list one by one, doing one of the following:*

(a) *Subcategorization Principle*: Match the symbol with a complement; or

(b) *Gap Introduction Principle*: Place the symbol on the mother's SLASH set.[21]

Thus, when some of the elements listed in SUBCAT does not match with a complement, then it is considered to be *displaced* and its specification is removed from SUBCAT and it is stored in the SLASH set of the mother, that is, its cancellation is delayed until SLASH is bound at the top of the dependency.

But we still need something else to account for the middle of the dependency. Just as in GPSG, HPSG resorts to a principle to *pass up* SLASH information: the Binding Inheritance Principle (BIP):

(43) *Binding Inheritance Principle*

For each BIND feature, the value of that feature on a phrase is the union of the values on the daughters less those values that are explicitly discharged.[22]

---

[21]I introduced a couple of modifications in these definitions. Pollard's version of the GIP is as follows: "place the symbol on the head daughter's SLASH list". First, I substituted the word "list" for "set" because, as we saw in the previous footnote, set-valued SLASH seems to be more appropriate that list-valued SLASH. Second, I changed "head daughter" by "mother"; this is necessary because, if we maintained Pollard's version, we would licence representations where SLASH in lexical head daughter is not empty, which, under any reasonable interpretation of SLASH, is inconsistent, since this would mean that the gap is within the lexical head, and not a sister to it. This seems moreover to be Pollard's intended interpretation, given the tree representations he provides as exemplification in both papers.

[22]This is the version of the BIP given in [Pollock, 1989]. I have only changed the name which in the paper is *Nonlocal Principle*.

With the BIP we have all the necessary mechanisms to handle unbounded dependencies. There are a few problems, though. Note that we have not written the principles in the format we have been using so far, i.e. as implicative feature structures. The reason is very simple, it cannot be done. Let us examine them a bit closer to see why this is impossible. Consider first the SP and the GIP. What these principles are supposed to do can be paraphrased as a clause (the SP proper) followed by an if-then statement to handle the exception, since the GIP is something like the default case of the SP:

- Discharge any element in the SUBCAT list of the head daughter, which matches an element in the COMP-DTRS list; if some element is not matched, then put it in the SLASH set of the mother.

There are two problems here. On the one hand, the if-then clause explicitly requires that we use (existential) quantification over a list, but recall that in our discussion of the formalism we never introduced quantification as one of the possible operations of our formal language. On the other hand, the principle as it is fails to prevent the subject, which in declarative clauses is never discharged at the same level as the rest of the complements, to go into the SLASH list, producing representations like that in Figure 11.[23]

Similarly, we can look at the BIP as the combination of two clauses, a main if-then statement and a default clause:

- If some element in the SLASH set of the head daughter matches an

---

[23]Note that the representation in Figure 11 would be rejected in English on independent grounds, since there is no rule in the grammar of English which sanctions a flat structure where a saturated sign immediately dominates its lexical head without it being marked as inverted. The problem remains however. Consider a null subject language like Spanish where subject inversion is possible:

(i)

a. Juan quiere a María (J loves M)

b. quiere Juan a María (loves J M)

c. quiere a María (loves M)

d. es el tipo de persona que nunca sé a quién quiere (is the kind of person that I never know who loves)

(ia) is a simple declarative. (ib) has the subject inverted and it could be the yes-no question version of (ia), but it could also be part of an embedded indirect interrogative like *no sé si quiere Juan a María* (I do not know whether J loves M), where inversion is not obligatory. (ic) could be the null subject version of either (ia) or (ib). Finally, (id) shows that extraction of the subject is possible from embedded direct interrogatives, where subject inversion is obligatory. Now, it is generally assumed that the structure of inverted sentences is flat, but inversion in null subject languages is rather free and it is possible with any verb, so that we cannot rely on a lexical feature marking verbs as invertible and non-invertible; it is likely then that Spanish has a rule licensing flat structures like the one which will sanction a substructure like that of Figure 11. Thus, a sequence like *quiere a María* can be analyzed as being flat with one extracted complement, in which case nothing prevents the grammar to provide for (ia) an analysis like that of Figure 11. Borsley ([Borsley, 1987]) offers a similar argument with reference to this problem to which I will return in the next section.

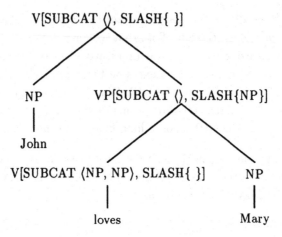

Figure 11: The GIP does not prevent subjects to go into the SLASH

element in the FILLER-DTR list, then discharge it. The value of the SLASH set of the mother is the union of the SLASH sets of all its daughters.

Again, we find the same problem. In that case we need quantification over a set to get the desired results.

We have identified a couple of dubious features in the HPSG framework, one in the formal side, the other in the linguistic side. In the next section we will see that if we introduce some refinements in the formalism, and give up some linguistic assumptions, there is a straightforward solution which may have some interesting consequences for the theory.

2.2.4   Other Possible Extensions and Refinements

As we have seen, the HPSG theory of IBSS and further developments suffers of some inadequacies with relation to certain formal aspects (i.e. the impossibility to express quantification), and certain linguistic aspects concerning the interaction of the principles designed to account for unbounded dependencies and the less oblique element in SUBCAT lists (i.e. the subject).

As for quantification, there seem to be good arguments for this extension of the formalism. This extension has been in fact carried out within the CLG formalism, a formalism in which complex constraints — like the linguistic principles we discussed in the previous section — can be expressed in a slightly restricted form of first order predicate logic. These properties make CLG well suited for expressing, among others, HPSG-style of grammars. I will not enter into the formal details of the introduction of quantification in such a complex-feature-based formalism, which are discussed at length by Damas and Varile ([Damas and Varile, 1989]) and Balari, Damas, Moreira and Varile ([Balari *et al.*, 1990]) [24]. I will however assume that this possibility is available to us and that some formalized version of the SP+GIP and the BIP in the preceding section are possible; on this particular matter see [Balari *et al.*, 1990].

I will concentrate then on the problem of the interaction between unbounded dependencies and subject selection, which calls for other solutions than just refinements of the formalism. This interaction has always been a source of lots of publications concerned with the following facts about English:

(44)

a. who do you think left

b. *who do you think that left

(45)

a. who do you believe to have left

b. *who do you believe for to have left

(46)

a. who did you complain that John hates

b. *who did you complain John hates

c. *who did you complain that hates Mary

d. *who did you complain hates Mary

e. *who did Mary quip (that) left

f. *who did it disturb John (that) left

In (44) and (45) we have examples of constructions with the so-called bridge verbs, which under certain circumstances allow for the extraction of the subject of their clausal complement, and for which Chomsky and Lasnik ([Chomsky and Lasnik, 1977]) proposed the *that-trace* and *for-to* Filters. The examples in (46) show construction with non-bridge verbs, in which subject extraction of the complement is always impossible, while the extraction of other complements is possible.

---

[24] Part of the contents of this section is an extension of the work reported in ([Balari *et al.*, 1990]), and it is the result of close interaction with my colleagues to whom I am very grateful for many helpful suggestions and criticisms.

To see how this construction can be handled within HPSG, I will first briefly sketch the GPSG analysis, just to have a source of comparison. In GPSG, the termination of unbounded dependencies is handled by metarules; the metarule designed for subject extraction is SLASH Termination Metarule 2 (STM2):[25]

(47) STM2 $\qquad$ $X \rightarrow W, V^2[+\text{SUBJ}, \text{FIN}]$
$$\Downarrow$$
$$X/NP \rightarrow W, V^2[-\text{SUBJ}]$$

STM2 says that for every rule in the grammar introducing a finite sentential complement, there is another rule introducing a finite VP immediately dominated by a category having an NP value for SLASH. Thus, (44a) is analyzed as a special case of extraction without a gap in the subject position of the complement, such that the relation between the SLASH specification on the mother node and the complement missing a subject is accounted for by the CAP, which requires that the value of SLASH and the AGR^{26} value of the VP be the same; for a more detailed discussion of SLASH and AGR agreement, see [Hukari and Levine, 1987]. On the other hand, (44b) is blocked from two different sources. The first source is related to the impossibility of STM2 to apply to a rule like (48), even if it matches the right-hand side of the metarule:

(48) $\qquad$ $S[\text{COMP that}] \rightarrow [\text{SUBCAT that}], H[\text{COMP NIL}]$

STM2 cannot apply to this rule because it would be a violation of one of GPSG's global constraints, the Lexical Head Constraint which prevents metarules from taking as input those rules not introducing a lexical head, as it is the case in (48) where H[COMP NIL] is phrasal. This rule is the responsible of admitting the top of that-clauses like the local tree in Figure 12.

Thanks to the following FCRs we force the presence of the SUBJ and FIN features:

(49) $\quad$ *a.* $\quad$ FCR15: $\quad$ $[\text{COMP}] \equiv [+\text{SUBJ}]$

$\quad$ *b.* $\quad$ FCR17: $\quad$ $[\text{COMP that}] \supset ([\text{FIN}] \lor [\text{BSE}])$

which are the core of the second source. STM2 can apply to the following rule:

---

[25]I use the same notational conventions as GPSG here. V^2 is an abbreviation for $[-N, +V, BAR\ 2]$, i.e. verbal projections with two bars. The SUBJ feature is a boolean feature which distinguishes VPs ($[-SUBJ]$ categories) from Ss ($[+SUBJ]$ categories), since both are analyzed as V^2s.

[26]AGR is also a category valued feature that we find in all verbs. This is how subject selection is handled in GPSG. Note that the analysis of missing subjects in GPSG embodies a rather interesting assumption, namely, that subjects, not being directly selected, cannot be source of gaps in unbounded dependencies, they have the power to give rise to long-distance agreement with the verb they are a subject of. As we will see below, the incorporation of such an assumption has many interesting consequences for the HPSG theory of unbounded dependencies in particular and for the organization of linguistic information within signs in general.

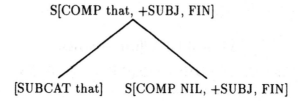

Figure 12: GPSG representation for the top local tree of a that-clause

(50)   VP → H[40], S[FIN]

which admits trees like the one in Figure 13.

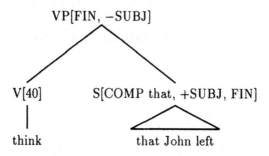

Figure 13: Local tree admitted by rule (50), introducing finite complements

But the output of STM2 to (50) would never admit the tree in Figure 13 without violating FCR15:

(51)   *VP/NP → H[40], V²[COMP that, -SUBJ, FIN]

This analysis is elegant since it moreover predicts the facts in (46), given the GPSG ID rules for non-bridge verbs:

(52) a.   VP → H[80], S[that]   (quip, complain)

     b.   VP[AGR NP[it]] → H[20], NP, S[that]   (disturb)[27]

These rules could be the input of STM2, but their output would violate FCR15.

---

[27]This second rule is itself the output of the Extraposition Metarule.

The *for-to* case is a bit different. *Believe* can be introduced by the following ID rule:

(53)   VP → H[14], V²[INF, +NORM]

Thanks to FCR15, FCR18: [COMP for] ⊃ [INF] and FSD9: [INF, +SUBJ] ⊃ [COMP for], we admit the trees in Figures 14 and 15.

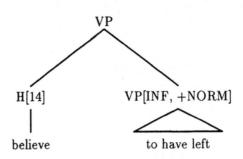

Figure 14: Rule (53) admits infinitival VPs...

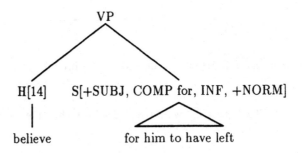

Figure 15: ... and infinitival Ss as complements

This explains the ungrammaticality of (45b), since STM2 only applies to rules introducing finite sentential complements. No rule like the following is possible:

(54)   *VP/NP → H[14], V²[INF, -SUBJ]

But this only accounts for the ungrammaticality of (45b), not the grammaticality of (45a), since there is no way to sanction SLASH in the rule. The answer is that believe is also a transitive verb introduced by the following rule:

(55)   VP → H[17], NP, VP[INF]

(55) can be the input to the other metarule for SLASH termination (STM1), which sanctions the extraction of the object NP, as shown in Figure 16.

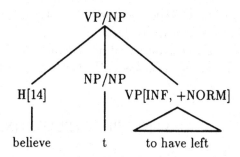

Figure 16: Local tree admitted by the rule produced after applying STM1 on rule (55)

Unfortunately, we know that the *that-trace* analysis is not general enough to extend it to other languages like Italian or Spanish where the pattern is exactly the opposite as in English:

(56)

a. chi pensi che verrà (who do you think that will come)

b. *chi pensi verrà (who do you think will come)

c. quién piensas que vendrá (who do you think that will come)

d. *quién piensas vendrá (who do you think will come)

This examples show that a radical revision of the GPSG analysis of missing subjects is called for, even though the idea that no actual subject gaps exist is an interesting one.[28] A first attempt to solve this problem is that of Pollard ([Pollard, 1985]), who, in an earlier version of HPSG, tries to reduce all GPSG metarules to HPSG lexical rules. STM2 is no exception in Pollard's account where the following lexical rule operating over the SUBCAT list of verbs taking sentential complements is proposed:

(57) $X[SUBCAT \langle \dots, S, \dots \rangle] \Rightarrow X[SLASH \langle NP \rangle, SUBCAT \langle \dots, VP, \dots \rangle]$

Perfectly aware of the problem with the interaction between subject selection and subject extraction, he adds the following constraint to the GIP (which is essentially the same we discussed in the previous section):

---

[28] Actually, the whole GPSG analysis of unbounded dependencies must be revised for those languages with multiple extractions, which cannot be handled by a category-valued SLASH.

(58) Subject Gap Prohibition (SGP)

>Gap introduction is disallowed in case the removal of the symbol from the
SUBCAT list emptied the list ([Pollard, 1985], p. 257).

He moreover suggests that this constraint would be absent from the grammar of those
languages which do not show *that-trace* effects.

Now, note that apart from the rather ad hoc character of the SGP, the lexical rule
for subject extraction is licensing local trees like that in Figure 17.

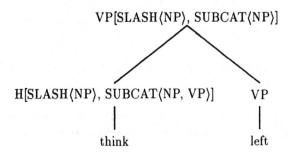

Figure 17: The values of SLASH in a VP when lexical rule (57) is applied

It is not clear what means to have SLASH in preterminal symbols not dominating a
trace (it is as if the gap were within *think*). On the other hand, it is not at all clear how
the NP in SLASH is going to be interpreted as the subject of the VP complement, unless
the rule be restated as in (59):

(59)   X[SUBCAT ⟨..., V[SUBCAT ⟨⟩], ...⟩] ⇒
         X[SLASH ⟨NP$_i$⟩, SUBCAT ⟨..., V[SUBCAT ⟨NP$_i$⟩], ...⟩]

That is, as a special case of control. But even in this case, we would have problems.
Pollard does not provide rules for introducing complementizers, but he assumes that the
lexical rule for subject extraction applies over lexical items taking complementizerless
sentential complements. This is tantamount saying that, for instance, *think* would have
the two following (schematic) lexical entries:

(60) *a.*   think1   [SUBCAT⟨S[that]⟩]

     b.   think2   [SUBCAT⟨S[¬COMP]⟩]

Apart from the inadequacy of this solution, which introduces unnecessary redundancy
in the lexicon, there is the problem of how is going to be captured the fact that an S

is complementizerless. In GPSG we have FCR15 which stipulates that any [+SUBJ] category must also be specified for COMP (and viceversa). COMP defaults to NIL through free instantiation as the only possible value when no other is instantiated. HPSG does not seem to have an equivalent mechanism, though.

Our problem is then how we can account for the English paradigms in (44-46) without imposing too many language particular constraints which disallow a smooth account for the Romance facts in (56).

To this end, we will consider a proposal by Borsley ([Borsley, 1987]) who, in a similar vein, points out some problems of the HPSG account of subject selection. Since Borsley's arguments are rather similar to ours — although he points out a few more deficiencies that we have not considered here — we will not repeat them here, and we will go directly into his solution which has recently been adopted (with modifications) in two recent papers by Carl Pollard ([Pollock, 1989]; [Pollard, 1990]).

Borsley notes that these problems disappear if instead of having just one SUBCAT feature, lexical entries are already specified for SUBCAT and a new SUBJECT feature. That is, separating subject selection from complement selection, as in GPSG. Thus, the SUBCAT and SUBJECT list of an intransitive, transitive, and ditransitive verbs would respectively look like in (61):

(61) *a.* [SUBJECT⟨NP⟩, SUBCAT⟨⟩]   intransitive

    b. [SUBJECT⟨NP⟩, SUBCAT⟨NP⟩]   transitive

    c. [SUBJECT⟨NP⟩, SUBCAT⟨NP, NP⟩]   ditransitive

And Rules 1 and 2 would be significantly modified as in (62):

(62) *a.* R1: $X[SUBCAT \langle\rangle] \rightarrow H[SUBCAT \langle \ldots, Y_n\rangle], C^*$

    b. R2: $X[SUBCAT \langle\rangle] \rightarrow H[SUBCAT \langle\rangle, SUBJECT \langle Y\rangle], C$

But Borsley's account is not without problems. First, the SP+GIP become much more complicated, since the principle must account for both complement and subject cancellation separately and, consequently, for gap introduction of complements and subjects also separately. Second, while Borsley correctly predicts that in English subject gaps cannot be introduced at the level in which complements are cancelled given R1 and R2, his SP is only disguising Pollard's SGP:

(63) Subcategorization Principle ([Borsley, 1987])

Any category that is in the SUBCAT list of a head and not on the SUB-CAT list of its mother or on the SUBJ list of a head and not in the SUBJ list of its mother must be matched by a sister of the head or *in the first case be on the SLASH list of its mother* [italics are mine, SB].

Thus subject gaps are forbidden by Borsley just as they were by Pollard. The account does not carry over to Romance languages then, since if we eliminate the phrase *in the first case* from the SP for Spanish and Italian, we are again back to the beginning where we were unable to distinguish subject extraction from simple subject cancellation.

A third problem with Borsley's account is that it neglects completely the role that complementizers play in *that-trace* effects, since subject extraction seems to correlate directly with the presence/absence of a complementizer.

In the next paragraphs I will try to sketch a solution to these problems having the advantage of being compatible with any of the languages we have considered here.

The first move will be to consider subject extraction. In this case, what seems to be required is something like what we had in GPSG, i.e. treat subject extraction as a subcase of subject-verb agreement. Thus, without giving up Borsley's idea that subjects are selected separately from complements, we will carry it to its ultimate consequences so as to have the SUBJECT feature away from the influence of the SP and the GIP. The best way to do that is to put SUBJECT within the BIND features, instead of LOCAL; thus it will be subject to the BIP and R2 becomes a subcase of R3, just that while in latter SLASH is bound, in the former SUBJECT is bound. That SUBJECT is a BIND feature is confirmed by the fact that subjects enter into many binding relations such as extractions, control of the subject of infinitive verbs, control of the subject of finite verbs (in null subject languages), etc.

The second step would be to consider the role of complementizers. In fact, it seems that complementizers play a much more important role in the facts we have been discussing; it seems that a complementizer in English cannot attach to a phrase which has not yet found its subject, a constraint that does not hold of Romance languages. The best way to capture this fact is to give complementizers the power to select complements just as other lexical items do, that is, as we pointed out before in this paper, the status of minor categories needs to be reconsidered.

Consider the following schematic lexical entries for *that* and *for*, where I use SELECT, a category-valued feature, instead of SUBCAT to encode the selectional properties of minor categories, and to capture the fact that minor categories, unlike major ones, select one element only:

(64) *a.* that [SYN|LOC|SELECT V[SUBJECT⟨⟩, SUBCAT ⟨⟩, FIN ∨ BSE]]]

　　　b. for [SYN|LOC|SELECT V[SUBJECT⟨⟩, SUBCAT ⟨⟩, INF]]]

Consider, moreover, the lexical entries for some bridge and non-bridge verbs (for typographical reasons I sometimes abbreviate SUBJECT as SB and SUBCAT as SC):

(65) a.

$$
\left[
\begin{array}{ll}
\text{PHON} & \textit{think} \\
\text{SYN} & \left[
\begin{array}{ll}
\text{LOC} & \left[
\begin{array}{ll}
\text{HEAD | MAJ} & \text{V} \\
\text{SUBCAT} & \langle\text{V[SUBCAT } \langle \rangle, \text{ FIN} \vee \text{BSE]}\rangle
\end{array}
\right] \\
\text{BIND} & \left[
\begin{array}{ll}
\text{SUBJECT} & \{\text{NP}\} \\
\text{SLASH} & \{\ \}
\end{array}
\right]
\end{array}
\right]
\end{array}
\right]
$$

b.

$$
\left[
\begin{array}{ll}
\text{PHON} & \textit{believe} \\
\text{SYN} & \left[
\begin{array}{ll}
\text{LOC} & \left[
\begin{array}{ll}
\text{HEAD | MAJ} & \text{V} \\
\text{SUBCAT} & \langle\text{V[SC }\langle \rangle, \text{ COMP for]} \vee \\
 & \quad \text{V[SB}\{\text{NP1}\},\text{SC}\langle \rangle, \text{ INF]}\rangle
\end{array}
\right] \\
\text{BIND} & \left[
\begin{array}{ll}
\text{SUBJECT} & \{\text{NP1}\} \\
\text{SLASH} & \{\ \}
\end{array}
\right]
\end{array}
\right]
\end{array}
\right]
$$

c.

$$
\left[
\begin{array}{ll}
\text{PHON} & \textit{complain} \\
\text{SYN} & \left[
\begin{array}{ll}
\text{LOC} & \left[
\begin{array}{ll}
\text{HEAD | MAJ} & \text{V} \\
\text{SUBCAT} & \langle\text{V[COMP that]}\rangle
\end{array}
\right] \\
\text{BIND} & \left[
\begin{array}{ll}
\text{SUBJECT} & \{\text{NP}\} \\
\text{SLASH} & \{\ \}
\end{array}
\right]
\end{array}
\right]
\end{array}
\right]
$$

Consider also Rule 4 introducing minor categories, where Y stands for the minor category:

(66) $\qquad$ X → Y[SELECT $\boxed{1}$], $\boxed{1}$ H[29]

Thus, for example, the combination of the rules and principles we have discussed so far with lexical entries (64a) and (65a) will give rise to the VPs in (67), but never to the VP in (68):

(67)

a. think that he left

b. think he left

c. think left

(68) think that left

---

[29]The fact that certain features like COMP must also be present in the mother category may be accounted for by extending the HFP, as in [Warner, 1989], or just by stipulating it directly in the rule as in [Balari *et al.*, 1990]. Note an important feature of this rule that even though the minor category has some head-like status, the head is still the major phrase to which it is attached, thus, unlike GB we do not have complementizer phrases, but just sentences with complementizers, as in GPSG.

Similarly, the other lexical entries also produce the desired results. In bridge verbs, missing subjects are impossible when the complementizer is present because in that case its selectional restrictions are violated, but are possible without the complementizer since no restriction is imposed by the verb on the presence of the subject of its complement. On the other hand, non-bridge verbs always disallow missing subjects: when the complementizer is present extraction is disallowed on the same grounds as in the case of bridge verbs; when no complementizer appears, the problem is not the missing subject, as the examples in (46) show, it is just that the selectional properties of the verb are violated. But the advantage of this analysis is that in the case of Romance languages we do not have to modify the principles of grammar, just the lexical entries for the complementizers in such a way that they do not impose any restriction of the SUBJECT list of the clause to which they attach, the rest remaining exactly the same (we just have to add a rule for subject inversion where all complements are cancelled and the subject is bound at the same level).

3   Conclusion and Further Issues

In this paper we have presented a theory of linguistic information, HPSG, and we have looked at its main aspects both on the formal side and the linguistic side. We have discussed some of its main aspects such as how is the grammar is organized in principles, rules and lexical entries and we have seen them work in the treatment of subcategorization and unbounded dependencies; we have also pointed at some problems of the theory with relation to the principles handling subcategorization and unbounded dependencies and we provided a solution for them.

However, we have left many questions undiscussed, which, for space reasons, we could not even consider. A very important one concerns the organization of the lexicon and the role of lexical rules in such constructions as passive and extraposition; this is treated in detail in chapter 8 of IBSS and in [Sag and Pollard, 1987] which is also a good review of the main aspects of the theory. Also a review of the theory is [Pollock, 1989]; there the possibility of having separate lists for COMPLEMENTS, SUBJECTS and SPECIFIERS selection is considered, but it seems to have been abandoned as it is shown in [Pollard, 1990].

Another important matter we left out is the role of the Grammatical Hierarchy in explaining many facts about the grammar of natural languages such as lexical rules, word order, control and binding phenomena. The interaction of lexical rules with the Grammatical Hierarchy is again discussed in chapter 8 of IBSS; word order and LP rules are analyzed in chapter 7 of IBSS, in [Sag, 1986], and in [Pollard, 1990], the latter with special reference to German. A semantics-based analysis of control is developed in [Sag and Pollard, 1988] and in chapter 3 of [Pollard and Sag, in prep.], which have circulated as unpublished drafts. Anaphoric dependencies are discussed in another unpublished paper, [Pollard and Sag, 1988a].

The problem of unbounded dependencies is first considered in [Pollard, 1985] and in [Pollard, 1988]; in IBSS it is just referred. In chapter 4 of [Pollard and Sag, in prep.], unbounded dependencies are discussed at length (although the version that has circulated is still incomplete) and totally different solutions to the problems we discussed in the previous section are proposed; in particular, a special sign for traces is introduced to handle gap introduction, and the BIP is modified so as to be sensitive to *inherited* SLASH values and *to-bind* SLASH values, in an attempt to prevent SLASH to percolate freely once it has been bound (this would be unnecessary if the BIP could use quantification and worked essentially like the SP in discharging bound elements).

Finally, there is also a paper on agreement, [Pollard and Sag, 1988b], where the phenomenon is analyzed as the interaction between syntactic and semantic principles.

What all this amount of work shows, to my view, is the potential of the information-based approach to linguistics for developing an adequate theory of human competence, with the advantage of being developed within a mathematically sound and quite well understood formalism. This has the additional advantage that HPSG-style of grammars can be fairly easily implemented, which makes them very good for the testing of linguistic hypotheses, and for the development of computer applications, be it on the purely applied side such as machine translation ([van Noord *et al.*, 1990]), or on the more theoretical side like the development of new grammar formalisms like, for example, CLG.

4 Acknowledgements

This work has been carried out within the framework of the Eurotra R&D program for machine translation financed by the European Communities. I am particularly grateful to Luís Damas and Giovanni B. Varile, who gave me the opportunity to work with them in the CLG formalism; most of what is good in this paper is due to the long discussions about grammar formalisms and about some of the ideas that appear at the end of section 2. I would also thank an anonymous reviewer for some helpful comments. All errors are of course my own.

Three Lectures on Situation Theoretic Grammar*

Robin Cooper

Centre for Cognitive Science, University of Edinburgh

2 Buccleuch Place — Edinburgh EH8 9LW — Scotland

1   Situation theoretic grammar: getting started

1.1   Introduction

We use sentences of our language to talk about situations. If I utter a declarative sentence like

Anna waved

I might be describing an actual or real situation temporally located some time before my utterance. For example, if I am using the name 'Anna' to refer to my daughter who is called Anna, I might well be describing a situation which actually took place.

An utterance of this sentence is itself a situation. This is a situation in which a middle-aged man manipulates his speech organs in a rather obscure way to produce a linguistically significant noise. Such a situation might be related to another rather different kind of situation perhaps located in an entirely different region of space and time and involving a little girl moving her arm in a particular way. The two situations are quite different in character but are related in a complex way involving among other things the grammar of English. We wish to construct a theory that will give some account of the nature of this relationship.

It would not be much use trying to create a precise account of the relationship between our uses of language and other situations if we did not have a precise theory of situations. Intuitive as the term "situation" might be, we have to have a theory which tells us what we mean by it in our technical work.

We will informally introduce various notions from situation theory. (For a more detailed survey of situation theory see [Barwise, 1989] and [Devlin, forthcoming]). Unlike pure set theory which constructs all set theoretic objects out of just one kind of object,

*The preparation of these notes was supported by DYANA, ESPRIT Basic Research Action project 3175. I am grateful to the STaGr group at Edinburgh, the STASS group at CSLI and particularly Jon Barwise for help with various aspects of the research that is reported here. Conversations with Hans Kamp and Bill Rounds have also contributed this research.

i.e. sets, situation theory introduces a rather rich collection of different kinds of situation theoretic objects in addition to situations. We will characterize some of these objects in what follows.

1.2 Basic situation theory

1.2.1 Relations

We first introduce situation-theoretic objects called RELATIONS. Among the objects we call relations will be objects such as **run** or **kiss** which correspond to English verbs. Each relation has certain ARGUMENT ROLES associated with it. Thus **run** has a single argument role, the role of runner. The relation **kiss** has two roles, the role of kisser and the role of kissed. The precise nature of argument roles is a matter that can be discussed. One might say that both **run** and **kiss** have agent roles (i.e. the runner and the kisser) and that **kiss** in addition has a patient role (i.e. the kissed). On this view there would be a small number of roles (which, in line with the linguistic literature, we might call THEMATIC roles rather than argument roles) which the various relations would either have or not have. Another view would be that each relation would have its own roles which it would not share with any other relation. Thus we would say that **run** has a runner role and **jump** has a jumper role rather than that they both have an agent role. We will sidestep the issue here and say that a relation which has one argument role has an A-role and that a relation that has two argument roles has an A-role and a B-role. We will arbitrarily decide that the A-role will be the role for the argument that we would normally consider to correspond to the subject of an active English sentence whose main verb represents the relation. Thus the A-role for **kiss** will be the kisser-role and the B-role for **kiss** will be the kissed-role.

Only certain kinds of situation-theoretic objects will be APPROPRIATE to FILL the argument roles of particular relations. For example, one might want to say that a relation would not be appropriate to fill the A-argument role of either **run** or **kiss**. This is reflected in the fact that it makes no sense to say 'run kissed Anna' or 'running kissed Anna' nor to say the negation of these sentences. It simply does not seem to be a reasonable issue to discuss whether running kissed Anna or not.

We will assume that associated with each argument role to a relation there is a MINIMAL APPROPRIATENESS CONDITION, i.e. a condition which must be fulfilled in order for an object to be appropriate for that role. It need not be a sufficient condition: there may be things which fulfill this condition but which nevertheless we can show to be inappropriate for the argument role (e.g. because, if they were appropriate, we would be led into a paradox). These minimal appropriateness conditions, we will assume, are not necessarily something that is given to us by a general theory of situations, but will be specified in connection with an application of situation theory to the specification of a particular fragment of a natural language. For example, if the fragment we are treating includes the verb 'kiss' then we will specify that any use of 'kiss' will represent the relation **kiss** with A-argument and B-argument roles both of which are associated with the condition that an appropriate argument be an individual. What counts as an individual will be something that is determined by our particular application rather than the general theory of situations.

Situation theory, then, tells us that there are relations, that relations have argument roles and that argument roles have appropriateness conditions associated with them. It does not, however, tell us precisely which relations there are or precisely what their argument roles or appropriateness conditions are.

1.2.2 Infons

The next kind of situation theoretic object we introduce is INFON (also called STATE OF AFFAIRS, SOA or POSSIBLE FACT in the literature).

Basic infons

We begin by characterizing BASIC INFONS in terms of the relations they stand in to other situation theoretic objects. There is an important relation that holds between any basic infon and exactly one relation. We will call this relation **relation-of**. Suppose that σ is the infon corresponding to the fact of Anna kissing Claire. Then **relation-of** will hold between σ and **kiss**. The relation **relation-of**, unlike **kiss**, is a relation whose minimal appropriateness conditions are specified by situation theory. The A-argument role of **relation-of** must be filled by a possible fact and the B-argument role must be filled by a relation. If σ stands in the relation **relation-of** to some relation r, we will use locutions like 'σ has the relation r', 'σ's relation is r' and so on.

We will represent basic infons as follows:

$$\langle\!\langle \text{run}, \text{c}; 1 \rangle\!\rangle$$
$$\langle\!\langle \text{kiss}, \text{a}, \text{c}; 1 \rangle\!\rangle$$

Assuming that c represents an individual named Claire and a represents an individual named Anna, let us say, Jon Barwise's and my daughter respectively, these pieces of notation represent the possible fact that Claire runs and the possible fact that Anna kisses Claire. The constituents and polarity of a possible fact are represented within the brackets '$\langle\!\langle \rangle\!\rangle$'. The constituents are represented to the left of the semi-colon and the polarity to the right of the semi-colon. We adopt the convention of representing the constituents in the order relation, A-argument, B-argument, etc. A '1' to the right of the semi-colon indicates that the infon is positive. A '0' indicates that it is negative. The corresponding negative possible facts would thus be represented by:

$$\langle\!\langle \text{run}, \text{c}; 0 \rangle\!\rangle$$
$$\langle\!\langle \text{kiss}, \text{a}, \text{c}; 0 \rangle\!\rangle$$

These are the possible facts that Claire does not run and that Anna does not kiss Claire. For each basic infon there is another infon which has exactly the same constituents but which has the opposite polarity. If σ is a basic infon we will use $\overline{\sigma}$ to represent the fact which is exactly like σ except that it has the opposite polarity, that is the DUAL of σ.

Our characterization of basic infons so far has left out an important constituent. Running and kissing do not just take place or not in the world — they take place at particular locations in space and time. Thus infons can also have space-time locations as constituents, though it is not the case that all infons must have a location. There are two ways that we can think of locations. One way is to introduce an additional defining relation for possible facts, location-of. Another way is to say that relations may have an argument role for locations. If we choose the first way, we might represent the location by ℓ as in the following:

$$\langle\!\langle \ell, \text{run}, c; 1 \rangle\!\rangle$$
$$\langle\!\langle \ell, \text{kiss}, a, c; 1 \rangle\!\rangle$$

If we choose the second, it is more normal to represent the location as an argument in the following way:

$$\langle\!\langle \text{run}, c, \ell; 1 \rangle\!\rangle$$
$$\langle\!\langle \text{kiss}, a, c, \ell; 1 \rangle\!\rangle$$

We will make the simplifying assumption that infons do not have locations since the role that locations play is not our concern here. It would have been very important to take locations into account if we were going to give a treatment of tense and aspect. For some work on tense and aspect in the framework we are going to develop see [Glasbey, 1990], [Glasbey, forth.].

Conjunctive and disjunctive infons

In addition to basic infons there are conjunctive and disjunctive infons. That is, if σ_1 and σ_2 are infons, then there are infons

$$\sigma_1 \wedge \sigma_2$$
$$\sigma_1 \vee \sigma_2$$

and their corresponding duals

$$\overline{\sigma_1 \wedge \sigma_2}$$
$$\overline{\sigma_1 \vee \sigma_2}$$

We will see the significance of these complex infons when we discuss situations below.

Unsaturated infons

Some uses of English sentences clearly contain uses of transitive verbs but do not provide any indication of what plays one of the argument roles of the relation involved. Examples include cases of "object deletion" such as 'Anna ate' and agentless passive sentences such as 'Anna was seen'. Situation theory allows for UNSATURATED INFONS, where not all of the argument roles of the relation are filled. We will represent these as follows:

$$\langle\!\langle \text{eat}, \text{a}, \_; 1 \rangle\!\rangle$$
$$\langle\!\langle \text{see}, \_, \text{a}; 1 \rangle\!\rangle$$

The '_' here represents an argument role of the relation which is not filled in the infon. We use it to mark the position of the unfilled role since we are using position in this notation to indicate argument roles. We will see what role is played by unsaturated infons when we discuss situations below.

1.2.3 Situations

Situations are situation-theoretic objects which stand in a certain relationship to infons. We talk either of a situation SUPPORTING an infon or of an infon HOLDING in a situation to mean in an intuitive sense that the infon is "true" in or of the situation, is a fact in the situation or that the situation makes the infon factual. The relation **support** has an A-argument role for a situation and a B-argument role for an infon. If a situation s supports an infon σ, we write

$$s \models \sigma$$

If s does not support σ, we write

$$s \not\models \sigma$$

Situations are completely defined by the collection of infons they support. There are no two distinct situations which support exactly the same infons.

If $\mathcal{S}$ is a collection of situations we use

$$\models_{\mathcal{S}} \sigma$$

to say that there is some situation $s \in \mathcal{S}$ such that

$$s \models \sigma$$

In this case we say that σ is ACTUAL with respect to $\mathcal{S}$ or supported in $\mathcal{S}$. We use

$$\not\models_{\mathcal{S}} \sigma$$

to say that there is no situation $s \in \mathcal{S}$ such that

$$s \models \sigma$$

If a collection of situations is COHERENT then

(i) There is no basic infon σ such that

$$\models_{\mathcal{S}} \sigma \text{ and } \models_{\mathcal{S}} \bar{\sigma}$$

(ii) If $\models_{\mathcal{S}} \sigma_1 \wedge \sigma_2$ then

$$\models_{\mathcal{S}} \sigma_1 \text{ and } \models_{\mathcal{S}} \sigma_2$$

If $\models_S \overline{\sigma_1 \wedge \sigma_2}$ then

$$\models_S \overline{\sigma_1} \text{ or } \models_S \overline{\sigma_2}$$

If $\models_S \sigma_1 \vee \sigma_2$ then

$$\models_S \sigma_1 \text{ or } \models_S \sigma_2$$

If $\models_S \overline{\sigma_1 \vee \sigma_2}$ then

$$\models_S \overline{\sigma_1} \text{ and } \models_S \overline{\sigma_2}$$

(iii) If $\sigma(\vec{\rho})$ is a positive basic infon which is unsaturated with respect to the argument roles $\vec{\rho}$ and

$$\models_S \sigma(\vec{\rho})$$

then there is some sequence of objects $\vec{a}$ such that

$$\models_S \sigma(\vec{\rho}/\vec{a})$$

i.e. the infon which is like $\sigma(\vec{\rho})$ except that the objects $\vec{a}$ play the roles $\vec{\rho}$, is supported in S.

If $\sigma(\vec{\rho})$ is a negative basic infon which is unsaturated with respect to the argument roles $\vec{\rho}$ and

$$\models_S \sigma(\vec{\rho})$$

then there is no sequence of objects $\vec{a}$ such that

$$\models_S \overline{\sigma}(\vec{\rho}/\vec{a})$$

i.e. the infon which is like the dual of $\sigma(\vec{\rho})$ except that the objects $\vec{a}$ play the roles $\vec{\rho}$, is not supported in S.

Some remarks are appropriate to clause (ii) and (iii) of this definition. It is normal in situation theory to require something stronger than (ii). (See, for example, [Barwise, 1989], Chapter 11 and [Barwise and Etchemendy, 1990].) One stronger formulation (leaving out the dual cases which can be treated straightforwardly in a similar manner) is:

for any $s \in S$

if $s \models \sigma_1 \wedge \sigma_2$ then
$$s \models \sigma_1 \text{ and } s \models \sigma_2$$

if $s \models \sigma_1 \vee \sigma_2$ then
$$s \models \sigma_1 \text{ or } s \models \sigma_2$$

This is stronger because it requires that any situation which supports a complex infon also supports the more basic infons which are required by it. The weaker formulation requires that the more basic infons be supported, but it does not require that they be supported by the same situation. There is a further strengthening of this requirement for complex infons which is also standardly assumed in situation theory, namely that the conditionals are strengthened to biconditionals:

for any $s \in S$

$s \models \sigma_1 \wedge \sigma_2$ iff
$\quad s \models \sigma_1$ and $s \models \sigma_2$

$s \models \sigma_1 \vee \sigma_2$ iff
$\quad s \models \sigma_1$ or $s \models \sigma_2$

Exactly parallel choices are presented to us in connection with clause (iii) concerning unsaturated infons. Suppose some situation supports the infon

$\langle\!\langle \text{eat}, \text{a}, \_; 1 \rangle\!\rangle$

corresponding to 'Anna eats'. If Anna eats, then Anna eats something. That is, for some x the infon

$\langle\!\langle \text{eat}, \text{a}, x; 1 \rangle\!\rangle$

is supported. Our weak formulation does not require that this infon is supported by the same situation as supports the unsaturated infon. Nor, since we have used a conditional rather than a biconditional, does it require that the unsaturated infon has to be supported if the saturated infon is supported.

What kind of intuitions might lead us to choose among these options? We will hold to the basic intuition that situations are parts of the world that we can perceive, basing ourselves on intuitions that motivated some of the original work on the situation semantics of perception complements in [Barwise, 1981] and [Barwise and Perry, 1983]. We might say that the strongest requirements are motivated in the case of conjunctive infons since it is hard to imagine someone seeing Anna smile and Anna jump without also seeing Anna smile and seeing Anna jump and vice versa. That is, you cannot have the conjunctive infon supported by a situation without having the two conjuncts supported by that situation and vice versa. With disjunctive infons things are perhaps not quite so clear. You presumably cannot see Anna smile or Anna jump without in addition seeing one or other of the disjuncts but it is perhaps not so clear that to see a situation which supports one of these disjuncts is to see a situation which supports the disjunction. One perhaps unsavoury consequence of having the biconditional here we would not be able to have situations s which support just one infon, since for every infon supported by s, s would support the disjunction of that infon with every other infon and furthermore the disjunction of that infon with every other infon and so on. Thus situations might be forced to be somewhat "larger" than we had first imagined. So for disjunction we might consider the middle possibility, the conditional which requires that if a situation supports a disjunctive infon, then it supports one of the disjuncts but not the other way around.

For unsaturated infons it seems like the weakest condition might be most appropriate. We can certainly imagine someone seeing Anna eat without seeing what it is she is eating so we should not require the saturated infon to be supported by any situation which supports the unsaturated infon. However, it is difficult to imagine someone seeing Anna eat a banana without seeing her eating. Taking this into account we might strengthen our original condition by adding

for all $s \in S$
if $\sigma(\vec{\rho})$ is a positive basic infon which is unsaturated with respect to the argument roles $\vec{\rho}$ and there is some sequence of objects $\vec{a}$ such that

$$s \models \sigma(\vec{\rho}/\vec{a})$$

then

$$s \models \sigma(\vec{\rho})$$

1.2.4 Some notation

We often have occasion to talk about certain facts being actual in some collection of situations S, i.e. to make statements such as

$$\models_S \langle\!\langle r, a_1, \ldots, a_n; 1 \rangle\!\rangle$$
or
$$\models_S \langle\!\langle r, a_1, \ldots, a_n; 0 \rangle\!\rangle$$

for some relation r and arguments $a_1, \ldots, a_n$. We are often not particularly concerned to make clear exactly which coherent collection of situations S we have in mind but assume that there is some background collection of general relevance. In this case we can suppress the subscript S and in order to make things more easily readable we will abbreviate such statements as

$$r(a_1, \ldots, a_n)$$
$$\sim r(a_1, \ldots, a_n)$$

respectively.

1.3 Using situation theory to talk about language

1.3.1 The relation gr

Our grammars will define a relation, gr, between situation-theoretic objects. In Fragment 1, the small grammar that we shall use in this section (see 1.3.6 below), we will characterize this relation as taking two arguments, a USE of a linguistic expression (a notion we will characterize shortly) and another situation theoretic object which may be either an individual or an infon which we will call a CONTENT of the use. Later on we will adjust our view of exactly what the arguments to grammar relations gr are. In displayed examples and our rules we will represent uses by underlining. Thus

<u>Anna smiles</u>

represents a use of the sentence

'Anna smiles'

Words and sentences as such we shall enclose in single quotation marks.

What kind of situation-theoretic object would be a good candidate for the content of such a use? Here we shall take the content to be an infon. The infon is perhaps ultimately not a sufficiently subtle notion to be taken as the content of a sentence and some notion of proposition as has been discussed in situation theory (e.g. by [Barwise, 1989]) might be needed. However, for the purposes of these lectures, infon will suffice. An obvious candidate for the content of the use <u>Anna smiles</u> would be the infon

$$\langle\!\langle \text{smile}, \text{a}; 1 \rangle\!\rangle$$

where a is my daughter, who happens to be named Anna. Then we would say:

$$gr(\underline{Anna\ smiles}, \langle\!\langle \text{smile}, \text{a}; 1 \rangle\!\rangle)$$

This says that some particular use of the sentence 'Anna smiles' has as its content the infon $\langle\!\langle \text{smile}, \text{a}; 1 \rangle\!\rangle$, according to a grammar (for English) which characterizes the relation gr.

A central idea behind situation semantics which goes back to the early presentation of the theory in [Barwise and Perry, 1983] is that meaning is characterized as a relation among situations[1]. In the case of simple declarative sentences the main situations to be related are the utterance situation and the described situation. We talk of one situation where a person makes subtle movements of the speech organs as describing another situation where something entirely different might be going on. We shall equate our notion of use with that of utterance situation. Thus we have a use which we consider to be a special kind of situation describing another situation. The situation it describes must be one that supports the infon which is the content of that use. Suppose that gr is the grammar relation for English[2], u is a use of an English sentence and s is a situation described by that use. Then the following two requirements must be met:

$$gr(u, \sigma)$$
$$s \models \sigma$$

---

[1] Or rather types of situations, a refinement we will not consider here.

[2] We make the simplifying assumption that there is exactly one grammar relation for English.

1.3.2 Uses

What kind of situations might uses of linguistic expressions be? We might partially characterize a use of the word 'Anna' as a situation u of which the following hold:

$$u \models \langle\!\langle \text{use-of}, u, \text{'Anna'}; 1 \rangle\!\rangle$$
$$u \models \langle\!\langle \text{category}, u, \text{noun}; 1 \rangle\!\rangle$$
$$u \models \langle\!\langle \text{person}, u, \text{third}; 1 \rangle\!\rangle$$
$$u \models \langle\!\langle \text{number}, u, \text{singular}; 1 \rangle\!\rangle$$

A use of a sentence whose constituents are themselves the uses $\underline{NP}$ and $\underline{VP}$ we might partially characterize as a situation u of which the following hold:

$$u \models \langle\!\langle \text{category}, u, \text{S}; 1 \rangle\!\rangle$$
$$u \models \langle\!\langle \text{constituents}, u, \{\underline{NP}, \underline{VP}\}; 1 \rangle\!\rangle$$
$$u \models \langle\!\langle \text{precede}, \underline{NP}, \underline{VP}; 1 \rangle\!\rangle$$

We are exploiting an important feature of situation theory in these characterizations, namely that situations need not be well-founded. That is, a situation s can support infons in which s occurs as an argument. For discussion and motivation of this for the analysis of common knowledge see [Barwise, 1989], Chapter 9.

1.3.3 Feature-value notation for uses

Note that a reasonable grammatical theory of many of the relations of the infons that uses support would say that they are functional. We could state this in the following way:

if S is a coherent collection of situations and

$$u \models \langle\!\langle r, u, v; 1 \rangle\!\rangle$$

then there can be no $v' \neq v$ such that

$$\models_S \langle\!\langle r, u, v'; 1 \rangle\!\rangle$$

We shall call such relations FEATURES OF UTTERANCES. If f is a feature of u and

$$u \models \langle\!\langle f, u, v; 1 \rangle\!\rangle$$

we shall say that v is the VALUE of f for u. It is convenient to adopt an abbreviatory notation. For

$$u \models \langle\!\langle f_1, u, v_1; 1 \rangle\!\rangle$$
$$\vdots$$
$$u \models \langle\!\langle f_n, u, v_n; 1 \rangle\!\rangle$$

we may write

$$u \models \begin{bmatrix} f_1 : & v_1 \\ \vdots & \\ f_n : & v_n \end{bmatrix}$$

1.3.4 Labelled bracketing notation for uses

We shall use labelled bracketings or their equivalent tree diagrams to represent uses. The notational convention is that

$$[A_1, \ldots, A_n]_X$$

stands for a use u such that

$u \models \langle\!\langle \text{category}, u, X; 1 \rangle\!\rangle$
$u \models \langle\!\langle \text{constituents}, u, \{\underline{A_1}, \ldots, \underline{A_n}\}; 1 \rangle\!\rangle$

$\underline{A_1} \models \langle\!\langle \text{category}, u, A_1; 1 \rangle\!\rangle$
$\qquad \vdots$
$\underline{A_n} \models \langle\!\langle \text{category}, u, A_n; 1 \rangle\!\rangle$

$u \models \langle\!\langle \text{precede}, \underline{A_1}, \underline{A_2}; 1 \rangle\!\rangle$
$\qquad \vdots$
$u \models \langle\!\langle \text{precede}, \underline{A_{n-1}}, \underline{A_n}; 1 \rangle\!\rangle$

1.3.5 Compositionality

The grammar relation gr holds not only between uses of sentences and their contents but also between constituents of uses and their contents. We will define gr in such a way that the content of a particular use depends on contents associated with its immediate constituents.

1.3.6 Fragment 1: Simple sentences

Sample domain

In defining our grammar we will need to make reference to certain individuals and relations which will use in the contents of words and phrases. This need to define a domain in order to define the grammar will be avoided when we get to the more sophisticated approach we will develop in the next section. We will make the following assumptions:

ind(a)
ind(c)
rel(smile, A-role)

$\sim$ rel(smile, B-role)
rel(like, A-role)
rel(like, B-role)
appr(smile, A-role, ind)
appr(like, A-role, ind)
appr(like, B-role, ind)

Grammar

It is useful in defining grammars to break the relation gr up into relations s, np, v, etc. corresponding to the categories we use in the grammar. We would then define gr in terms of these "smaller" relations defined by the grammar as follows:

$gr(u, o)$ iff
    either $s(u, o)$
    or $np(u, o)$
    or $v(u, o)$
    or ...

A grammar consists of a lexicon and a syntax. The lexicon is a list of words in the fragment being defined, characterizations of what situations are uses of those words and a characterization of the contents related to such uses by gr.

Lexicon

Anna:
$n(u, a)$ if
$$u \models \left[\begin{array}{ll} \text{use-of:} & \text{'Anna'} \\ \text{category:} & \text{N} \end{array} \right]$$

Claire:
$n(u, c)$ if
$$u \models \left[\begin{array}{ll} \text{use-of:} & \text{'Claire'} \\ \text{category:} & \text{N} \end{array} \right]$$

smiles:
$v(u, \text{smile})$ if
$$u \models \left[\begin{array}{ll} \text{use-of:} & \text{'smiles'} \\ \text{category:} & \text{V} \end{array} \right]$$

likes:
$v(u, \text{like})$ if
$$u \models \left[\begin{array}{ll} \text{use-of:} & \text{'likes'} \\ \text{category:} & \text{V} \end{array} \right]$$

Syntax

Lexical insertion

If $\underline{w}$ is a use of a word w listed in the lexicon, then

$$\frac{x([w]_{\underline{X}}, c) \text{ if}}{x(w, c)}$$

Phrase structure

1. $\dfrac{s([NP_1 \ V \ NP_2]_{\underline{S}}, \langle\!\langle r, x, y; 1\rangle\!\rangle) \text{ if}}{\begin{array}{l} np(\underline{NP_1}, x) \\ v(\underline{V}, r) \\ np(\underline{NP_2}, y) \end{array}}$

2. $\dfrac{s([NP \ V]_{\underline{S}}, \langle\!\langle r, x; 1\rangle\!\rangle) \text{ if}}{\begin{array}{l} np(\underline{NP}, x) \\ v(\underline{V}, r) \end{array}}$

3. $\dfrac{np([N]_{\underline{NP}}, x) \text{ if}}{n(\underline{N}, x)}$

Grammaticality

$\underline{S}$ is a grammatical sentence use of Fragment 1 if

$$s(\underline{S}, \sigma)$$

and σ is an infon. Thus $\underline{Anna \ smiles \ Claire}$ is not a grammatical sentence use since $\langle\!\langle smile, a, c; 1\rangle\!\rangle$ is not an infon because **smile** only has one argument role.

Description

$\underline{S}$ describes situation d according to Fragment 1 if $\underline{S}$ is a grammatical sentence use of Fragment 1, $s(\underline{S}, \sigma)$ and $d \models \sigma$.

2 Parametric objects

2.1 Introduction

There are two aspects of Fragment 1 which seem particularly unpromising:

i. It relates uses of expressions to their contents, i.e. situation theoretic objects, compositionally. That is, each constituent of a use is made to correspond to an object. Noun-phrases correspond to individuals; verbs correspond to relations and sentences correspond to infons. No verb-phrases were used in Fragment 1 and, indeed, none of the kinds of situation theoretic objects we introduced seem appropriate as objects to assign to verb-phrases.

ii. It provides an analysis of proper names which seems to require that all uses of some particular name have the same individual as content. This, however, is not the case. Many different people have the same name (John Perry and John Etchemendy, to name but two) and different uses of names can be related to different individuals. We do not want to be forced into a position where we have to say that there is a different word 'John' for each individual named John. Rather we want to say that different uses of the word 'John' can be related to different individuals depending on the context or the environment of the use. An adequate account of this phenomenon should allow us to give a description of the grammar without having to include reference to the particular domain of individuals that the language can be used to talk about, as we did in Fragment 1.

We will attack both these problems by introducing parametric objects into situation theory and characterizing situation theoretic grammar in terms of parametric objects and environments for them.

2.2 Parametric objects in situation theory

2.2.1 Parameters

A theory of parametric objects and parameters is central to any version of situation theory. However, it is not totally clear what is the best way to characterize such objects. The standard assumption in situation theory is that parameters are objects which are additional to the non-parametric universe and that they can be used as a kind of placeholder in parametric objects. For a recent careful discussion of this view of parameters see [Westerståhl, 1990]. In previous work ([Cooper, ms.]) I have called this kind of parameter OBJECT PARAMETER and have attempted to contrast it with an alternative which I called STRUCTURAL PARAMETER. The idea behind the notion of structural parameter is that parameters, rather than being additional objects, are dimensions along which certain types of object can vary, that is, for infons they are relations like **A-argument-of, relation-of**. We then introduce parametric objects of the type which are indeterminate with respect to such dimensions of variation. Here I will not attempt to spell out either of these views of parameters but hope that what I have to say about parametric objects and their environments will be neutral between the two ideas.

We shall be concerned here with parametric infons and shall use uppercase letters like 'X' and 'Y' to represent parameters. Thus

$$\langle\!\langle see, X, b; 1\rangle\!\rangle$$
$$\langle\!\langle see, X, Y; 1\rangle\!\rangle$$

are parametric infons which are indeterminate with respect to or parametric on the A-role and A-role and B-role respectively. We also allow parametric infons to be indeterminate with respect to relation and polarity. Thus we have the parametric infon

$$\langle\!\langle R, X, Y; I\rangle\!\rangle$$

We can have a single parameter corresponding to more than one structural role in an infon. Thus, for example, we have

$$\langle\!\langle see, X, X; 1\rangle\!\rangle$$

We can also have parameters embedded within infons which are arguments to relations in other infons. Thus parametric infon

$$\langle\!\langle seem, \langle\!\langle smile, X; 1\rangle\!\rangle; 1\rangle\!\rangle$$

is indeterminate with respect to the A-argument of its A-argument.

2.2.2 Environments for parametric objects

The idea behind parametric objects is that they are abstractions or generalizations over classes of non-parametric objects. Thus the parameters of a parametric object can be associated with objects, called ANCHORS, which, if they were to replace the parameters, would yield one of the objects in the class that the parametric object abstracts over. Such anchors are provided by environments. The notion of environments presented here is slightly different from that presented in [Cooper, 1989], [Cooper, 1990] but it represents, I hope, an improvement on the earlier version.

2.2.3 Environments for parametric objects

Environments are situations which support infons whose relation is **anchor**. Initially we will assume that the relation **anchor** has three argument roles, though we will see shortly that we need an additional one. The three roles that we will consider now are for a parametric object, a parameter and for another object which is to serve as the anchor for the parameter. As a preliminary definition, we will say that an ENVIRONMENT for a parametric object π is a situation which for any parameter p of π supports at most one infon

$$\langle\!\langle anchor, \pi, p, v; 1\rangle\!\rangle$$

The object v is the anchor or VALUE of the parameter. For example, an environment for π, where π is the parametric infon

$$\langle\!\langle \text{see}, X, Y; 1 \rangle\!\rangle$$

might be a situation env such that

$$env \models \langle\!\langle \text{anchor}, \pi, X, a; 1 \rangle\!\rangle$$
$$env \models \langle\!\langle \text{anchor}, \pi, Y, b; 1 \rangle\!\rangle$$

This situation env may support more facts than this, as long as it does not provide more than one value for any of the parameters.

This notion of environment where the relation **anchor** has just the three argument roles we have indicated is not quite right. We will want to talk of the same parametric object having its parameters anchored by different environments. This is particularly important if we take the structural view of parameters that I want to push. On the structural view we can have a parametric infon like π above which is indeterminate with respect to its A- and B-arguments. However, we cannot have a parametric infon which is like π except that it has different parameters for the A- and B-arguments. This means that on the structural view

$$\langle\!\langle \text{see}, X, Y; 1 \rangle\!\rangle$$
$$\langle\!\langle \text{see}, W, Z; 1 \rangle\!\rangle$$

would be different notations for the same object. Clearly we need to allow for the same parameters in this parametric infon to be anchored to different individuals in different environments. On the object view of parameters the need is not so great since we might be able to assume that there is a sufficient supply of parameters to allow us to say that a given parameter in a parametric object is only anchored to one object. However, this would seem to go against one of the basic intuitions that we have about parameters, namely that they can be anchored to different objects in different environments.

The problem arises when we consider this in the context of coherent collections of situations. Given the functional nature of the relation **anchor** we might expect to be able to conclude from

S is a coherent collection of situations

$env \in S$

$env \models \langle\!\langle \text{anchor}, \pi, p, v; 1 \rangle\!\rangle$

that for any $v' \neq v$

$\models_S \langle\!\langle \text{anchor}, \pi, p, v'; 0 \rangle\!\rangle$

However, this apparently reasonable characterization of functionality would allow at most one environment for a given parametric object within a coherent collection of situations.

We will avoid this problem by adding an additional argument role to the relation **anchor**. This argument role will be for a collection of LABELS or HANDLES that are used to point to the parameter. In our general theory of parametric objects we shall say that any kind of situation theoretic object might be used to label a parameter. Perhaps most intuitively we can think of particular situations or events as being labels for parameters in an environment, though we by no means wish to restrict labels to be such objects. We can now give the correct definition of environment.

> An ENVIRONMENT for a parametric object π is a situation which for any parameter p of π supports at most one infon of the form
>
> $$\langle\!\langle \text{anchor}, \pi, p, \{lab_1, \ldots, lab_n\}, v; 1 \rangle\!\rangle$$

We now require the relation **anchor** to be functional in the following sense:

> if
>
> > S is a coherent collection of situations
> >
> > $env \in S$
> >
> > $env \models \langle\!\langle \text{anchor}, \pi, p, \{lab_1, \ldots, lab_n\}, v; 1 \rangle\!\rangle$
>
> then for any $v' \neq v$
>
> > $\models_S \langle\!\langle \text{anchor}, \pi, p, \{lab_1, \ldots, lab_n\}, v'; 0 \rangle\!\rangle$

As an example of two different environments consider the parametric infon

$$\pi = \langle\!\langle \text{called}, \text{X}, \text{`Hesperus'}; 1 \rangle\!\rangle$$

and the two environments

$$env_1 \models \langle\!\langle \text{anchor}, \pi, \text{X}, \{s_1\}, v; 1 \rangle\!\rangle$$
$$env_2 \models \langle\!\langle \text{anchor}, \pi, \text{X}, \{s_2\}, v; 1 \rangle\!\rangle$$

where

$$s_1 \models \langle\!\langle \text{see}, a, v, \ell_1; 1 \rangle\!\rangle$$
$$s_2 \models \langle\!\langle \text{see}, a, v, \ell_2; 1 \rangle\!\rangle$$

and the location ℓ_1 is in the evening and the location ℓ_2 is in the morning. We can see that we might be able to build an analysis of knowledge in terms of parametric infons and environments where an agent could be aware of env_1 but not env_2. (For discussion of Frege's puzzle in terms of this kind of framework see [Cooper, 1989].)

On this view environments are not so much ways of relating parameters to their anchors, but rather ways of relating parts of the world (the labels) to other parts of the world (the anchors) mediated by the parametric objects. We are most interested here in cases where situations which are uses of linguistic expressions are used to label parameters. Therefore we can see the environments we shall characterize as ways of relating utterances to other objects in the world mediated by parametric infons.

Notation for environments

We introduce an abbreviatory notation for environments by means of an example. Suppose that

$$\pi = \langle\!\langle \text{like}, X, Y; 1 \rangle\!\rangle$$

and that *env* is a situation which supports the following infons and no others:

$$\langle\!\langle \text{anchor}, \pi, X, \{\underline{Anna}\}, a; 1 \rangle\!\rangle$$
$$\langle\!\langle \text{anchor}, \pi, Y, \{\underline{Claire}\}, c; 1 \rangle\!\rangle$$

Then we will represent *env* as

$$_\pi[[\underline{Anna}] : X/a, [\underline{Claire}] : Y/c]$$

When it is obvious from the context we will sometimes suppress the subscript π which indicates what parametric infon the environments provides labels and anchors for. The notation otherwise consists of a list of terms of the form

$$[lab_1, \ldots, lab_n] : p/v$$

corresponding to the infon

$$\langle\!\langle \text{anchor}, \pi, p, \{lab_1, \ldots, lab_n\}, v; 1 \rangle\!\rangle$$

2.2.4 Relating parametric infons and environments to non-parametric infons

For each parametric infon, π, and environment for π, *env*, there is a unique corresponding non-parametric object obtained from the parametric infon by removing the parameters and letting the anchors of the parameters given by the environment play the role of the corresponding parameter in the infon. We will call this the BASIS for π with respect to *env*. For example, the basis for

$$\langle\!\langle \text{see}, X, Y; 1 \rangle\!\rangle$$

with respect to

$$[[\underline{Anna}] : X/a, [\underline{Claire}] : Y/b]$$

is

$$\langle\!\langle \text{see}, a, b; 1 \rangle\!\rangle$$

2.2.5 Incorporating restrictions into environments

We have said that environments may support other infons in addition to the infons with the relation **anchor**. In particular they may support infons which have the anchors of parameters as arguments. Thus for some environment env we might have

$$env \models \langle\!\langle \text{anchor}, \pi, \text{X}, \{\underline{Anna}\}, a; 1 \rangle\!\rangle$$
$$env \models \langle\!\langle \text{named}, a, \text{`Anna'}; 1 \rangle\!\rangle$$
$$env \models \langle\!\langle \text{female}, a; 1 \rangle\!\rangle$$

The infons that do not have the relation **anchor** are called restrictions. This is because they are important when we are specifying what kind of environments may be associated with parametric infons in given applications. Thus in our fragment we will say that environments are allowed which associate uses of 'Anna' with individuals and which in addition must support the restrictions given here but we will not in our definition of the fragment make any reference to the particular individuals which a parameter labelled by a use of 'Anna' can be anchored to. By characterizing the allowable environments in this way we are in effect restricting the possible anchors for parameters labelled by a use of 'Anna' to females named Anna.

This approach to restrictions is different to the standard view of restrictions in situation theory. It has normally been assumed that there are objects which are restricted parameters. So, for example, we might have the following two variant notations for a parametric infon with a restricted parameter

$$\langle\!\langle \text{smile}, \text{X} | \langle\!\langle \text{named}, \text{X}, \text{`Anna'}; 1 \rangle\!\rangle; 1 \rangle\!\rangle$$
$$\langle\!\langle \text{smile}, \text{X}_{\langle\!\langle \text{named}, \text{X}, \text{`Anna'}; 1 \rangle\!\rangle}; 1 \rangle\!\rangle$$

The idea behind a restricted parameter is that it can only be anchored to something which meets the restriction. The notion has been used to great effect for linguistic analysis by Gawron and Peters ([Gawron and Peters, 1990a], [Gawron and Peters, 1990b]). Westerståhl ([Westerståhl, 1990]) discusses restricted parameters from the perspective of formalizing situation theory and suggests some potential problems that might arise. He elects to avoid them and takes up an alternative suggested by Plotkin which involves a restriction connective between propositions. The reasons that I have decided to use environments with restrictions rather than restricted parameters are the following:

i. restricted parameters have a dubious ontological status even on the object view of parameters. It is difficult to see what kind of situation theoretic object they could be unless we think of them in formal terms, e.g. as an ordered pair consisting of a parameter and an infon. On the structural view of parameters which I would like to promote where the parameters are thought of as dimensions of variation like **A-argument-of** it is even more difficult to see what it means to restrict the parameter in the required sense.

ii. restricted parameters are normally represented with just an infon to represent the restriction but it is not obvious which situation should support the restriction. It may not be enough simply to say that the restriction is supported somewhere in the coherent collection of situations under consideration. It may not be sufficient to require that a use of 'Anna' can be used to refer to Anna in all circumstances simply because there are situations where she is called Anna. For example, in some contexts she might be referred to by her other name 'Julia' or 'Miss Cooper' and it might be inappropriate to use 'Anna' to refer to her in those contexts. Saying that the restriction must be supported by the environment places a locality condition on the restriction. It is the very situation which provides the anchor which also supports the restriction that she is named Anna.

iii. it is quite inconvenient to state restrictions that involve more than one parameter in the parametric object in terms of restricted parameters. Does the restriction go on one of the parameters? If so, which one? Do we have a different parametric object if we choose to put the restriction on one of the parameters as opposed to another? Or do we have to require that such restrictions occur on all parameters involved in the restriction?

iv. in terms of computation where we might gradually build up information about more and more restrictions on parameters on the basis of, for example, parsing a sentence, several occurrences of the same parameter prove quite inconvenient. We might naturally associate one restriction with one occurrence of the parameter and another restriction with another occurrence of the parameter. The intention should be that we associate both restrictions with the parameter and that properly in the notation both restrictions should be associated with both occurrences. Clearly, from a combinatorial point of view it is preferable to have one place where the restrictions are kept (namely the environment) rather than to have to update the notation for each occurrence of the parameter.

2.2.6   Classifying environments

In using environments in our theory of grammar we will have need of some specific kinds of environments. An environment env for a parametric object π is

1. COMPLETE iff for each parameter p of π there is some $lab_1, \ldots, lab_n, v$ such that

$$env \models \langle\!\langle \text{anchor}, \pi, p, \{lab_1, \ldots, lab_n\}, v; 1 \rangle\!\rangle$$

2. a UNIQUE LABELLING iff for any lab_i there is at most one parameter p of π such that there is some $lab_1, \ldots, lab_n$ and v such that

$$env \models \langle\!\langle \text{anchor}, \pi, p, \{lab_1, \ldots, lab_i, \ldots, lab_n\}, v; 1 \rangle\!\rangle$$

3. RESTRICTED iff there is no p not a parameter of π such that for some $lab_1, \ldots, lab_n, v$ and polarity i

$$env \models \langle\!\langle \text{anchor}, \pi, p, \{lab_1, \ldots, lab_n\}, v; i \rangle\!\rangle$$

4. CONFINED TO A LINGUISTIC USE u iff for any $u', lab_1, \ldots, lab_n, p$ and v

$$env \models \langle\!\langle \text{anchor}, \pi, p, \{lab_1, \ldots, u', \ldots, lab_n\}, v; 1 \rangle\!\rangle$$

implies $u' = u$ or u' is a subconstituent of u (where subconstituent is defined in the obvious recursive manner given the notion of constituent we have introduced).

2.3 Parametric infons and environments in situation theoretic grammar

2.3.1 The relation gr

We will now think of the grammar relation gr as having three or four argument roles. We can either think of the relation as being polyadic or we can say that there is more than one relation. Which option we choose is not of importance for this application, though we will talk as if we have a single polyadic relation.

When the relation gr holds between three arguments those arguments are: a linguistic use, a parametric infon and an environment for that parametric infon. Thus we can make statements of the following form:

$$gr(u, \pi, env)$$

If _Anna smiles_ is a use of 'Anna smiles' we will require that the relation gr holds in the following kind of case:

$$gr(\underline{Anna\,smiles}, \langle\!\langle R, X; 1 \rangle\!\rangle, env)$$

where

$env \models [[\underline{smiles}, \text{pred}] : R/\text{smile}, [\underline{Anna}, \text{subj}] : X/x]$
$env \models \langle\!\langle \text{named}, x, \text{`Anna'}; 1 \rangle\!\rangle$
$env \models \langle\!\langle \text{female}, x; 1 \rangle\!\rangle$

That is, the relation gr holds between a use of 'Anna smiles', the parametric infon $\langle\!\langle R, X; 1 \rangle\!\rangle$ and any environment which:

i. labels the relation parameter R with the use of 'smiles' which is a subconstituent of the sentence use and anchors it to the relation **smile**

ii. labels the parameter X with the use of 'Anna' which is a subconstituent of the sentence use and anchors to some object x such that env supports the fact the x is named by the word 'Anna' and the fact that x is female.

In fact we require a little bit more than this. We require that each parameter have another label besides the use. This second label is a grammatical function. We will say more about grammatical functions below.

This, then, is the solution to the problem of proper names that we mentioned at the beginning of this section. Our statement of the grammar will not make reference to any particular individuals and there is no requirement that a use of a proper name refers to any particular individual. It is only required that a use of a proper name refers to an individual named by that proper name.

The other problem we mentioned at the beginning of this section concerned the treatment of constituents like VPs for which we did not have a situation theoretic object to act as content. The approach we take to this is to let verbs introduce complete parametric infons and have the various constituents place restrictions on what kind of environment the use can be associated with. Thus for a use *likes* of the verb 'likes' we will have

$$gr(\underline{likes}, \langle\langle R, X, Y; 1\rangle\rangle, env)$$

where for some uses u_1 and u_2 and objects x and y

$$env \models [[\underline{likes}, \text{pred}] : R/\text{like}, [u_1, \text{subj}] : X/x, [u_2, \text{obj}] : Y/y]$$
$$u_1 \models [\ \text{person:}\quad \text{third}\ ]$$

For a use *likes Claire* we will have

$$gr(\underline{likes\ Claire}, \langle\langle R, X, Y; 1\rangle\rangle, env)$$

where for some uses u_1 and u_2 and objects x and y

$$env \models [[\underline{likes}, \text{pred}] : R/\text{like}, [u_1, \text{subj}] : X/x, [\underline{Claire}, \text{obj}] : Y/y]$$
$$env \models \langle\langle \text{named}, y, \text{'Claire'}; 1\rangle\rangle$$
$$env \models \langle\langle \text{female}, y; 1\rangle\rangle$$
$$u_1 \models [\ \text{person:}\quad \text{third}\ ]$$

For an utterance u to be a grammatical sentence use we must require that the environment for the parametric infon is complete, a unique labelling, restricted and confined to u. We can recover the notion of content that we had in Fragment 1 at least for grammatical sentence uses. If u is a grammatical sentence use and

$$gr(u, \pi, env)$$

then a content for u is σ where

$$\text{basis}(\pi, env, \sigma)$$

2.3.2 Grammatical functions

Grammatical functions we take to be relations (in the situation theoretic sense) which hold between uses. Thus, for example, in English, if we have a sentence use $[NP\ VP]_S$ we might say

$$\text{subj}([NP\ VP]_S, \underline{NP})$$

In Fragment 2 we do not make any use of the particular characterization of the grammatical function relations but use the grammatical functions as labels for parameters in order to make sure that appropriate consituents of uses get associated with the right parameters. Our use of grammatical functions here seems very similar to their use in Lexical Functional Grammar. For example, with active verbs it is important that the label **subj** be associated with the A-argument parameter. For passive verbs, on the other hand, it is important that the label **subj** be associated with the B-argument parameter.

2.3.3 Fragment 2: Proper names

Lexicon

Anna:
$n(u, gr, \pi(X), env)$ if

$$u \models \left[\begin{array}{ll} \text{use-of:} & \text{`Anna'} \\ \text{category:} & \text{N} \\ \text{person:} & \text{third} \end{array} \right]$$

$env \models [[u, gr] : X/x]$
$env \models \langle\!\langle \text{named}, x, \text{`Anna'}; 1 \rangle\!\rangle$
$env \models \langle\!\langle \text{female}, x; 1 \rangle\!\rangle$

Claire:
$n(u, gr, \pi(X), env)$ if

$$u \models \left[\begin{array}{ll} \text{use-of:} & \text{`Claire'} \\ \text{category:} & \text{N} \\ \text{person:} & \text{third} \end{array} \right]$$

$env \models [[u, gr] : X/x]$
$env \models \langle\!\langle \text{named}, x, \text{`Claire'}; 1 \rangle\!\rangle$
$env \models \langle\!\langle \text{female}, x; 1 \rangle\!\rangle$

Jon:
$n(u, gr, \pi(X), env)$ if

$$u \models \left[\begin{array}{ll} \text{use-of:} & \text{`Jon'} \\ \text{category:} & \text{N} \\ \text{person:} & \text{third} \end{array} \right]$$

$env \models [[u, gr] : X/x]$
$env \models \langle\!\langle \text{named}, x, \text{`Jon'}; 1 \rangle\!\rangle$
$env \models \langle\!\langle \text{male}, x; 1 \rangle\!\rangle$

Robin:

$n(u, gr, \pi(X), env)$ if

$$u \models \begin{bmatrix} \text{use-of:} & \text{`Robin'} \\ \text{category:} & \text{N} \\ \text{person:} & \text{third} \end{bmatrix}$$

$env \models [[u, gr] : X/x]$

$env \models \langle\langle \text{named}, x, \text{`Robin'}; 1 \rangle\rangle$

she:

$n(u, gr, \pi(X), env)$ if

$$u \models \begin{bmatrix} \text{use-of:} & \text{`she'} \\ \text{category:} & \text{N} \\ \text{person:} & \text{third} \\ \text{case:} & \text{nom} \end{bmatrix}$$

$env \models [[u, gr] : X/x]$

$env \models \langle\langle \text{female}, x; 1 \rangle\rangle$

her:

$n(u, gr, \pi(X), env)$ if

$$u \models \begin{bmatrix} \text{use-of:} & \text{`her'} \\ \text{category:} & \text{N} \\ \text{person:} & \text{third} \\ \text{case:} & \text{acc} \end{bmatrix}$$

$env \models [[u, gr] : X/x]$

$env \models \langle\langle \text{female}, x; 1 \rangle\rangle$

I:

$n(u, gr, \pi(X), env)$ if

$$u \models \begin{bmatrix} \text{use-of:} & \text{`I'} \\ \text{category:} & \text{N} \\ \text{person:} & \text{first} \\ \text{case:} & \text{nom} \\ \text{speaker:} & x \end{bmatrix}$$

$env \models [[u, gr] : X/x]$

herself:

$n(u, gr, \pi(X,Y), env)$ if

$$u \models \begin{bmatrix} \text{use-of:} & \text{`herself'} \\ \text{category:} & \text{N} \\ \text{person:} & \text{third} \\ \text{case:} & \text{acc} \end{bmatrix}$$

$env \models [[u, gr] : X/x, [u', gr'] : Y/x]$

$env \models \langle\langle \text{female}, x; 1 \rangle\rangle$

$u' \models [\text{person:} \quad \text{third}]$

Note: In a more complete treatment of reflexives we may place restrictions on gr' (e.g. that it is **subj** for a language like German) or on the syntactic relationship between u and u' (e.g. precede(u', u), command(u, u')).

smiles:
$v(u, \langle\langle R, X; 1\rangle\rangle, env)$ if

$$u \models \begin{bmatrix} \text{use-of:} & \text{'smiles'} \\ \text{category:} & V \end{bmatrix}$$

$env \models [[u, \text{pred}] : R/\text{smile}, [u', \text{subj}] : X/x]$

$u' \models [\text{ person: third }]$

smile:
$v(u, \langle\langle R, X; 1\rangle\rangle, env)$ if

$$u \models \begin{bmatrix} \text{use-of:} & \text{'smile'} \\ \text{category:} & V \end{bmatrix}$$

$env \models [[u, \text{pred}] : R/\text{smile}, [u', \text{subj}] : X/x]$

$u' \models [\text{ person: first }]$

likes:
$v(u, \langle\langle R, X, Y; 1\rangle\rangle, env)$ if

$$u \models \begin{bmatrix} \text{use-of:} & \text{'likes'} \\ \text{category:} & V \end{bmatrix}$$

$env \models [[u, \text{pred}] : R/\text{like}, [u_1, \text{subj}] : X/x, [u_2, \text{obj}] : Y/y]$

$u_1 \models [\text{ person: third }]$

like:
$v(u, \langle\langle R, X, Y; 1\rangle\rangle, env)$ if

$$u \models \begin{bmatrix} \text{use-of:} & \text{'like'} \\ \text{category:} & V \end{bmatrix}$$

$env \models [[u, \text{pred}] : R/\text{like}, [u_1, \text{subj}] : X/x, [u_2, \text{obj}] : Y/y]$

$u_1 \models [\text{ person: first }]$

is-liked:
$v(u, \langle\langle R, \_, X; 1\rangle\rangle, env)$ if

$$u \models \begin{bmatrix} \text{use-of:} & \text{'is-liked'} \\ \text{category:} & V \end{bmatrix}$$

$env \models [[u, \text{pred}] : R/\text{like}, [u', \text{subj}] : X/x]$

$u' \models [\text{ person: third }]$

Lexical insertion

If $\underline{w}$ is a use of a word w listed in the lexicon, then

$x([w]_X, \pi, env)$ if
$\quad x(\underline{w}, \pi, env)$

$x([w]_X, gr, \pi, env)$ if
$\quad x(\underline{w}, gr, \pi, env)$

Phrase structure

1. $s([NP\ VP]_S, \pi, env)$ if
   $\quad np(\underline{NP}, \text{subj}, \pi, env)$
   $\quad vp(\underline{VP}, \pi, env)$
   $\quad \underline{NP} \models [\ \text{case:}\quad \text{nom}\ ]$

2. $vp([V\ NP]_{VP}, \pi, env)$ if
   $\quad v(\underline{V}, \pi, env)$
   $\quad np(\underline{NP}, \text{obj}, \pi, env)$
   $\quad \underline{NP} \models [\ \text{case:}\quad \text{acc}\ ]$

3. $vp([V]_{VP}, \pi, env)$ if
   $\quad v(\underline{V}, \pi, env)$

4. $np([N]_{NP}, gr, \pi, env)$ if
   $\quad n(\underline{N}, gr, \pi, env)$
   $\quad \underline{N} \models [\ \text{case:}\quad \alpha\ ]$
   $\quad \underline{NP} \models [\ \text{case:}\quad \alpha\ ]$

Grammaticality

φ is a grammatical sentence utterance according to Fragment 2 if

$\quad s(\varphi, \pi, env)$

and env is a complete, restricted environment for π which is a unique labelling confined to φ.

Description

φ describes situation s according to Fragment 2 if φ is a grammatical sentence utterance according to Fragment 2 and

$\quad circ(\varphi, \pi, env)$
$\quad s(\varphi, \pi, env)$
$\quad basis(\pi, env, \sigma)$
$\quad s \models \sigma$

Here we use the relation **circ** for "circumstances" to indicate the actual π and *env* associated with the utterance φ of the many which could have been associated with according to the constraints expressed by the grammar.

3 Quantification

3.1 Introduction

In this section we will look at how generalized quantifiers can be incorporated into situation theoretic grammar in a way that seems to preserve much of classical generalized quantifier theory (see, for example, [Barwise and Cooper, 1981], [Gärdenfors,1987])[3]. At the same time it provides us with some novel additions to the traditional approach which result from the use of situations in the analysis.

We will also look at a basic treatment of quantifier scope and see how the environments used in situation theoretic grammar provide us with a level of information about an utterance where quantifier scope is not resolved.

We will conclude by making some remarks about computational implications of situation theoretic grammar as presented here.

3.2 Generalized quantifiers

3.2.1 Quantifier relations

In classical generalized quantifier theory natural language determiners are considered to denote relations between sets. Here we will introduce QUANTIFIER RELATIONS corresponding to determiners. Quantifier relations are relations which have two argument roles for properties. Let us suppose that P and Q are the properties of being a man and running respectively. We will say what properties are in the next section. We will have quantificational infons of the form

$$\langle\!\langle \text{every}, P, Q; 1 \rangle\!\rangle$$
$$\langle\!\langle \text{every}, P, Q; 0 \rangle\!\rangle$$
$$\langle\!\langle \text{most}, P, Q; 1 \rangle\!\rangle$$

corresponding respectively to

> every man runs
> not every man runs
> most men run

We will also treat 'a' and 'the' as corresponding to quantifier relations of this kind, although this is not standard in situation semantics. [Barwise and Perry, 1983] make a

---

[3]For an illuminating discussion of a number of alternatives for treating generalized quantifiers in situation theory see [Richard Cooper, 1990].

distinction between singular noun-phrases (i.e. indefinite and definite descriptions) which essentially pick out an individual and general noun-phrases such as 'no fish' and 'every man' which must be analysed as quantifiers. [Gawron and Peters, 1990a] follow Barwise and Perry and make the distinction by analysing the singular noun-phrases in terms of restricted parameters and the general noun-phrases in terms of generalized quantifiers. For some discussion of the alternatives see [Cooper and Kamp, forth.].

3.2.2   Properties

In order to give an account of generalized quantifiers we have to introduce properties into our situation theory. Properties involve abstraction over parameters in a parametric infon. We shall consider properties like the following

$$[X \,|\, s \models \pi(X)]$$
$$[X,Y \,|\, s \models \pi(X,Y)]$$
$$[X,S \,|\, S \models \pi(X)]$$

where $\pi(X)$ and $\pi(X,Y)$ are parametric infons with parameters X and X,Y respectively. We will say that a has the property

$$[X \,|\, s \models \pi(X)]$$

just in case

$$s \models \pi(X/a)$$

that is, s supports the infon obtained by replacing the parameter X in $\pi(X)$ with a. Similarly we say that a and b have the property or stand in the relation

$$[X,Y \,|\, s \models \pi(X,Y)]$$

just in case

$$s \models \pi(X/a, Y/b)$$

and that a and s have the property (stand in the relation)

$$[X,S \,|\, S \models \pi(X)]$$

just in case

$$s \models \pi(X/a)$$

So, for example, we might read the property

$$[X \,|\, s \models \langle\!\langle \mathrm{man}, X; 1 \rangle\!\rangle]$$

as "the property of being a man in situation s". When a property is defined in terms of a specific situation in this way, we will call it a SPECIFIC PROPERTY. We can think of

$$[X,S \mid S \models \langle\!\langle man, X; 1 \rangle\!\rangle]$$

as the generic property of being a man, actually a relation that holds between an individual and a situation just in case the individual is a man in the situation.

The notion of properties obtained by abstraction is similar in some respects to the kind of notion which one finds in other systems such as Montague's semantics [Dowty *et al.*, 1981] or property theory [Chierchia et al.,1989] except that here the notion of situation is playing a role which has no precise correspondence in the other theories. We shall explore some of the consequences of defining properties in terms of situations for natural language semantics.

3.2.3 Resource situations

Barwise and Perry in [Barwise and Perry, 1983] introduced the notion of resource situation in order to be able to treat definite descriptions. They wanted to preserve the intuition that definite descriptions have a uniqueness requirement, even though it is quite clear that a sentence like 'the dog ran away' does not require that there only be one dog in the universe. At first blush one might think that a situation semantics would be able to treat such sentences easily since they could be analysed as describing situations (i.e. parts of the world) which contain exactly one dog. However, other examples (due originally to [Lewis, 1979] show that it cannot be the described situation in which there is a unique dog. Consider the discourse

> We have a dog and a cat and I think we are going to have to keep them under better control. Yesterday the dog got into a fight with the neightbour's dog and bit it and the neighbour is thinking of reporting us to the police.

Here it is clear that the sentence

> Yesterday the dog got into a fight with the neighbour's dog

describes a situation in which there are two dogs and so there is no way that we could analyse the description as giving us a unique dog in that situation. Barwise and Perry suggested that the intuition that definite descriptions require uniqueness can be preserved if we introduce the notion of resource situation. They suggested that each use of definite description could be related to a different resource situation in which there is exactly one dog. For them, this resource situation was used to determine the singular referent of the use of the definite description. Since resource situations are related to uses of definite descriptions it could be the çase that we could have two occurrences of the same definite description in the same sentence which nevertheless have a different referent. Thus under certain circumstances the situation described above could be described by

> the dog bit the dog

Admittedly two occurrences of the same definite description within the same sentence are a bit difficult to understand in this way. However, I do not believe that it is impossible given the right circumstances.

On the generalized quantifier analysis it is the situation in the property which is the resource situation. Thus an infon corresponding to 'the dog barked' would be

$$\langle\!\langle \text{the}, [X \mid s \models \langle\!\langle \text{dog}, X; 1 \rangle\!\rangle], [X \mid s' \models \langle\!\langle \text{bark}, X; 1 \rangle\!\rangle]; 1 \rangle\!\rangle$$

The fact that the property

$$[X \mid s \models \langle\!\langle \text{dog}, X; 1 \rangle\!\rangle]$$

is the first argument to the relation **the** means that it will be required that there is exactly one object which has this property, that is that there is exactly one object a of which the following holds

$$s \models \langle\!\langle \text{dog}, a; 1 \rangle\!\rangle$$

Thus s will be the situation which provides the unique referent for the definite description. It will be the resource situation for the use of the noun-phrase 'the dog'.

Although resource situations were introduced by Barwise and Perry to account for definite descriptions this is not the only use to which they can be put. Our analysis of generalized quantifiers predicts that there might be a resource situation for any quantified noun-phrase. Consider, for example, the sentence 'everybody came to the party'. It is a well-known fact that the quantification here is not over the entire universe of people, or even all the people in the domain of discourse. It is generally assumed that the range of quantification for any quantifier has to be limited in some way by the context of use. Just as with definite descriptions, we can argue that the range of quantification is not determined by the described situation. Consider the sentence 'everything is on the table'. This describes a situation in which there is a table and "everything" is on it. However, "everything" cannot include everything in the situation since the table is in the situation and the sentence does not mean that the table is on itself. Hence we need a resource situation distinct from the described situation which determines the range of quantification for the use of 'everything'.

3.2.4 Constraints on quantifier relations

We need to say more about quantifier relations before we can be said to have given a reasonable analysis of quantification. It is not enough to say that quantifier relations are relations between properties. We also need to say what else must hold if a quantificational infon is supported. It is at this point that we can import the classical set-theoretic analysis of generalized quantifiers into situation theory. It is still an open question whether this is the most appropriate thing to do for a situation semantics. However, it is a rather conservative move and I think it is important to show that it is possible and to make precise exactly how it might be done. We do it here by defining constraints on quantifier relations by adding further clauses to the characterization of coherent collections of situations given in Section 1. We give constraints for the quantifier relations **every**,**the** and **a**[4].

If S is a coherent collection of situations and $s, s' \in S$ then

i. $\models_S \langle\!\langle \text{every}, [X \mid s \models \pi(X)], [Y \mid s' \models \pi'(Y)]; 1 \rangle\!\rangle$ iff
$\forall x[s \models \pi(X/x) \rightarrow s' \models \pi'(Y/x)]$

ii. $\models_S \langle\!\langle \text{the}, [X \mid s \models \pi(X)], [Y \mid s' \models \pi'(Y)]; 1 \rangle\!\rangle$ iff
$\exists x[s \models \pi(X/x) \wedge \forall y[s \models \pi(X/y) \rightarrow x = y]]$
$\wedge \forall x[s \models \pi(X/x) \rightarrow s' \models \pi'(Y/x)]$

iii. $\models_S \langle\!\langle \text{a}, [X \mid s \models \pi(X)], [Y \mid s' \models \pi'(Y)]; 1 \rangle\!\rangle$ iff
$\exists x[s \models \pi(X/x) \wedge s' \models \pi'(Y/x)]$

These definitions use a resource situation in both the first and second arguments of the quantifier relations. It is an open question whether this option is required for natural language semantics. (See the discussion of 'each' below for a suggestion of how the specific property in the second argument might be used.) We can also give constraints which use a generic property (i.e. one abstracting both over individuals and situations) in the second argument. This we might think of as either an alternative analysis for natural language quantification or as providing an additional reading. The basic strategy of the following constraints is to say that a quantifier relation holds between a specific property P and a generic property Q just in case there is some situation s such that the relation holds between P and the specific property obtained by fixing s to be the situation for Q. Thus we get the effect of existential quantification over resource situations in the second argument.

Here is the precise definition for **every**, **the** and **a**:

If S is a coherent collection of situations and $s, s' \in S$ then

i. $\models_S \langle\!\langle \text{every}, [X \mid s \models \pi(X)], [Y,S \mid S \models \pi'(Y)]; 1 \rangle\!\rangle$ iff
$\forall x[s \models \pi(X/x) \rightarrow \exists s' \in S \; s' \models \pi'(Y/x)]$

ii. $\models_S \langle\!\langle \text{the}, [X \mid s \models \pi(X)], [Y,S \mid S \models \pi'(Y)]; 1 \rangle\!\rangle$ iff
$\exists x[s \models \pi(X/x) \wedge \forall y[s \models \pi(X/y) \rightarrow x = y]]$
$\wedge \forall x[s \models \pi(X/x) \rightarrow \exists s' \in S \; s' \models \pi'(Y/x)]$

iii. $\models_S \langle\!\langle \text{a}, [X \mid s \models \pi(X)], [Y,S \mid S \models \pi'(Y)]; 1 \rangle\!\rangle$ iff
$\exists x[s \models \pi(X/x) \wedge \exists s' \in S \; s' \models \pi'(Y/x)]$

3.2.5 Generic quantification

Now that we have seen what it means for a quantifier relation to hold between two specific properties and between a specific and generic property the question arises as to what

---

[4]To make this complete we would need to give constraints not only for the positive infons as we do here but also for the corresponding negative infons. There are a number of alternatives for doing this and we will not discuss them here or for any of the other conditions that we introduce below.

might be the case if a quantifier relation holds between two generic properties. This we will interpret as universal quantification over situations corresponding to the first argument. This will give us a kind of generic reading. This proposal is not meant to be a complete analysis of genericity. However, I think that some additional specification of the range of situations being universally quantified over might go a long way towards providing an account of why singular indefinite and definite descriptions in natural language can have generic force. This limiting of the range of situations might be tied to an account of precisely which collection of coherent situations we are talking about.

The general claim here is that the quantification over individuals in these cases is not essentially different from the non-generic cases. It is the fact that we have used universal quantification over situations which gives the effect of universality.

Here are the clauses for **every, the** and **a**:

If S is a coherent collection of situations and $s, s' \in S$ then

i. $\models_S \langle\!\langle \text{every}, [X,S \mid S \models \pi(X)], [Y,S' \mid S' \models \pi'(Y)]; 1 \rangle\!\rangle$ iff
$\forall s \in S[\forall x[s \models \pi(X/x) \rightarrow \exists s' \in S \, s' \models \pi'(Y/x)]]$

ii. $\models_S \langle\!\langle \text{the}, [X,S \mid S \models \pi(X)], [Y,S' \mid S' \models \pi'(Y)]; 1 \rangle\!\rangle$ iff
$\forall s \in S[\exists x[s \models \pi(X/x) \wedge \forall y[s \models \pi(X/y) \rightarrow x = y]]$
$\rightarrow \forall x[s \models \pi(X/x) \rightarrow \exists s' \in S \, s' \models \pi'(Y/x)]]$

iii. $\models_S \langle\!\langle \text{a}, [X,S \mid S \models \pi(X)], [Y,S' \mid S' \models \pi'(Y)]; 1 \rangle\!\rangle$ iff
$\forall s \in S[\exists x[s \models \pi(X/x)] \rightarrow \exists x[s \models \pi(X/x) \wedge \exists s' \in S \, s' \models \pi'(Y/x)]]$

It seems from this that the addition of resource situations to classical generalized quantifier theory might give us a powerful tool for analysing the kind of quantification we find in natural language.

3.2.6   Distinguishing 'each' and 'every'

In this section we discuss a way in which the addition of resource situations to the classical theory of generalized quantifiers can help us to make a distinction which is difficult or impossible to make in a standard truth conditional analysis. Our pretheoretic intuitions about the difference between 'each' and 'every' is that 'each' forces us to consider each thing being quantified over individually whereas 'every' allows us to consider the things being quantified over as a whole. To make this intuition more concrete let us consider the following two sentences with perception complements.

John saw every person in the room leave
John saw each person in the room leave

It seems to me that the first sentence could report that John saw a situation in which everybody rushed out of the room, perhaps in the case of a fire alarm going off. It may well be that he saw a room full of people, followed by a mad scramble to get to the door and then an empty room and that he need not have seen each individual person leave the room. The second sentence, on the other hand, does not allow this general reading. It requires that John saw each person person leave the room individually.

We could capture this difference in the following way. Suppose that s is the situation that John saw and that r is the resource situation which determines the range of the quantifier. (We do not rule out the possibility that r is identical with s.) Then we might say that the first sentence requires

$$s \models \langle\!\langle \text{every}, [X \mid r \models \langle\!\langle \text{person}, X; 1\rangle\!\rangle], [X, S \mid S \models \langle\!\langle \text{leave}, X; 1\rangle\!\rangle]; 1\rangle\!\rangle$$

Here the situation s is required to support the quantificational fact but it is not required to support each of the individual facts of leaving. For the sentence with 'each' we might require

$$s \models \langle\!\langle \text{every}, [X \mid r \models \langle\!\langle \text{person}, X; 1\rangle\!\rangle], [X \mid s \models \langle\!\langle \text{leave}, X; 1\rangle\!\rangle]; 1\rangle\!\rangle$$

Here it is required that s support not only the quantificational fact but also each of the individual facts of leaving, since the resource situation for the second argument to **every** is s itself. The difference between 'each' and 'every' on this view is that 'each' does not allow generic properties in the second argument and requires the resource situation to be identical with s[5].

3.3 Quantifier scope and environments

3.3.1 Quantification and anchoring

In our previous discussion of environments for parametric infons we analysed environments as situations which provide both anchors and labels for parameters. We said that environments supported infons of the form

$$\langle\!\langle \text{anchor}, \pi, p, \{lab_1, \ldots, lab_n\}, v; 1\rangle\!\rangle$$

for parametric object π, parameter p, labels $\{lab_1, \ldots, lab_n\}$ and anchor (value) v. Now we shall consider environments which also provide information about quantification over parameters. By this we mean that they support infons of the form

$$\langle\!\langle \text{quantify}, \pi, p, \{lab_1, \ldots, lab_n\}, q; 1\rangle\!\rangle$$

where q is a quantifier. What we mean by a quantifier is an infon with a quantifier relation which is unsaturated with respect to its B-argument role. For example,

$$\langle\!\langle \text{every}, [X \mid s \models \langle\!\langle \text{man}, X; 1\rangle\!\rangle], \_; 1\rangle\!\rangle$$

In our abbreviatory notation for environments we shall use '//' to represent quantification in a similar way to our use of '/' to represent anchoring. Suppose that

$$\pi = \langle\!\langle \text{like}, X, Y; 1\rangle\!\rangle$$

---

[5]It is at this point not totally clear to me what is the best way to achieve this in a compositional treatment. It requires a little more mechanism than we will detail here.

and that *env* is a situation which supports the following infons and no others:

$\langle\!\langle \text{quantify}, \pi, X, \{\underline{Anna}\}, \langle\!\langle \text{every}, [X \mid s \models \langle\!\langle \text{girl}, X; 1\rangle\!\rangle], \_; 1\rangle\!\rangle; 1\rangle\!\rangle$
$\langle\!\langle \text{anchor}, \pi, Y, \{\underline{Claire}\}, c; 1\rangle\!\rangle$

Then we will represent *env* as

$_\pi[[\underline{every\ girl}] : X /\!/ \langle\!\langle \text{every}, [X \mid s \models \langle\!\langle \text{girl}, X; 1\rangle\!\rangle], \_; 1\rangle\!\rangle, [\underline{Claire}] : Y/c]$

Similarly if *env* supports

$\langle\!\langle \text{quantify}, \pi, X, \{\underline{every\ girl}\}, \langle\!\langle \text{every}, [X \mid s \models \langle\!\langle \text{girl}, X; 1\rangle\!\rangle], \_; 1\rangle\!\rangle; 1\rangle\!\rangle$
$\langle\!\langle \text{quantify}, \pi, Y, \{\underline{a\ doll}\}, \langle\!\langle \text{a}, [X \mid s \models \langle\!\langle \text{doll}, X; 1\rangle\!\rangle], \_; 1\rangle\!\rangle; 1\rangle\!\rangle$

we will represent *env* as

$_\pi[[\underline{every\ girl}] : X /\!/ \langle\!\langle \text{every}, [X \mid s \models \langle\!\langle \text{girl}, X; 1\rangle\!\rangle], \_; 1\rangle\!\rangle,$
$[\underline{a\ doll}] : Y /\!/ \langle\!\langle \text{a}, [X \mid s \models \langle\!\langle \text{doll}, X; 1\rangle\!\rangle], \_; 1\rangle\!\rangle]$

3.3.2 The basis relation

Environments as characterized above do not provide any information about quantifier scope. It is as if each quantifier were entered into storage, except that there is no explicit storage mechanism. The notion of basis which we characterized in the previous section and which we use to obtain the content of a use now involves something more complicated than simply replacing parameters with their anchors. In the case of a quantified parameter we have to quantify in the quantifier in order to obtain a basis. An important aspect of this is that **basis** is now a relation rather than a function as it was when we only had anchoring. This is because the quantifiers can be quantified in varying orders. The definition of the basis relation corresponds quite closely to the kind of quantifier scope algorithms that have been proposed in the computational literature (e.g. [Hobbs and Shieber, 1987], [Lewin, 1990]). Here is the most straightforward characterization of a basis relation:

1. if $env \models {}_\pi[[lab_1, \ldots, lab_n] : X /\!/ \langle\!\langle q, p, \_; 1\rangle\!\rangle]$ then

   $\text{basis}(\pi, env, \sigma)$ if
   $\text{basis}(\langle\!\langle q, p, [X, S \mid S \models \pi]; 1\rangle\!\rangle, env - {}_\pi[[lab_1, \ldots, lab_n] : X /\!/ \langle\!\langle q, p, \_; 1\rangle\!\rangle], \sigma)$

2. if $env \models {}_\pi[[lab_1, \ldots, lab_n] : X/v]$ then

   $\text{basis}(\pi, env, \sigma)$ if
   $\text{basis}(\pi(X/v), env - {}_\pi[[lab_1, \ldots, lab_n] : X/v], \sigma)$

3. $\text{basis}(\pi, [\ ], \pi)$

In this definition we use notation such as

$env - {}_\pi[[lab_1, \ldots, lab_n] : X /\!/ \langle\!\langle q, p, \_; 1\rangle\!\rangle]$

to represent that situation like *env* except that it does not support the infons represented by

$$_\pi[[lab_1, \ldots, lab_n] : X // \langle\!\langle q, p, \_; 1 \rangle\!\rangle]$$

We also use '[ ]' to represent the empty environment (situation)[6].

3.3.3 Quantifiers and reference

Nothing in our characterization of environments so far prevented the possibility that parameters can be simultaneously quantified and anchored. One view that we might take is that parameters can either be quantified or anchored but not both. We might call environments that respect this, "classical" environments since this is what corresponds most closely to the view of quantification and reference that we inherit from the logical approach to semantics. However, we need not require that environments be classical in this sense and I think an interesting possibility is raised by this approach. We can allow environments in which a single parameter is simultaneously quantified and anchored. A basic constraint on any such environment *env* is that for any parametric object π and parameter p if *env* supports both

$$\langle\!\langle \text{quantify}, \pi, p, \{lab_1, \ldots, lab_n\}, q; 1 \rangle\!\rangle$$

and

$$\langle\!\langle \text{anchor}, \pi, p, \{lab'_1, \ldots, lab'_m\}, v; 1 \rangle\!\rangle$$

then $\{lab_1, \ldots, lab_n\} = \{lab'_1, \ldots, lab'_m\}$.

If we allow parameters to be simultaneously quantified and anchored (e.g. by a witness to the quantifier, in something like the sense of [Barwise and Cooper, 1981]) then we can in effect analyse indefinites and definites both as generalized quantifiers and singular terms at the same time and perhaps take advantage of both analyses. I have in mind that uses of indefinite and definite descriptions would always require the parameter they label to be quantified and that they may in addition be optionally anchored to a witness for the quantifier. When the parameter is anchored we would say that the use is referential. This anchoring must be used to constrain the basis relation. For example, a referential description must take wide scope over a universal quantifier.

If we take the view that quantified parameters in general may also be anchored, referential uses are not limited to definite and indefinite descriptions. For example, we could think of a parameter labelled by a use of 'every girl' as being anchored to a witness set for the quantifier. Barwise and Perry [Barwise and Perry, 1983] distinguished between what they called singular (i.e. singular definites and indefinites) and general noun-phrases in essentially the same manner as classical discourse representation theory (DRT) [Kamp, 1981] and Heim's file-change semantics [Heim, 1982]. The distinction

---

[6]The empty situation is, as far as I know, not usually included in the ontology of standard situation theory. However, it might be convenient to introduce it, or its representative for such recursive definitions.

they drew could be characterized as: singular noun-phrases refer whereas general noun-phrases quantify. On the view we are suggesting this distinction would be replaced by: singular noun-phrases quantify and may refer to individuals whereas general noun-phrases quantify and may refer to sets.

3.4   Conclusion

I conclude these lectures with some remarks on what I see as the computational relevance of the theory we have developed.

3.4.1   Situation theoretic grammar and discourse

A leading concern of computational linguistics is to develop systems that can process and construct discourse. A problem that has received a great deal of attention is anaphora resolution. Broadly, there are two approaches that can be taken. We can look at previous syntactic structure to determine what the possible antecedents of a pronoun might be or we can construct some representation of the content such as a discourse representation structure and look there for potential antecedents. I would like to explore the possibility that discourse processing of this kind takes place on environments of the kind we have discussed, where both syntactic and semantic information and the relationship between utterance and reference is expressed, rather than at a purely syntactic level (in our terms, the situation which is the use) or a purely semantic level (in our terms, the content of the use).

The discussion of referential quantifiers provides us with an example of how this view might give different processing predictions than a classical DRT account. Consider the following data:

1. A child came in. She sat down.

2. Every child came in. $\left\{ \begin{array}{c} \text{*She} \\ \text{They} \end{array} \right\}$ sat down.

3. Every child had a hat. They were made of paper.

4. Only nine of the ten balls are in the bag. $^?$It's under the sofa.

Discourse 1 is clearly a case where there is an anaphoric relation between an antecedent noun-phrase and the pronoun. Partee's example in discourse 4, if it is possible at all, (Partee's original suggestion was that it was not) is pretty clearly a case where we have to reason our way to a referent for the pronoun based on the information from the previous discourse. There is no noun-phrase that the pronoun could be anaphoric to. How do the discourses 2 and 3 relate to these extremes? The analysis of discourse 2 in DRT is that the unacceptable version is ruled out because of the quantificational nature of 'every'. The acceptable version with the plural pronoun involves constructing an additional set on the basis of the discourse representation for the first sentence. A similar account is given of discourse 3. On the account that I am proposing discourse 1 and the acceptable version of discourse 2 fall together. The pronoun is simply picking up the referent of the quantifier. The unacceptable version of discourse 2 is ruled out because the singular pronoun refers to an individual and not a witness set. On the proposal that the reference of quantifier uses are always witnesses for the quantifier discourse 3 is closer to discourse 4 in that we have to do some additional reasoning on the basis of the content of the previous sentence in order to figure out the reference of the pronoun.

DRT draws a line between discourse 1, which requires no additional reasoning beyond the content of the first sentence to provide the referent for the pronoun and the others which do need such reasoning. The proposal here is that the line should be drawn between discourse 2 and discourse 3.

3.4.2   Quantifier scope and computation

The computation of quantifier scope is one of the central problems of computational linguistics. There is not just the problem of obtaining all and only the correct scopings of quantifiers but also of deciding what to do with them once you have got them. For example, it does not seem all that useful to question the naive user about which of several alternative logical forms they had in mind. It can be useful to compute a scope-neutral representation as is suggested for example by [Hobbs and Shieber, 1987]. However, their scope neutral representation is uninterpreted. (See [Lewin, 1990], for discussion of this.)

The kind of environments we have suggested here may be seen as providing partial information about the content of a sentence and its relationship to the utterance. It need not determine quantifier scope, though we have seen that, for example, anchoring a quantified parameter might place restrictions on the scoping and one can imagine other constraints on scope that could be expressed in such an environment. It may be that later sentences in a discourse may fill in further information concerning the environment of earlier sentences. Thus, for example, an occurrence of a singular pronoun might determine that an indefinite description in a previous sentence to which it is anaphorically related was referential and hence that the quantifier has wider scope than some other quantifier.

It is important here that we are adding information to partial information that we have, rather than generating all possible scopings and then ruling out certain readings because of what comes later in the discourse. Thus at the level of environments we would have a monotonic increase of information as the discourse progresses and would approach a determination of a content. We could, of course, compute contents at any stage in the discourse but there would not be any general guarantee that a non-deterministic choice of content would not be something that we would have to go back and revise in the light of information coming further along in the discourse. If, as is quite likely to be the case, there is not enough information in the discourse to completely determine quantifier scope then we have a meaningful representation of an environment with which we can reason rather than a quasi-logical form which needs to be subjected to a scoping algorithm before we can interpret it.

3.4.3 Translation from the perspective of situation theoretic grammar

I have done some preliminary work on translation in the framework of situation theoretic grammar. The basic intuition behind a situation semantics approach to translation is as follows. If we regard meaning as characterized in terms of the relationship between utterance situations and described situations (the intuition we started with in the first section), then translation can be regarded as a relation between an utterance situation, u, of one language and an utterance situation, u', of another language such that u and u' both describe the same situation. Note firstly that this does not necessarily mean that u and u' have precisely the same content. In fact it seems quite often to be the case that translations do not have the same content. This is conceptually important though a difficult problem to say anything precise about.

More technically, I think that the notion of environment provides us with a great deal of the right kind of mix of syntactic and semantic information to do something like the "multi-level" transfer which is recommended in[Kaplan *et al.*, 1989]. I have done some initial experiments using paraphrasing within the same language which allows us to partially specify the environment for the target by doing transfer from the environment for the source and then generate the paraphrase from the target environment. The results are encouraging since it does seem possible to generate several of the structural variants discussed in [Kaplan *et al.*, 1989] from a partially-specified environment. The trick is to not make the transfer specify too much of the target environment so that the structural variants which are needed are not ruled out by the constraints expressed in the environment. The advantages I see for this approach are

i. it takes semantic analysis more seriously than the LFG approach

ii. the transfer is stated as a relation between environments and is not seen as an addition to either of the grammars

iii. the transfer statements are relatively simple and intuitive and lead one to suspect that it might be possible to develop an interface that would allow the end user to specify transfer statements of her own.

3.4.4 Situated linguistic agents - a long term goal

I have a suspicion that in order to get machines to understand and use natural language in anything approaching general conversation it will be necessary to rethink natural language processing in terms of some robotic architecture, rather than building an abstract natural language system of the kind we are used to today and possibly bolting it on to some autonomous vehicle. I would like to think that the view of grammar we have presented might point in some small way towards an understanding of what such a project might be. From the beginning of work on situation semantics, Barwise and

Perry have stressed the view that understanding language is similar in crucial respects to the way that agents in a given environment exploit information in one situation to gain information about another situation or potential situation. An autonomous vehicle which observes an obstacle has to be able to predict a crash situation on the basis of its perception. A linguistic agent has to predict the nature of a described situation on the basis of a situation which is an utterance by another agent. In both cases it is crucial to the information obtained how the agent is situated in its environment.

Basic Aspects of the Theory of Generalized Quantifiers

João Peres

Departamento de Linguística, Universidade de Lisboa

Alameda da Universidade — 1699 Lisboa Codex — Portugal

1 Quantification in Natural Languages

Quantification is a fundamental operation in the formation of natural language sentences. In fact, the vast majority of sentences in any human language exhibit *quantifying operators* — more shortly, *quantifiers* — by means of which some notion of *quantity* is expressed. In this elementary introduction to some aspects of a theory about natural language quantification, we will exclusively concentrate on those quantifiers that constitute an essential semantic component of noun phrases. A discussion pointing to a broader view of quantifying structures can be found in [Loebner, 1987a] and [Loebner, 1987b]. The following sentences, where the element inducing a quantification value appears underlined, all illustrate cases of quantifying structures that do not involve noun phrases:

(1) *Mary is very tall.*

(2) *This book is rather expensive.*

(3) *This box is twice as heavy as that one.*

(4) *I can hardly hear you.*

(5) *Could you speak up, please?*

(6) *I strongly support your position.*

(7) *Peter worked hard.*

(8) *It always rains this time of the year.*

(9) *Mary comes to visit Peter frequently.*

(10) *The topic was partially covered in the report.*

2 Montague's PTQ

The leading ideas concerning noun phrase quantification stem from the work of Richard Montague, namely from his 1970/1973 paper *The Proper Treatment of Quantification in Ordinary English* (henceforth, PTQ, [Montague, 1970]). One of his most relevant contributions to the understanding of nominal natural language quantification was the claim that different sorts of noun phrases, including proper nouns, definite descriptions, and explicitly quantified noun phrases — *every N* and *a N* are those that appear in the PTQ — behave in a similar way with respect to their role in the meaning composition of the formulas of which they are constituents. In this unified view, a noun phrase is taken to denote a set of properties of individuals (extensionally, a family of sets of individuals). Accordingly, and, for the sake of simplicity, in extensional terms, the noun phrase *Peter* is taken to denote the set of sets of individuals that contain the individual Peter, the noun phrase *every man* is taken to denote the set of sets of individuals that contain all men, and the noun phrase *a woman* is taken to denote the set of sets of individuals that contain at least one woman. Taking the symbol $\Longrightarrow$ to represent the translation function between the expressions of English and the expressions of the logical language, the syntactic structures of English on the left side would correspond to the logical (extensional) expressions on the right side, where p is the individual constant that denotes the individual named Peter and the primed nouns are the logical equivalents of English common nouns:

(11) $[_{NP}$ Peter$]$ $\Longrightarrow$ $\lambda P.[P(p)]$

(12) $[_{NP}$ every man$]$ $\Longrightarrow$ $\lambda P.[\forall x.[man'(x) \rightarrow P(x)]]$

(13) $[_{NP}$ a woman$]$ $\Longrightarrow$ $\lambda P.[\exists x.[woman'(x) \wedge P(x)]]$

Taking run' to be the translation of $[_{VP}$ run$]$, the sentences *Peter runs*, *every man runs* and *a woman runs* would translate, respectively, into the equivalent formulas in (14)a, (15)a and (16)a, each of which is equivalent, by lambda-conversion, to the corresponding b. formula:

(14) a. $\lambda P.[P(p)]$ (run')

  b.   run'(p)

(15) a. $\lambda P.[\forall x.[man'(x) \rightarrow P(x)]]$ (run')

  b. $\forall x.[man'(x) \rightarrow run'(x)]$

(16) a. $\lambda P.[\exists x.[woman'(x) \wedge P(x)]]$ (run')

  b. $\exists x.[woman'(x) \wedge run'(x)]$

Many important aspects of nominal natural language quantification were open for further research after Montague's initial steps. A major one was the extension of a semantics of natural language quantifiers from the small set that Montague had accounted for to the total range of expressions used in human languages to express quantification. It should be reminded that Montague's system exhibited a serious restriction from a linguistic — both theoretic and descriptive — point of view. As a matter of fact, he had limited his treatment of noun phrases to those that either could be translated into lambda-expressions without any of the quantifiers of the predicate calculus (as was the case of proper nouns) or could be translated into expressions involving only the quantifiers available in this calculus. Besides, the syntactic categorial status of the natural language quantifying operators — in the PTQ fragment, *a*, *every*, and *the* — was not fully clarified, since Montague had introduced these expressions syncategorematically in the syntax, that is, without assigning them to a syntactic category in the lexicon. It therefore remained to be proven that a consistent general semantics could be found for all the expressions that, considering certain linguistic properties, apparently should be considered as members of one syntactic class — expressions like *ten*, *two thirds*, *many* and *most*.

3   The Initial Theory of Generalized Quantifiers

After Montague, [Barwise and Cooper, 1981] represents the first major step towards an enriched approach to the semantics of nominal quantification. Their proposals, which derive directly from Montague's basic ideas, were also inspired by the work of the Polish logician Mostowski, who, in a sense, faced in logic and mathematics the same kind of problem that would later, after Montague, be formulated for the semantics of natural language quantification. That was the problem of integrating in a single system — ideally, as axiomatically reliable as the traditional predicate calculus — both the existential and universal quantifiers and the multitude of other quantifiers used in common mathematical discourse, which he considered to "represent a natural generalization of the logical quantifiers" ([Mostowski, 1957], p. 12) — the reason why, in the next line, he calls them *generalized quantifiers*. In the logician's own words, his discussion

> "centers around the problem whether it is possible to set up a formal calculus that would enable us to prove all true propositions involving the new quantifiers" (ib.).

The system devised by Barwise and Cooper ([Barwise and Cooper, 1981]) — which has become known as Generalized Quantifier Theory (henceforth, GQT), as a direct consequence of the title of the paper, and, indirectly, as a fair tribute to Mostowski — has achieved several important improvements in what concerns the semantics of nominal quantification. In the first place, a general semantics for natural language nominal quantifiers is devised, which takes into account both syntactic and semantic categorial issues. As Westerståhl ([Westerståhl, 1986]) points out, the notion of a *syntactic class of quantifiers* did not appear in logic before [Mostowski, 1957]. Regarding the linguistic literature, the same observation can roughly be made, with the difference that the temporal reference now derives from the 1981 paper that has just been mentioned. In relation to this categorial approach, some interesting proposals of linguistic universals are advanced in the paper. In the second place, important mathematical properties exhibited by natural language quantifiers are brought to light, as a result of the clear set-theoretic definition that each natural language quantifier is assigned.

A third improvement produced by GQT has to do with the logical language being used. While sticking to Montague's choice — in the PTQ — of interpreting the natural language via an intermediate logic, Barwise and Cooper resorted to a language — named Logic with Generalized Quantifiers, L(GQ) for short —, which undoubtedly is — using computer science slang — much more user friendly than the predicate calculus. This is, of course, partly due to the fact that L(GQ) does not contain the artificial quantifiers of this logical language. The reason for this absence is not one of friendliness improvement; instead, it lies in the fact that not all natural language quantifiers can be translated by means of the existential and universal quantifiers of the predicate calculus (e.g., *many* and *most*), which naturally invites an attempt to dispense with these quantifiers, while systematically translating all natural language quantifiers in a similar and new way. Another reason for the simplicity of the logical language is that, for the sake of avoiding levels of complexity that would be rather irrelevant for the main points at stake, it is conceived of as a purely extensional language.

In what follows, I will summarize those of the ingredients of GQT, basically as it stands in [Barwise and Cooper, 1981], that I believe to be crucial for capturing the main characteristics of the semantics the theory provides for natural language nominal quantification:

i. In the syntax of English, expressions like *some, every, ten, most* and *many* are assigned the category **determiner**; they combine with **nouns** to form **noun phrases**; the latter combine with **verb phrases** to form **sentences**;

ii. **nouns** and **verb phrases** translate into expressions of L(GQ) of the category **set term** (the equivalent of the extensional type $\langle e, t \rangle$ in the PTQ), which denote sets of individuals;

iii. the **determiners** *some, every,* (the *exactly ten* version of) *ten* and *most* are translated into the **logical determiners some', every', !10** (to be read as *exactly ten*) and **most'** of L(GQ)[1]; the **determiner** *many* is translated into the **non-logical determiner many'**; all L(GQ) **determiners** — both **logical** and **non-logical** — denote functions from sets of individuals (i.e., denotations of **set terms**, which translate **nouns** and **verb phrases**) to families of sets of individuals (i.e., denotations of the translations of **noun phrases**);

iv. **noun phrases** translate into expressions the authors name **quantifiers**; although acceptable arguments can be invoked for this terminological idiosyncrasy, I will

---

[1] I am arbitrarily using primes as the convention for distinguishing, in most cases, natural and logical language expressions.

use the more neutral label **second-order set terms**, while keeping the label **quantifier** for determiners, as has been standard in the literature subsequent to the paper we have been referring to; all **second-order set terms** denote families of sets of individuals;

v. proper nouns, a particular kind of **noun phrases**, when taken as syntactic constituents, are translated into **second-order set terms**, regularly formed by a **logical determiner** (corresponding to the singular definite article in natural languages) and a **set term**, which is a lambda-abstract denoting the (unit) set of individuals that are identical to the individual involved in the denotation of the proper noun; this individual is denoted by an individual constant that translates the proper noun as a lexical item; e.g., *Peter* as a lexical item translates into an individual constant (say, **p**), while [$_{\text{NP}}$ **Peter**] translates into a **second-order set term** which contains a lambda-abstract involving that constant, as described above (say, **the 1** λx.[x=p], where **the 1** is the normal translation for the singular definite article); this solution, besides being quite adequate for unifying the translation of all noun phrases into a single logical category, does perfectly account for those languages — of which Portuguese is an example — where proper nouns can be preceded by the definite article;

vi. examples of formal semantic definitions of L(GQ) **logical determiners** are as follows (where [[a]] is to be read as "the denotation of a (in a given model)" and E is taken to be the set of individuals in the universe):

- [[**some'**]] is the function which assigns to each A $\subseteq$ E the family of sets

$$[\![\text{some'}]\!](A) = \{X \subseteq E : X \cap A \neq \emptyset\}$$

- [[**every'**]] is the function which assigns to each A $\subseteq$ E the family of sets

$$[\![\text{every'}]\!](A) = \{X \subseteq E : A \subseteq X\}$$

- [[**!10**]] is the function which assigns to each A $\subseteq$ E the family of sets

$$[\![!10]\!](A) = \{X \subseteq E : \#(X \cap A) = 10\}$$

- [[**most'**]] is the function which assigns to each A $\subseteq$ E the family of sets

$$[\![\text{most'}]\!](A) = \{X \subseteq E : \#(X \cap A) > \#(A)/2\}$$

vii. the semantic definitions of **non-logical determiners** — like *many* and *few* (and, according to the authors, *most*) — can only be contextually determined, in accordance with what they call the *fixed context assumption*.

Let us exemplify the computation of the truth value of sentence (17)a below, whose translation into L(GQ) is (17)b:

(17)   a.   *Every student swims.*
       b.   `every'(student') λx.[swim'(x)]`

According to the semantic definition of **every'** given in **vi.** above, together with the rule for computing the semantic value of sentences (i.e. a truth value) — which says that a sentence is true if and only if the set of individuals denoted by the verb phrase is in the family of sets denoted by the subject noun phrase —, sentence (17)a is true if and only if the set of swimmers is a member of the family of sets each of which has the set of students as its subset, or, more simply, if and only if the set of students is a subset of the set of swimmers; in formal representation, the condition is as follows:

(17)   c. $[\![λx.[swim'(x)]]\!] ∈ [\![every'(student')]\!]$
            $[\![λx.[swim'(x)]]\!] ∈ [\![every']\!]([\![student']\!])$
            $[\![λx.[swim'(x)]]\!] ∈ \{X ⊆ E : [\![student']\!] ⊆ X\}$
            $[\![student']\!] ⊆ [\![λx.[swim'(x)]]\!]$
            $[\![student']\!] ⊆ [\![swim']\!]$

Let us now see an example with a proper noun, in (19). Beforehand, we need to define the denotation of **the 1** in the following terms:

(18) $[\![the\ 1]\!](A) = [\![every']\!](A)$ if #(A) = 1;
       undefined otherwise.

(19)   a.   *Peter is Danish.*
       b.   `the 1 (λx.[x = p]) (danish')`
       c. $[\![danish']\!] ∈ [\![the\ 1\ (λx.[x = p])]\!]$
            $[\![danish']\!] ∈ [\![the\ 1]\!]([\![λx.[x = p]]\!])$
            $[\![danish']\!] ∈ \{X ⊆ E : [\![λx.[x = p]]\!] ⊆ X\}$
            $[\![danish']\!] ∈ \{X ⊆ E : \{[\![p]\!]\} ⊆ X\}$
            $[\![danish']\!] ∈ \{X ⊆ E : [\![p]\!] ∈ X\}$
            $[\![p]\!] ∈ [\![danish']\!]$

Having briefly gone through the main features of the interpretation system that constitutes GQT, we may now wonder what progress the theory has originated with respect to *a general theoretical definition of a natural language nominal quantifier*. Namely, the question arises whether or not GQT can rigorously tell what can and what cannot be a natural language quantifier. In the 1981 version of GQT, the property "**live on**" — which is now more currently named *Conservativity* — was the most serious candidate to a distinctive feature of natural language nominal quantifiers. It was defined in the following terms:

"in a model $M=\langle E, [\![\ ]\!] \rangle$, a quantifier [read: a denotation of a noun phrase] Q *lives on* a set $A \subseteq E$ if Q is a set of subsets of E with the property that, for any $X \subseteq E$, $X \in Q$ iff $(X \cap A) \in Q$" (cf. p. 178).

Keenan ([Keenan, 1987]) considers conservativity to be an essential — possibly the most general — property of natural language quantifiers. However, as had already been pointed out in [Keenan and Stavi, 1986], even with a universe of just two individuals there are $2^{16} = 65536$ possible (binary) quantifiers. Of these, according to the same authors, only $2^9 = 512$ are conservative. Obviously, conservativity is not the only general condition on natural language quantifiers.

Besides conservativity, several other general conditions on natural language quantifiers have been extensively studied (cf. [van Benthem, 1986], [Westerståhl, 1986], and [Partee *et al.*, 1990]). Among them are *Extension* (or *Constancy*), *Quantity* and *Variation*, which, together with conservativity, appear to define a class containing all natural language quantifiers. In what follows, conditions are given that express each of the properties at stake. D is to be taken as the denotation of a determiner, D_X is to be taken as the denotation of a determiner with respect to a domain X, A and B are subsets of the domain, and, accordingly, DA (or $D_X A$) is a set of sets of individuals (or, equivalently and — considering the syntax of the conditions — preferably, a characteristic function of a set of sets of individuals) — in Barwise and Cooper's terminology, a quantifier:

(20) **Conservativity**

$DAB \leftrightarrow DA(A \cap B)$

(21) **Extension**

If $A, B \subseteq E \subseteq E'$, then $D_E AB \leftrightarrow D_{E'} AB$

(22) **Quantity**

If F is a bijection from $M1$ to $M2$, then $D_{E1} AB \leftrightarrow D_{E2} F(A) F(B)$,

where M_1 and M_2 are models and E_1 and E_2 are their corresponding domains.

(23) **Variation**

For each domain E there is a domain E' such that $E \subseteq E'$, $A, B, C \subseteq E'$ such that $D_{E'} AB$ and $\neg D_{E'} AC$

Conservativity states that the set $A \cap B$ is the relevant set for determining the value of DAB (intuitively: in order to compute the semantic value of the sentence *every student swims* all that is required is that we check the truth of the sentence *every student is a student that swims*, because the two are equivalent). Notice that, if quantifiers are to be conservative, an expression like *only* cannot be taken as a quantifier (notice that the sentence *only women bear children* implies *only women are women that bear children*, but the second does not imply the first). As for extension, a quantifier holding this property is not sensitive to extensions of the domain, which, for example, is not the case with at least one instance of *many* (in a sentence like *there are many planets*, where the set that constitutes the domain may be involved in the meaning computation). Quantity asserts that interpretations are preserved up to isomorphic models, or, in other words, that quantifiers are sensitive to the number of individuals, not to a particular selection of them. As Mostowski put it, "quantifiers should not allow us to distinguish between different elements of I" (where I is the domain) (cf. [Mostowski, 1957], p. 13). Finally, variation requires that quantifiers be effective regarding different domains, that is that, given a set A and a family of sets DEA assigned by DE to A, there has to be in E', for $E \subseteq E'$, some $C \subseteq E'$ such that C is not in $D_{E'}A$. Accordingly, variation excludes from the family of natural language quantifiers an otherwise (binary) quantifier that would relate any two sets. Considered together, these four properties state that only the cardinalities of the sets $A - B$ and $A \cap B$ are relevant for the meaning computation of any formula DAB. As a consequence of this restriction, and if we confine ourselves to finite domains, D can be seen as corresponding to a mapping from natural numbers into sets of natural numbers, or, more perspicuously, given a relational view on quantifiers — to be explored in the next section —, as corresponding to a relation R between natural numbers defined as in (21) (from [Zwarts, 1983], p. 39):

(24) $R(x, y) \leftrightarrow$ there are A, B, E with $\#(A - B) = x$ and $\#(A \cap B) = y$
    such that $D_E AB$.

Given these facts, it is possible to represent natural language quantifiers in a tree of numbers, which is extensively analysed in [van Benthem, 1986] and [Westerståhl, 1986], and in earlier papers by the same authors. These trees not only contain abundant information regarding properties of quantifiers but also can constitute an interesting tool for determining the relation between mathematically expressible quantifiers — given the four above mentioned conditions — and linguistically expressed quantifiers in a given language.

At this point, it should be said that several challenges have been opposed to the unified treatment of the semantics of noun phrases in GQT. Skipping the details, I will just mention three of them. The first is [Hoeksema, 1983], where a proposal is made for the transfer of the numerals, together with operators like *many* and *few*, from the class of determiners to a class of adjectives. A second one comes froms Partee ([Partee, 1987]), who argues against a uniform treatment of noun phrases as denoting families of sets of individuals, insisting instead on the idea that a distinction should be maintained between *referring*, *predicative* and *quantificational noun phrases*. Finally, a reference is due to Loebner ([Loebner, 1987a]), who considers that definite noun phrases and at least certain occurrences of indefinite noun phrases should not be treated in terms of quantification, as it is done in GQT. Regarding definites, the same suggestion appears in [Westerståhl, 1986]. As for indefinites, the line of thought developed in [Kamp, 1981] and [Heim, 1982] goes in the same direction. Presenting and discussing the arguments of all these proposals that challenge the trend followed by Montague and by Barwise and Cooper lies well beyond the scope of the present elementary introduction to GQT.

4   The Relational View on Determiners

In GQT, the expressions that were classified as natural language determiners were taken to denote functions from sets of individuals to sets of sets of individuals. Given that such functions are in a one-to-one correspondence with binary relations between sets of individuals, if one moves from the initial GQT perspective to considering the denotations of determiners to be (for the moment binary) relations between sets of individuals, nothing really crucial changes in the theoretical conception of nominal quantification. However, such a change in perspective, which dislocates the emphasis regarding the quantifying role from the noun phrases to the determiners themselves, allows a straightforward analysis of interesting properties of relations involved in natural language quantification. In a series of papers whose publication started in 1983, van Benthem has given continuing attention to this subject. These papers were collected in [van Benthem, 1986].

All the properties that will be presented below — which appear to be, among those that have been studied, the most interesting from a linguistic point of view — can be directly inferred from the semantic definition of the determiners (which, ignoring some relevant distinctions, I will henceforth call *quantifiers*). Some of these properties may turn out to be a fundamental part of the human cognitive architecture, in that they constitute inferential patterns that can give rise to the extension of information states.

Let us now turn to other relevant properties of quantifiers. They will be given with a simplified definition and some examples of quantifiers holding them.

(25)   PERSISTENCE (OR LEFT INCREASING MONOTONICITY)

   $Q\,XY\ \&\ X \subseteq Z \to Q\,ZY$
   Exs.:   *a, some, at least $\underline{n}$, more than $\underline{n}$*

(26)   ANTI-PERSISTENCE (OR LEFT DECREASING MONOTONICITY)

   $Q\,XY\ \&\ Z \subseteq X \to Q\,ZY$
   Exs.:   *every, no, the, less than $\underline{n}$, at most $\underline{n}$*

(27)   (RIGHT) INCREASING MONOTONICITY

   $Q\,XY\ \&\ Y \subseteq Z \to Q\,XZ$
   Exs.:   *every, all, the, a, at least $\underline{m/n}$, more than $\underline{m/n}$, most, both, some, at least $\underline{n}$, more than $\underline{n}$*

(28) (RIGHT) DECREASING MONOTONICITY

$Q\,XY\ \&\ Z \subseteq Y \rightarrow Q\,XZ$
Exs.: *no, less than $\underline{m/n}$, at most $\underline{m/n}$, less than $\underline{n}$, at most $\underline{n}$*

(29) REFLEXIVITY

$Q\,XX$
Exs.: *every, all, the, both, at least $\underline{m/n}$*

(30) IRREFLEXIVITY

$\neg Q\,XX$
Exs.: *less than $\underline{m/n}$, nearly all*

(31) QUASIREFLEXIVITY

$Q\,XY \rightarrow Q\,XX$
Exs.: *a, more than $\underline{m/n}$, most, some, at least $\underline{n}$, more than $\underline{n}$* (plus all
the reflexives)

(32) WEAK REFLEXIVITY

$Q\,XY \rightarrow Q\,YY$
Exs.: *every, all, a, at least $\underline{m/n}$, more than $\underline{m/n}$, some, at least $\underline{n}$, more
than $\underline{n}$*

(33) SYMMETRY

$Q\,XY \rightarrow Q\,YX$
Exs.: *a, no, some, less than $\underline{n}$, at most $\underline{n}$, exactly $\underline{n}$, at least $\underline{n}$, more
than $\underline{n}$*

(34) ANTISYMMETRY

$Q\,XY\ \&\ Q\,YX \rightarrow X = Y$
Exs.: *every, all, the, both*

Although they exhibit other inferential properties besides those listed above, natural language quantifiers do not exhibit many other definable properties of quantifiers. For example, it appears that no human language has *asymmetric quantifiers*
($Q\,AB \rightarrow \neg Q\,BA$) or *circular quantifiers* ($Q\,AB\ \&\ Q\,BC \rightarrow Q\,CA$) or *Euclidean*

quantifiers (Q AB & Q AC → Q BC). I believe that two main interesting results can arise from a deep investigation of this sort of properties. The first is related to the possibility of a rigorous mathematical characterization of the quantifiers of the human languages. The second has to do with the possibility of clusters of this kind of properties playing a crucial role in some sorts of semantic behaviour of noun phrases, namely in the selection of possible readings (e.g., group and distributive readings). This idea was explored in [Peres, 1987].

5 The Semantics of Plurals

Although Montague has not included plurals in the PTQ, they are of paramount importance in natural languages and raise very interesting issues. One of these has to do with a formal definition of ontological plurality. In a sense, the crucial question to be asked in this respect concerns what changes have to be imposed on the traditional plain set-theoretical definition of the universe of discourse of first-order predicate calculus in order to account for natural language plurals. Another important issue regards a clear characterization of natural language expressions in terms of the role of ontological plurality in the definition of their denotations. Let us look at some examples where some notion of plurality is at stake in different ways.

(35)   *The Portuguese did not enter the Second World War.*

(36)   *Elephants will be extinct within a few decades.*

(37)   *American cars have Japanese engines.*

(38)   *Five of the girls are good swimmers.*

(39)   *Some of the visitors rented a car.*

(40)   *All the researchers gathered to discuss the project.*

(41)   *All the teams gathered to discuss the project.*

Sentences (35)-(37) are examples of the sort of problems involving the interpretation of plurals that we will not be concerned with here, the reason being that, to my knowledge, no clear connection has as yet been established between GQT and the solutions that have been suggested for them. In sentences (35) and (36), the Subject noun phrase — a definite plural in the first case and a bare plural in the second — is semantically related to a sort of entity that can be considered a *natural kind*. Such variety of structures has been paid considerable attention by different authors, after the initial discussion has been triggered in [Carlson, 1977a] — see also [Carlson, 1977b], [Carlson, 1989], and the bibliography in the latter reference. As for sentence (37), while its first noun phrase is still a kind denoting one, its second noun phrase is an illustration of the structures that Sjaak de Mey named *dependent plurals* (given, of course, the assumption that each regular American car has only one engine).

The remaining four sentences all exhibit the sort of plural noun phrases occurrences that bear upon the opposition *distributive reading / group reading*. In sentence (37), only a distributive reading makes sense, which means that the predicate *be a good swimmer* is being applied to each of the (semantically) singular individuals involved in the denotation of the noun phrase *five of the girls*. As for sentence (39), it is ambiguous between a group and a distributive reading, which is partly due to the fact that a predicate like *rent* is not specified as to the (semantic) singular or plural character of the individuals related to its subject noun phrase denotation. Sentence (40) can only be assigned a group reading. This derives from the fact that a predicate like *gather* only admits collective individuals in its denotation, which obviously is not the case with each of the single individuals — *the researchers* — supplied by the denotation of the noun phrase *all of the researchers*. Differently, sentence (41) is ambiguous between a distributive reading and a group reading. The ambiguity arises from the fact that *team* is a collective common noun, which, together with a collective predicate like *gather*, can support both readings.

The first attempt to incorporate plurals in an extended PTQ framework can be found in [Bennett, 1974], where a strictly set-theoretical approach to the definition of plural objects was adopted. Bennett's system contains a rather heavy syntax, due to the fact that the semantic distinctions between singular and plural entities are fully reflected in the syntax, by means of categorial distinctions in the lexicon. On the semantic side, a major shortcoming of the system is the asymmetric ontology chosen for — using Bennett's terms — "individual-level" and "group-level" common nouns and verb phrases. In fact, these subclasses of "individual-level" expressions are taken to have members of the universe in their denotations, while the latter are taken to have sets of members of the universe, which means that there are no group-level individuals. This perspective certainly does not do justice to the common behaviour of all nouns — collective or not — in natural languages.

Link's work ([Link, 1983]) constitutes an important step in the understanding of the semantics of plurality. From the semantic point of view, the main feature of his system consists of a boolean definition of the universe of discourse, where no individuals, singular or plural, are taken to be sets. The first major advantage of his proposal is precisely that plural individuals can be defined without being identified with purely abstract mathematical entities like sets. Another one is that, while a merely set-theoretical approach does not appear to be adequate for the semantics of mass nouns, a boolean one does. This brings together in a unified system the semantics of quantification with both count and mass nouns. In [Link, 1984] and [Link, 1987], new developments were made towards an extended treatment of quantified nominal structures involving common nouns. In the latter paper, Link adduces evidence in favour of the compatibility between his boolean approach and GQT. In what follows I will briefly present some issues involving count nouns for which Link's system (henceforth LP, for Logic with Plurals) appears to offer at least part of a satisfactory solution.

The universe of LP is a structured domain where the traditional individuals in the domain of a first-order predicate calculus are the atoms that generate a lattice-theoretical structure. If we take E to be the universe, a `join` operation is defined on E which forms individual sums (henceforth, *i-sums*) out of any subset of individuals, the atoms included. Consequently, the universe constitutes a join-semilattice, which is complete (that is, closed under the `join` operation). The `join` operation induces a partial order relation on E, represented by $\leq_i$. A one-to-one correspondence (I believe, rather than a one-to-one function, as Link ([Link, 1984], p. 250) puts it) is defined between the i-sums built up from the "pure atoms" that constitute the singular entities of traditional universes and a set of what we could name "complex atoms". The union set of the sets of pure and complex atoms generates a new join-semilattice, which constitutes the domain of discourse.

Singular nouns are taken to denote sets of atoms. Plural nouns are taken to denote complete join-subsemilattices generated by the set of atoms in the denotation of their singular counterparts. Accordingly, given the singular noun *girl*, translated into `girl'` in the logic and in whose denotation there are three pure atoms, that is, such that $\#([\![\text{girl'}]\!]) = 3$, the corresponding plural noun *girls*, to be translated into `*girl'`, where $*$ is the semantic counterpart of the natural language pluralization, denotes the set $[\![*\text{girl'}]\!]$ of cardinality $2^3 - 1 = 7$ (the subtraction being due to the "zero" element of the lattice, which is apparently irrelevant for the semantics of natural languages). The members of such set are the three atomic girls, the three i-sums of girls with two atomic parts and the single i-sum of girls with three atomic parts, which is the supremum of the lattice-theoretical structure $[\![*\text{girl'}]\!]$. If the translations of the girls names are **a**, **b**, and **c** and if we take $+$ to be the logical symbol for the lattice-theoretical operation `join`, we have $[\![*\text{girl'}]\!] = \{\,[\![a]\!],\,[\![b]\!],\,[\![c]\!],\,[\![a\text{+}b]\!],\,[\![a\text{+}c]\!],\,[\![b\text{+}c]\!],\,[\![a\text{+}b\text{+}c]\!]\,\}$. Now suppose that the three girls at stake are the only members of some committee. This complex atom would be the value of the i-sum $[\![a\text{+}b\text{+}c]\!]$ in the above mentioned one-to-one correspondence between the i-sums built up from the "pure atoms" and the complex atoms. We could represent it by $[\![\langle a\text{+}b\text{+}c\rangle]\!]$. This complex atom would then be in the denotation of *committee*.

Such a rich universe admits an interesting variety of predicates with respect to their possible denotations. For example, a predicate like *gather* can only have its denotation defined in the union set of the sets of i-sums and complex atoms, while a predicate like *rent* can denote any subset of the universe. This last fact is illustrated by the following sentences:

(42) *The boy rented a car.*   (pure atom)

(43) *The boys rented a car.*   (i-sum, the supremum)

(44) *The group rented a car.*   (complex atom)

One of the most interesting problems that Link ([Link, 1984]) aimed at solving was the one raised by relative clauses with multiple heads, which he named *hydras*, as the (underlined) one occurring in (45):

(45)   *The man and the woman <u>who met yesterday</u> have just married.*

The basic idea behind Link's rendering of the interpretation of the sentence is that the predicate (say, *met yesterday*, for the sake of simplicity) is being applied to an individual sum formed by a man-atom and a woman-atom. On the syntactic side, his suggestion is that from the nouns *man* and *woman* a "complex nominal" man and woman is built up, "which denotes the set of all sums consisting of one man and one woman" (cf. [Link, 1987], p. 153). The next step is the application of the relative clause to the complex nominal, whereby in the semantics a group denoting predicate is applied to an expression denoting a set of i-sums. Finally, the determiner is applied twice in the syntax of the natural language, despite the fact that it corresponds to a single operator in the semantic representation. I think that this strategy is quite arguable both on syntactic grounds and in view of the preservation of some notion of compositionality. In [Peres, 1989], I have tried to show that hydras can be dealt with in a rather straightforward way with a canonical syntax of coordinated noun phrases and a compositionality preserving translation. In any case, beyond possible shortcomings in particular strategies, Link's LP remains a strong and inspiring system that can account for numerous kinds of structures, namely hydras as complex as (46) — due to Link —, which serves as a closing example of recent advances in the semantics of plurals:

(46)   *All the students and some of the professors who had met in secret joined in underground activities after the coup d'état.*

As an exercise, I invite the reader to substitute *teams* and *committees* for, respectively, *students* and *professors* in the above sentence, and to answer the following questions: what theoretically possible readings are elicited and which of these do we reject as unnatural (whatever this may mean)?

6   Monadic, Polyadic and n-ary Quantifiers

As was previously said, all the natural language quantifiers we have mentioned so far can, in an exclusively extensional approach, be taken to denote relations between sets of individuals. However, nominal quantifying structures exist which cannot be semantically tackled by simply defining a condition on the intersection of two relevant sets. Take the following sentence:

(47)   *Every student read a different paper.*

What is special about sentence (47) is that the quantifying structure does not simply put a condition on the intersection of two sets of individuals — which would be, in this case, that the intersection between the set of students and some other set (which?) be the set of students itself. Instead, it requires not only that two sets be defined (the set of students and a set of papers) but also that the relation *read* operates a particular kind of mapping — a one-to-one function — between the two sets.

It appears that some variation can still be found in the literature with respect to terminology on these matters. Hence, I will choose to adopt what I believe to be Westerståhl's ([Westerståhl, 1986]) terminology. The other relevant papers are [Keenan, 1987] and [van Benthem, 1989]. All the authors consider [Mostowski, 1957] and [Lindström, 1966] to be the major inspiring sources. [Hamm, 1989] constitutes an excellent general introduction to this and all the other topics focussed on in this text.

Following my interpretation of [Westerståhl, 1986], a *monadic quantifier* is one that only relates sets of individuals, in the way we have seen in the previous sections, that is, without putting any condition on a relation between sets (in other words, without requiring a particular kind of mapping). Given a universe E, such quantifiers just state conditions on the intersection of two subsets of E (which is also represented as E^1, as opposed to E^2, an alternative symbol for the cartesian product $E \times E$). Accordingly, they are assigned the label $\langle 1, 1 \rangle$, the label for *binary monadic quantifiers*. As for the quantifiers of the predicate calculus, they are *unary monadic quantifiers*, that is type $\langle 1 \rangle$ quantifiers. As for the relevant quantifying operator in sentence (47), it really ties together two sets of individuals (subsets of E^1) and a relation between individuals (a subset of E^2). The involvement of this relation in the quantifying process makes the relevant quantifying structure a *polyadic quantifier*, the conventional type label being $\langle 1, 1, 2 \rangle$, which applies to binary polyadic quantifiers. Following [Keenan, 1987], in a sentence like (47) the complete quantifying structure is a discontinuous one, as appearing in the following semantic representation of the sentence:

(48)   (EVERY, DIFFERENT$_{sg}$) (STUDENT, PAPER, READ)

The truth conditions for the sentence read as follows, where $[\![R]\!]_x$ represents the image of $\{x\}$ under the relation R:

(49) $[\![$ (EVERY, DIFFERENT$_{sg}$) (STUDENT, PAPER, READ)$]\!]$ = 1

if and only if:

i.   ($[\![$ PAPER $]\!] \cap [\![$ READ $]\!]_a$) $\neq$ ($[\![$ PAPER $]\!] \cap [\![$ READ $]\!]_b$),
     for all $a \neq b$ in $[\![$ STUDENT $]\!]$

ii.   for all $a \in [\![STUDENT]\!]$ #($[\![$ PAPER $]\!] \cap [\![$ READ $]\!]_a$) = 1

The notion of polyadic n-ary quantifiers appears to be a most promising one for the treatment of several structures that have hitherto remained rather puzzling. Among them are quantifiers like *each*, comparative quantifiers, structures involving cumulative readings and reciprocal constructions. Examples of these occur, respectively, in the following sentences:

(50) *Each computer is assigned a different serial number.*

(51) *More men than women read the same novel.*

(52) *Five students bought twenty books.*

(53) *The two women date men who dislike each other.*

In sentence (52), the relevant reading, as opposed to a group and a distributive reading, is the one where there are five students (individually or not) involved in the act of buying books and there is a total number of twenty books bought. As for (53), the other ambiguous sentence, which appears in [Keenan, 1987] (p. 119), the relevant reading is the one where each of the two women dates one man and the two men dislike each other.

It is important to clarify what structures have been considered as — sticking to the terminology I have adopted — polyadic quantifiers with an n-arity higher than binary. Sentence (54) below is Keenan's (cf. [Keenan, 1987], p. 123) example for the occurrence of a type $\langle 1, 1, 1, 1, 1, 5 \rangle$ quantifier. In (55), an example is given of a sentence with a quaternary polyadic quantifier — type $\langle 1, 1, 1, 1, 4 \rangle$ —, together with the corresponding formal representation in Keenan's style. Sentence (56) contains an example of a ternary polyadic quantifier — type $\langle 1, 1, 1, 3 \rangle$.

(54) *At least two counselors told the same story to the same camper*
      on the same day in different tents.

(55) a. *Five students read the same paper for different exams at the same time*
      b. (FIVE, SAME, DIFFERENT, SAME)
          (STUDENT, PAPER, EXAM, TIME, READ)

(56) *Peter always wears the same tie.*

It is clear that in (55)b the predicate READ is being taken as denoting a quaternary relation, which obviously raises the question of how one can, in a consistent and elegant manner, account for what appears to be the possibility of contextually increasing or decreasing the n-arity of a predicate. In fact, it seems that not only the (obligatory) arguments of a predicate but also space and time adverbials and all other verb phrase modifiers — like *for different exams* in (55)a — would have to be taken, in the formal representation, as defining projections of the same relation.

The clarification of the above problem in the context of a reasonable syntax will not suffice to make polyadic quantification an unproblematic area. As a matter of fact, some new data will very likely require a revision of the initial proposals. The following are examples of such data:

(57)   *Every time Paul asked Mary to speak to the same person.*

(58)   *Peter read the same book as Mary.*

In (57), the noun phrases that identify the sets that are relevant for the polyadic structure are not in the same sentential domain. As for (58), if Keenan's proposal were to be extended to this sort of cases, the following formal representation should be obtained, where p and m are the set-theoretical constants corresponding to the individuals Peter and Mary:

(59)   (EVERY, SAME) ($\{p, m\}$, BOOK, READ)

If we compare the semantic representation in (59) with a standard syntactic structure of (58), it becomes obvious that a discrepancy exists between a semantic fact and a syntactic one. The first is the fact that the set $\{p, m\}$ is one of the arguments of the binary polyadic quantifier. The second is the fact that the proper nouns that identify the individuals Peter and Mary do not form a constituent, and have a rather different configurational status. This is certainly a problem for the definition of a mapping between the syntax and the semantics that complies with an acceptable degree of compositionality.

The Semantics of Tense and Aspect

Frank Van Eynde

Departement Linguistiek, Katholieke Universiteit Leuven

Maria-Theresiastraat 21 — 3000 Leuven — Belgium

The expressions of tense and aspect in natural language have received much attention in the recent past, both from linguists and logicians. However, when you want to develop an NLP system which includes a component for the analysis or understanding of temporal expressions, it is hard to find a theory or a description which can be taken off the shelf and turned into an implementation without major problems.

As a matter of fact, when I got the task a couple of years ago to develop a semantic analysis of tense and aspect for Eurotra, the machine translation project of the European Community, I found a lot of interesting ideas in the literature and a large number of detailed descriptions of individual temporal expressions, but none of them was sufficiently comprehensive or sufficiently precise to support the development of an MT system for the nine official EC languages, viz. German, French, Italian, Dutch, English, Danish, Greek, Portuguese and Spanish. It therefore took a lot of research and experimentation to construct a semantic treatment of tense and aspect which can be used for multilingual MT.

The treatment which finally emerged from the research will be presented in this paper. It consists of four parts. The first section gives a general survey of the expressions of tense and aspect in the EC languages. The second section introduces the conceptual framework in which the meanings of these expressions will be described. The third section discusses some constraints on the mappings between forms and meanings, and the last section is about applications.

1   The Forms

One of the more surprising facts about the literature on tense and aspect is that no two authors seem to agree on the contents of these terms. For that reason, I will not use them as primitives but rather as composites of more basic notions and distinctions. Those basic notions will be presented in the first six paragraphs of this section. The seventh paragraph is about temporal modifiers. The reason for including the latter is that both types of expressions, i.e. the forms of tense and aspect and the temporal adverbials express the same kind of information and that their semantics are, hence, closely interrelated. Examples will be drawn from all the EC languages.

1.1 The Present and The Past

The distinction between the present and the past is made in all of the EC languages, and in all of them it is expressed by morphological means, i.e. by different forms of the same verb. Some examples:

	present	past
	present	past
EN.	*I speak*	*I spoke*
DE.	*ich spreche*	*ich sprach*

1.2 The Imperfective

In the Romance languages and in Greek there is also a morphological distinction between the perfective and the imperfective. This distinction cross-classifies with the distinction between the present and the past, but it is only made explicit in the past; in the present it gets neutralised:

	present	past perf	past imperf
FR.	*je parle*	*je parlai*	*je parlais*
PO.	*eu falo*	*eu falei*	*eu falava*
GR.	*trexo*	*étreksa*	*étrexa*
		"I ran"	"I was running"

Since there is no present imperfective, the term *imparfait* refers unambiguously to the past imperfective in French. Also in Spanish and Italian grammars the past imperfective is simply called *imperfecto*, c.q. *imperfetto*. Only in Portuguese grammars one finds the full-fledged terms *pretérito imperfeito* and *pretérito perfeito*.

1.3 The Future and The Conditional

All of the EC languages have forms for the future and the conditional, but they express them in rather different ways.

In the Romance languages they are marked by affixes which are attached to the stem of the verb:

	future	conditional
FR.	*parl-erai*	*parl-erais*
PO.	*fal-arei*	*fal-aria*
IT.	*parl-ero*	*parl-erei*

Common to these forms is the presence of an -*r*-morpheme in the suffix. this -*r* is also present in the infinitive. The second part of the suffix is derived from a finite form of the auxiliary *have*. For the future it is the present tense of the auxiliary which is taken as a starting point:

FR.	*j'ai*	$\longrightarrow$	*parler-ai*	*nous av-ons*	$\longrightarrow$	*parler-ons*
	tu as	$\longrightarrow$	*parler-as*	*vous av-ez*	$\longrightarrow$	*parler-ez*
	il a	$\longrightarrow$	*parler-a*	*ils ont*	$\longrightarrow$	*parler-ont*
PO.	*eu h-ei*	$\longrightarrow$	*falar-ei*	*nós hav-emos*	$\longrightarrow$	*falar-emos*
	ele h-á	$\longrightarrow$	*falar-á*	*eles h-ão*	$\longrightarrow$	*falar-ão*

For the conditional the starting point is the past tense of the auxiliary, more specifically the imperfective past in French and Portuguese and the perfective past in Italian:

PO.	*eu hav-ia*	$\longrightarrow$	*falar-ia*	*nós hav-íamos*	$\longrightarrow$	*falar-íamos*
	ele hav-ia	$\longrightarrow$	*falar-ia*	*eles hav-iam*	$\longrightarrow$	*falar-iam*
IT.	*ebbi*	$\longrightarrow$	*parler-ei*	*av-emmo*	$\longrightarrow$	*parler-emmo*
	av-esti	$\longrightarrow$	*parler-esti*	*av-este*	$\longrightarrow$	*parler-este*
	ebbe	$\longrightarrow$	*parler-ebbe*	*ebbero*	$\longrightarrow$	*parler-ebbero*

In Greek the future and the conditional are expressed by an invariant particle *tha* which is followed by a finite form of the main verb. For the future it is the present form of the verb, for the conditional it is the past form. In contrast to the Romance languages Greek does not neutralise the distinction between perfective and imperfective for these forms. As a consequence, there are two forms for the future and two forms for the conditional:

GR.	*tha trexo*	*tha trekso*	(future)
	"will be running"	"will run"	
	tha étrexa	*tha étreksa*	(conditional)
	"would be running"	"would run"	
	(imperf)	(perf)	

In the Germanic languages the future and the conditional are expressed by means of an auxiliary followed by the main verb in the infinitive. The relevant auxiliaries are

EN. *will (shall)*　DA. *vil (skal)*　NL. *zullen*　DE. *werden*

For the future one uses the present tense of the auxiliary; for the conditional one uses the subjunctive past in german, and the indicative past in the other Germanic languages:

EN. *would*　DA. *ville (skulle)*　NL. *zouden*　DE. *würden*

1.4 The Perfect

In all EC-languages the perfect is expressed by an auxiliary followed by a non-finite form of the verb, usually a past participle. In some of the languages the auxiliary is always the same:

EN. *have*   SP. *haber*   GR. *exo*

In the other languages there is a choice between two forms:

FR. *avoir/être*   IT. *avere/essere*   PO. *ter/haver*
DE. *haben/sein*   NL. *hebben/zijn*   DA. *have/være*

The choice usually depends on the properties of the main verb: some verbs require *avoir/avere/...*, others require *être/essere/...*. The choice is language specific and rather arbitrary: it has to be specified in the lexicon whether a given verb requires the one or the other.

There is one case in which the perfect is not formed with an auxiliary. It concerns the (perfective) past perfect in Portuguese, which is expressed by means of an inflectional affix: *jogara* ("he had played").

1.5 The Progressive

The progressive is expressed by the auxiliary *be*, followed by a non-finite form of the verb, usually the gerund. As for its use one should make a distinction between languages which have an imperfective and languages which do not. In the former the progressive is used quite often, since it —more or less— takes over the function of the imperfective; in the latter the progressive is used less frequently.

An example of the former type is English:

EN. *be + gerund*

Examples of the latter type are Spanish and Italian:

IT. *stare + gerundio*
SP. *estar + gerundio*

In these languages the progressive is used to emphasize the notion of duration.

A typical property of the progressive, and one which also distinguishes it from the imperfective, is that it cannot be combined with all types of verbs. Stative verbs, like *know*, *own*, and *resemble*, for instance, do not take the progressive, and the same is true for their equivalents in the Romance languages.

The languages which have not been mentioned above do not have a progressive. They have periphrastic constructions which bear some resemblance to the progressive, but these constructions are more complex and, above all, far less commonly used than the *real* progressive. The relevant constructions are

FR.   *être en train de + inf*
NL.   *zijn aan het + inf*
DE.   *sein am/beim + inf*
DA.   *være ved at + inf*

Since the distinction between languages which have a progressive and languages which do not, does not coincide with any well-known distinction between language families it would be interesting to find out why the distinction is as it is.

1.6   The *Futur Proche*

As is suggested by its name, the *futur proche* is best known from French. It is expressed by the verb *aller* followed by an infinitive. Similar constructions exist in some of the other Romance and Germanic languages:

PO.   *ir + inf*
NL.   *gaan + inf*
EN.   *be going to +inf*

In Danish, German and Italian the equivalents of *go* are only used as verbs of movement, and not as temporal auxiliaries.

A good test for checking whether (the equivalent of) *aller* can be used as an auxiliary is to combine it with an inanimate subject, i.e. a subject whose referent cannot make movements. If the result is grammatical, as in

(1)   FR.   *il va pleuvoir*

(2)   EN.   *it is going to rain*

the language has a *futur proche*; if it is ungrammatical, as in

(3)   DE.   **es geht regnen*

the language has no *futur proche*.

An important difference between the auxiliaries of the future and the auxiliaries of the *futur proche* is that the former can be combined with all kinds of main verbs, whereas the latter cannot: *aller/ir/gaan* do not combine very well with most stative verbs. In that sense the *futur proche* resembles the progressive.

1.7 Temporal Modifiers

In the previous paragraphs I have presented the most important grammatical means for expressing temporal information, viz. the verbal affixes and auxiliaries. Like all grammaticalised expressions they are few in number and belong to a closed class.

Next to these grammatical means natural languages also dispose of lexical means for expressing temporal information, such as nouns, adverbs, conjunctions and prepositions. They do not belong to a closed class, and it is therefore impossible to present them all. Instead I will give a short survey of the different types of temporal modifiers.

From a morpho-syntactic point of view they can be classified as

- adverbial phrases: *yesterday, tomorrow, next, ...*

- prepositional phrases: *in two weeks, at 2 o'clock, ...*

- noun phrases: *the whole week, every day, ...*

- subordinate clauses: *before he went to Japan, while he was in Canada, ...*

From a semantic point of view one can distinguish two types of temporal modifiers: those which specify when something takes place, such as *tomorrow*, and *at two o'clock*, and those which specify the duration of an event, or the time it takes for a situation to originate, such as *for an hour* and *in a week*. The former will further be called time adverbials and the latter aspectual adverbials.

For completeness' sake I also mention the temporal quantifiers, i.e. the adverbials which specify how often or how many times a given situation obtains, such as *every day*, *often* and *twice*. They will not be treated in this paper, though.

2 The Meanings

In the previous section I have given a brief survey of the forms which the ec languages use to express temporal information. These expressions range from inflectional affixes over auxiliaries and periphrastic constructions to adverbs, nouns and other elements of open classes. I have taken care to keep this survey as neutral and uncontroversial as possible. It is simply a set of facts about a number of languages.

In this section I will leave the safe shore-side of morphological form and set out for a semantic analysis of the expressions. This is where the controversies start. For, whereas there is little disagreement on the description of the morpho-syntactic forms, there is no such thing as a commonly accepted view on how to investigate their meanings. Instead, one finds a variety of different approaches, theories, treatments and descriptions. Rather than presenting and comparing (some of) these different approaches, as I have done in [Eynde, 1985], I will simply choose one and follow it all the way through.

The framework in which the analysis will be cast is the one of formal semantics, more specifically a discourse-oriented version of it. As usual in this framework I will distinguish a number of levels (see Figure 1).

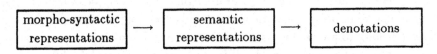

Figure 1: Representation levels

The representations at the morpho-syntactic level encode the distinctions which were discussed in the previous section, and their relation to the semantic representations will be discussed in the next section.

In this section I will concentrate on the semantic representations and their denotation, i.e. their interpretation in a model. The first paragraph presents the temporal structure of the model. The second one uses that model for the definition of a set of tense and aspect meanings which can be used for the semantic analysis of temporal expressions in isolated clauses, and the third paragraph shows how the analysis can be generalised so that it can also cope with temporal expressions in discourse.

2.1 A Temporal Structure

The ontological basis of the model is a temporal structure $< T, \cap, <>$, where

- T is a set of intervals

- $\cap$ is a binary operation on intervals (intersection)

- $<$ is a binary relation that linearly orders time (precedence).

An interval is a continuous subpart of the time line (Figure 2-a). It may consist of one single moment of time (Figure 2-b), but it cannot contain any gaps (Figure 2-c).

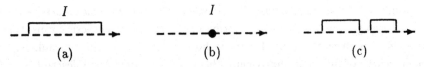

Figure 2: Time intervals

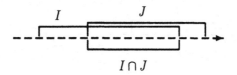

Figure 3: Intersection of intervals

The intersection of two intervals is that subpart of the intervals which they have in common (Figure 3).

Given the temporal structure $< T, \cap, <>$, the number of possible relations between intervals can be determined in a principled way: for any ordered pair of intervals (I and J), it will be the case that either $I \cap J = \emptyset$ and then $I < J$ or $I > J$ (top of Figure 4), or $I \cap J \neq \emptyset$ and then one of the last 5 cases in Figure 4 holds.

For any ordered pair of intervals on a one-dimensional time axis there is one and only one of these seven relations which can hold between them.

It would, of course, be possible to define more relations, such as "immediate precedence", "final part-of" or "initial part-of", but these are all special cases of the seven relations defined above.

It would also be possible to work with fewer relations. One could, for instance, require that one of the intervals, say J, be a moment of time, rather than a stretch of time. In that case the first interval (I) cannot be part of J, nor can it overlap with J, so that the only remaining possibilities are those in Figure 5.

Adding the requirement that both intervals have to be moments leads to a further reduction, for in that case proper inclusion is not possible either.

2.2 A Classical Model

A sentence such as

(4)   *elle travaille à Porto depuis 1980*

can be seen as the combination of a basic clause, *elle travailler à Porto*, with some temporal information, i.e. the *présent simple* and the modifier *depuis 1980*. The basic clause denotes some timeless state of affairs and the function of the temporal expressions is to specify at which moment or period this state of affairs obtains. In conformity with a well-known terminology I will call this period the time of event (E). In this case E is the period of her working in Porto.

The temporal expressions further specify that this period started in 1980 and that it includes the time of speech (S). The time of speech is the moment at which the utterance

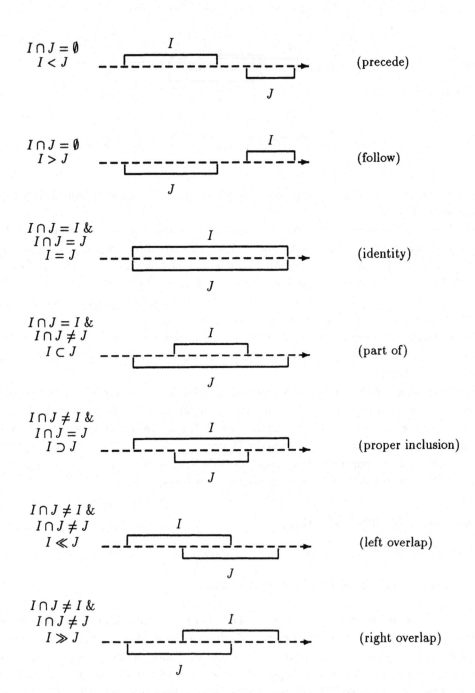

Figure 4: Relations between two intervals

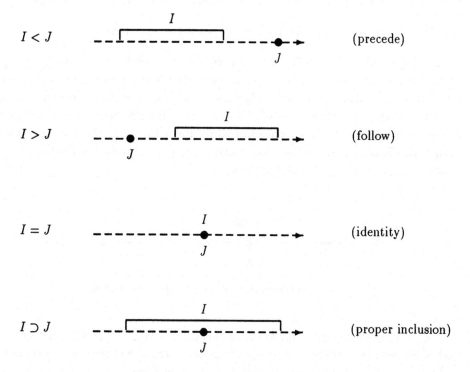

Figure 5: Relations when one interval is a moment of time

takes place. This moment is never specified explicitly; it is left implicit, but it provides a starting point for the interpretation of the temporal information.

A commonly held assumption is that the time of event is directly related to the time of speech, but Reichenbach has demonstrated in his "Elements of Symbolic Logic"[Reichenbach, 1947] that there is a third element in the relation, the so-called time of reference (R). To appreciate the need for this third element, consider

(5)   *at ten o'clock he had already eaten five sandwiches*

The basic clause of (5) is *he eat five sandwiches*; the temporal information is expressed by the pluperfect, and the adverbials *at ten o'clock* and *already*. The interesting thing now is that the adverbial *at ten o'clock* specifies a moment which precedes the time of speech, but which is not the time of event: *10.00h* is not the moment at which he ate the five sandwiches, but rather a moment at which the eating of the sandwiches had already been done. This moment is the time of reference, and the temporal relations in (5) can, hence, be represented as in the Figure 6.

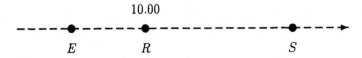

Figure 6: Representation of the temporal relations in (5)

One of the best known applications of this three-fold model is Reichenbach's description of the semantic difference between the present perfect and the simple past in English. In both cases the time of event precedes the time of speech, but in the former the time of reference coincides with the time of speech, whereas in the latter it coincides with the time of event as shown in Figure 7.

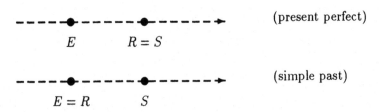

Figure 7: Difference between the present perfect and the simple past in English

Temporal expressions are, hence, analysed as pairs of relations between intervals, more specifically of the relation between the time of event and the time of reference —

Rel(E,R) —, and the relation between the time of reference and the time of speech — *Rel(R,S)*.

Following a proposal by Marion Johnson I will regard the former as aspect meanings and the latter as tense meanings [Johnson, 1981] p. 135. Combining this proposal with the derivation in the first paragraph of the possible relations between pairs of intervals, it becomes possible to determine the possible tense and aspect meanings in a non-arbitrary way. This will be done in the rest of the paragraph.

Tense meanings are relations between the time of reference and the time of speech — *Rel(R,S)*. In the case of

(5)   *at ten o'clock he had already eaten five sandwiches*

the relation is one of precedence: *ten o'clock* precedes the time of speech. Notice that the time of reference need not necessarily be a moment of time; it can also be a period of time, as in

(6)   *we were in Washington last week*

where the time of reference is the whole of last week. The time of speech, on the other hand, is generally assumed to be a moment. This implies that the number of possible relations between R and S is four: precede, follow, identity and inclusion (cf. section 2.1).

Furthermore, there seems to be no linguistic evidence for making a distinction between proper inclusion $\supset$ and identity $=$, since:

> "... languages do not have distinct grammatical categories of tense indicating location in time at a particular point vs. location in time surrounding a particular point." [Comrie, 1985] p. 123.

As a consequence, the number of possible relations between R and S can be reduced to the following three:

$$> (R, S) \quad = \quad posteriority$$
$$< (R, S) \quad = \quad anteriority$$
$$\supseteq (R, S) \quad = \quad simultaneity$$

These correspond to the traditional temporal concepts of future, past and present. Notice, however, that the latter is not defined in terms of identity, but in terms of improper inclusion. The reason for using a term like *anteriority* instead of *past* is that I want to make a clear distinction between tense forms and tense meanings. Since *past* is already used as the name of a tense form, it is better not to use it as the name of a tense meaning as well, since the relation between both is not necessarily one-to-one (cf. section 3.2).

As for the aspect meanings they are relations between a time of event and a time of reference — *Rel(E,R)*. In the case of

(5) *at ten o'clock he had already eaten five sandwiches*

the relation is one of precedence: the time of event precedes the time of reference.

Since both the time of reference and the time of event can be periods of a certain length, the number of possible relations between them amounts to seven (cf. section 2.1). It follows then that there are seven possible aspectual relations. I will now show how these relations can be used as formal definitions of the concepts which are often used for describing aspect meanings.

A well-known aspectual distinction is the one between the perfective and the imperfective. The perfective presents a situation as a single unanalysable whole, whereas the imperfective looks at a situation from the inside and focusses on the beginning, ending or continuation of it [Comrie, 1976] p. 3-4.

As formal counterparts of these definitions I propose the relations $\subset$ (E, R) and $= (E, R)$ for the perfective as in Figure 8.

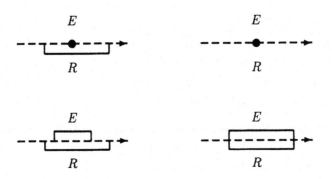

Figure 8: Possible cases for the perfective

These relations express the intuition that the time of event (E) is seen as one unanalysable whole from the point of view of the reference time. The formal definition of the perfective is, hence, $\subseteq (E, R)$.

For the imperfective I will make a distinction between three types. If the focus is on the continuation, the aspect is durative. For its representation I use the relation of proper inclusion: $\supset (E, R)$. The situation is clearly looked at from the inside: *R is in E* (Figure 9).

The two other types of imperfectivity will be represented as overlap relations (Figure 10).

In the case of left overlap the focus is on the end of the situation. This aspect will be called the terminative. In the case of right overlap the focus is on the beginning of the situation. This aspect will be called the inchoative.

Figure 9: Possible cases for the imperfective, durative

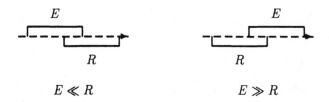

Figure 10: Imperfective: terminative and inchoative

Another aspect that is often mentioned in the literature is the so called perfect ($\neq$ perfective !). In conformity with Reichenbach, Johnson and others I will analyse it in terms of precedence: $< (E, R)$. I will, however, not use the term *perfect* for it, but rather the term *retrospective*. The reason for this is that the perfect aspect form should be distinguished from the retrospective aspect meaning.

Finally, there is the inverse of the retrospective, i.e. the prospective: $> (E, R)$. It is one of the meanings of the *futur proche*.

2.3   A Discourse Model

The model which has been presented in the previous paragraph is useful for the analysis of single clauses. For the analysis of texts I need an extension, or rather a generalisation of the original model.

The main extensions concern the introduction of another kind of interval, the point of perspective P (the term is borrowed from [Rohrer, 1985]), and the addition of indices to the intervals.

Instead of defining a time of reference with respect to the time of speech I will now define its position with respect to a point of perspective. For any clause i which is part of a discourse, there will be one point of perspective P_i and one time of reference R_i. If the clause is the first main clause of the discourse, then its point of perspective is anchored to the time of speech. In other cases the point of perspective will be anchored to the time of reference of a dominating or preceding clause. An example (see Figure 11):

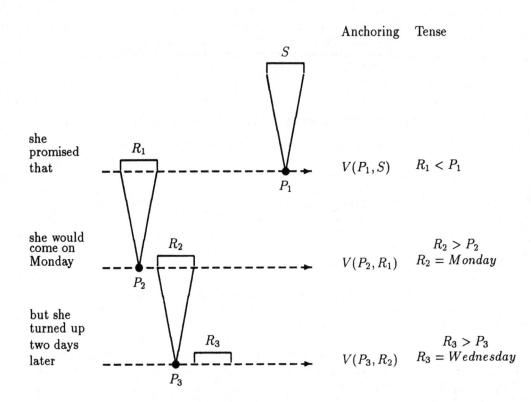

Figure 11: An example of anchoring and tense

(7)   *she promised that she would come on Monday, but she turned up two days later*

The notation $V(P_i, R_j)$ means that P_i is anchored to R_j. The interval R_j which anchors P_i is the temporal antecedent of the clause with point of perspective P_i. In the example the temporal antecedent of the first clause is the time of speech (S), the temporal antecedent of the second clause is the time of her promising ($R1$), and the temporal antecedent of the third clause is *Monday* ($R2$).

The differences between this discourse model and the Reichenbachian model are minor: the tense meanings are now relations between R_i and P_i (instead of between R and S), but since P_i is always a moment of time (just like S), the number of possible tense meanings remains the same. For the aspect meanings the changes are even smaller; they are now defined as relations between E_i and R_i (instead of between E and R), but this does not change anything to the range of possible aspect meanings.

In spite of the fact that the changes are minor, the expressive power of the formalism has increased considerably. It now provides a formalism for the temporal analysis of all types of clauses - whether embedded or not, whether isolated or in context.

3 The Relation Between Form and Meaning

In the previous section I have defined a vocabulary for the semantic analysis of the temporal expressions in the EC languages, but I have not yet demonstrated how this language independent vocabulary can be applied to the individual languages. This will be done in this section. I will start with the analysis of the time adverbials and the tense forms and then proceed with the aspect forms and the aspectual adverbials.

3.1 The Time Adverbials

The time adverbials are temporal modifiers which can be used as answers to when-questions. In terms of the model they specify the location of the time of reference, such as *at ten o'clock* in

(5) *at ten o'clock he had already eaten five sandwiches*

Notice that this adverbial does not give any information about the relation between the time of reference and the point of perspective: *at ten o'clock* can just as well denote some moment in the future as in the past. It is only because of the combination with a past tense in (5) that we know that it is ten o'clock in the past. Adverbials like these will further be called locational time adverbials.

Next to the locational time adverbials there are the relational ones, i.e. the adverbials which contain information about the relation between the time of reference and the point of perspective. If the point of perspective is directly derived from the time of speech, the time adverbial is deictic. Some examples are *now*, *tomorrow*, and *two weeks ago*. Depending on the kind of relation they express they can be characterised as

- simultaneous: *now, ...*

- anterior: *yesterday, two weeks ago, ...*

- posterior: *tomorrow, next summer, ...*

If the point of perspective is not derived from the time of speech, but from the reference time of a dominating or preceding clause, the time adverbial is anaphoric. Just like the deictic adverbials, they can be grouped in three subclasses

- simultaneous: *the same time, at that moment, ...*

- anterior: *two weeks before, previously, ...*

- posterior: *one week later, then, ...*

For a similar classification of the time adverbials, see [Smith, 1980].

3.2 Tense Forms and Tense Meanings

Tense forms are inflectional affixes and auxiliaries which express tense meanings. They include the

	present	past	future	conditional
FR.	*joue*	*joua*	*jouera*	*jouerait*
PO.	*joga*	*jogou*	*jogará*	*jogaria*
EN.	*plays*	*played*	*will play*	*would play*

Notice that the tense forms are combinations of bound morphemes and auxiliaries. They cannot appear in isolation, but only in combination with a given verb and a given aspect form. In the examples above the verb is *play* and the aspect form is the simple (cf. section 3.3). The same tense forms can be combined with other aspect forms to form the corresponding perfect, imperfective and progressive forms.

As to the meanings of the tense forms they will be defined as elements of the power set of possible tense meanings [1]. This power set contains eight elements:

{∅,
{anterior},
{posterior},
{simultaneous},
{anterior, posterior},
{anterior, simultaneous},
{posterior, simultaneous},
{anterior, posterior, simultaneous} }

Not all of these combinations can be assigned to particular tense forms, though, for there are a few constraints.

Bernard Comrie has argued, for instance, that "in a tense system, the time reference of each tense is a continuity" [Comrie, 1985] p. 50.

In practice this means that there are no tense forms which can express posteriority and anteriority without expressing simultaneity as well. The combination {*anterior, posterior*} can, hence, be discarded a priori.

---

[1] In this article I will only discuss the temporal meanings of the tense and the aspect forms. Their modal meanings will not be analysed.

A second restriction concerns the two combinations {*anterior, simultaneous*}and {*posterior, simultaneous*}. The former is a possible combination in languages which make a basic distinction between future (i.e., {*posterior*}) and non-future (i.e., {*anterior, simultaneous*}); the latter is a possible combination in languages which make a basic distinction between past ({*anterior*}) and non-past ({*posterior, simultaneous*}). Since a language cannot belong to both types at the same time, it follows that for any given language either the combination {*posterior, simultaneous*} or the combination {*anterior, simultaneous*} is ruled out. As it appears that the EC languages all belong to the languages which make a basic distinction between past and non-past, we can also discard the combination {*anterior, simultaneous*}.

In order to find out which of the six remaining combinations can be assigned to the tense forms I start from the following scheme:

$$
\begin{array}{lcl}
present & \Longleftrightarrow & simultaneous \\
past & \Longleftrightarrow & anterior \\
future & \Longleftrightarrow & posterior
\end{array}
$$

For the further refinement of this scheme I make use of a compatibility test: a tense form X can have a meaning Y, where Y is any of {*simultaneous, anterior, posterior*}, if and only if X can co-occur with a deictic adverbial of type Y in one and the same clause.

Let us take the English present as an example. This tense can be combined with simultaneous adverbials as in

(8)   *now I know*

but also with posterior adverbials as in

(9)   *he is coming tomorrow*

With anterior adverbials, though, one gets an ungrammatical result:

(10)   **he is coming last week*

The inability of the English present to express anteriority also appears from the fact that the clauses in which it is combined with a locational adverbial have a posterior interpretation:

(11)   *he is coming on Thursday*

means that he is coming on the next Thursday and not on some previous Thursday. It follows that the English present is a typical non-past tense: {*simultaneous, posterior*}.

The application of similar tests to the other tense forms yields the following results:

$$\begin{array}{rcl}
present & \Longleftrightarrow & \{posterior,\ simultaneous\} \\
past & \Longleftrightarrow & \{anterior\} \\
future & \Longleftrightarrow & \{posterior\} \\
conditional & \Longleftrightarrow & \emptyset
\end{array}$$

The conditional tense gets the value $\emptyset$ since it does not have a temporal meaning in isolated clauses. It can have a temporal meaning in subclauses, as will be pointed out immediately, but in simple isolated clauses it has a modal meaning.

All of the above is fairly simple and straightforward. There is one complicating factor, though: the use of the tense forms in texts is somewhat different from their use in isolated clauses. This is due to the fact that in anterior contexts the present is often replaced by the past and the future by the conditional. This phenomenon, which I will call "transposition" (after [Rohrer, 1985]), can be seen at work in the following sentences:

(12)   *he said that he was ill*

(13)   *he entered the room and fell on the carpet*

In (12) the time of his being ill is simultaneous with his saying that he is ill, and in (13) the time of his falling on the carpet is posterior to the time of his entering the room. In both cases one would expect a present tense in the second clause, but since the first clause is in the past, transposition applies and results in the use of a past tense in the second clause.

The discourse diagrams for these sentences are in Figure 12.

Similar remarks can be made about the use of the conditional in

(14)   *we all hoped that he would soon recover*

There are at least two possible ways of dealing with the phenomenon of transposition: it can be treated as a syntactic transformation or as an irregularity in the relation between form and meaning. In the former case one first maps the past on the present and the conditional on the future, and then applies the normal rules for relating forms to meanings. In the latter case one defines extra rules for the assignment of meanings to the past and the conditional.

The former alternative is more constrained than the latter and, hence, more attractive, but the choice for the one or the other might be language dependent. As for Dutch I have provided some evidence that it can be treated as a syntactic transformation (cf. [Eynde, 1989]).

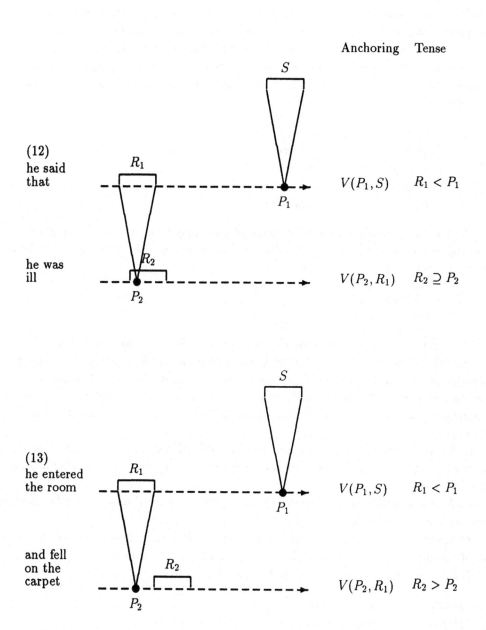

Figure 12: Diagrams for sentences (12) and (13)

3.3 Aspect Forms and Aspect Meanings

Aspect forms in my terminology are combinations of inflectional affixes and auxiliaries which express aspect meanings. The relevant forms are the imperfective, the perfect, the progressive and the *futur proche*. Since these forms do not exist in all of the EC languages, the systems of aspect forms differ from language to language.

An important distinction in this respect is the one between languages with and languages without an imperfective. Of the languages without an imperfective English has the richest system:

EN.	simple	*rain*
	perfect	*have rained*
	progressive	*be raining*
	perfect progr	*have been raining*
	futur proche	*be going to rain*

German and Danish, on the other hand, do not only lack the imperfective, but also the progressive and the *futur proche*. The only remaining aspectual distinction is the one between the simple and the perfect:

DE.	simple	*regnen*
	perfect	*geregnet haben*

For the languages with an imperfective the story is a bit more complex. The language with the most elaborate imperfective paradigm is Greek: it marks the perfective-imperfective distinction in all tenses except for the present. On the other hand, it does not mark the distinction in the perfect forms, and it lacks both the *futur proche* and the progressive. As a result, its aspectual system contains three paradigms: the perfective, the imperfective and the perfect.

In the Romance languages the perfective-imperfective distinction is only marked in the past tense, but unlike Greek it cross-classifies with the perfect and the other aspectual paradigms.

As for the assignment of meanings to the aspect forms I will follow roughly the same procedure as for the tense meanings.

At the most general level the meaning of an aspect form is an element of the power set of possible aspect meanings. This set contains $2^6 (= 64)$ elements.

For the definition of the mappings I start from the following scheme:

simple	$\Longleftrightarrow$	*perfective*
perfect	$\Longleftrightarrow$	*retrospective*
futur proche	$\Longleftrightarrow$	*inchoative*
imperfective	$\Longleftrightarrow$	*durative*

Languages which do not have an imperfective use the progressive for expressing durativity and if they do not have a progressive either, they choose another aspect form. The choice of this alternative form is governed by a principle, which I will call "the principle of minimal semantic distance".

For the measurement of semantic distance I start from a linear ordering of the aspect meanings:

retro	term	perf,dur	incho	pro
$<$	$\ll$	$\subseteq, \supseteq$	$\gg$	$>$
1	2	3	4	5

The distance between any two aspect meanings is the difference between the numbers with which they are associated. The distance between retrospectivity and prospectivity, for instance, is 4: $|1 - 5| = 4$. And the distance between terminativity and perfectivity is 1: $|2 - 3| = 1$.

The principle of minimal distance can now be formulated as follows: if a language lacks a special form for the expression of a given meaning, then it will use the form whose basic meaning is least distant from the meaning to be expressed.

An application: a language which has neither a progressive nor an imperfective will express durativity by means of the form whose basic meaning is the perfective, since the perfective is least distant from the durative: $|3-3| = 0$. Hence, we predict that languages like German, Dutch and Danish, will express the durative by means of the simple form, and this prediction is indeed born out !

The principle of minimal semantic distance also guides the choice of a form for the expression of terminativity. Some languages have a special form for this aspect. English, for instance, has the perfect progressive. Most languages, however, do not have such a form and in those cases the principle predicts which forms are available for the expression of terminativity, i.e. the (retrospective) perfect form, the (perfective) simple form or the (durative) imperfective form; in all of these cases the semantic distance equals 1: $|2-1| = |2-3| = 1$. The (inchoative) *futur proche*, on the other hand, is not available for this use, since its basic meaning is more distant from the one to be expressed: $|2-4| = 2$.

Taking into account the general scheme and the principle of minimal distance, and complementing it with language specific observations one can derive the following mappings for English:

EN.	*simple*	$\Longleftrightarrow$	{*perfective*}
	perfect	$\Longleftrightarrow$	{*retrospective, terminative*}
	progressive	$\Longleftrightarrow$	{*durative, perfective*}
	perfect progr	$\Longleftrightarrow$	{*terminative*}
	futur proche	$\Longleftrightarrow$	{*inchoative, prospective*}

Similar mappings can be defined for the other languages.

3.4 Aspectual Adverbials

The aspectual adverbials include the duration adverbials and the boundary adverbials.

The duration adverbials specify the length of the time of event. Depending on whether the basic clause is an event or a state/process they are expressed by an *in*-adverbial or a *for*-adverbial:

(15) *she ran the mile in five minutes* (event)

(16) *he has been sleeping for ten hours* (process)

(17) *we have been in France for a month* (state)

They do not express any relational information. Hence, they cannot be marked for any of the aspectual relations, such as perfectivity or durativity.

The boundary adverbials specify the beginning and/or the end of the time of event. They are prepositional phrases introduced by *since, from, until, till, from ... till.*

One of these expresses relational information: the *since*-adverbials denote an interval which begins in the past at some specified time (e.g. *Christmas* in *since Christmas*) and ends at a time which is not specified by the adverbial, but which is normally taken to be included in the time of reference. The relation between time of event and time of reference is, hence, one of left overlap as shown in Figure 13.

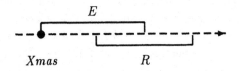

Figure 13: Relational information from *since Christmas*

It follows that *since*-adverbials express terminativity and that the compatibility of these adverbials with the aspect forms can be used as a test for deciding whether a given aspect form can be terminative.

(18) *she has been sleeping since 10.00* (perf prog)

(19) **she is sleeping since 10.00* (progressive)

(20) *he has been in trouble ever since he lost his nerve* (perfect)

(21) **he is/was in trouble ever since he lost his nerve* (simple)

3.5 Compositionality

Tense and aspect forms do not occur in isolation: finite verbs have both a tense form and an aspect form.

The meaning of their combination is the product of the meanings of their parts. An example: the meaning of the English present perfect progressive is the relational product of the meanings of the present with the meanings of the perfect progressive. In other words, the meaning of the present perfect progressive is compositional.

Not all combinations of tense and aspect are compositional, though. As an example let us take the present perfect in French, Dutch and German. Since the present expresses simultaneity or posteriority, a compositional analysis of the present perfect would assign it a {*simultaneous, posterior*} meaning as well, but the following examples show that the present perfect can be combined with an anterior time adverbial:

(22) FR. *je l'ai vu hier*
      NL. *ik heb hem gisteren gezien*
      DE. *ich habe ihn gestern gesehen*

It follows that the present perfect in these languages has an anterior meaning; as a matter of fact, it has the same meaning in these sentences as the simple past in English:

(23) EN. **I have seen him yesterday*
           I saw him yesterday

In French this special status of the present perfect is made explicit in its name; instead of calling it the *présent antérieur*, after the analogy with *passé antérieur* and *futur antérieur*, it is called the *passé composé*, thus emphasizing the fact that the present perfect is actually a past tense.

Depending on how many of these irregularities there are, the tense and aspect system of a given language will be more or less compositional. In case of a low degree of compositionality one could decide to assign meanings to combinations of tense and aspect forms, rather than to the tense and aspect forms separately.

4 Applications

An obvious application for my semantic analysis of tense and aspect is the one for which it was made in the first place, i.e. machine translation.

The reason why tense and aspect are a problem for MT is that the systems of tense and aspect forms are so different for the various languages that it is not possible to state one-to-one relations between the corresponding forms. As an example, take the translation of the French *présent simple* into English:

(24) *elle fume des cigares*
      she smokes cigars   (simple present)

(25)   *attention, il s'évanouit*
       take care, he faints
       take care, he is fainting   (present progressive)

(26)   *il vit à Paris depuis 1968*
       he lives in Paris since 1968
       he has lived in Paris since 1968   (present perfect)

(27)   *elle travaille à Louvain depuis 1980*
       she works in Leuven since 1980
       she has been working in Leuven since 1980   (present perfect progressive)

It appears that the French *présent simple* has at least four translational equivalents in English: the simple present, the present progressive, the present perfect and the present perfect progressive. Notice, furthermore, that the choice between these forms is not free: the simple present is a good equivalent for the *présent simple* in (24), but not in the other sentences.

One way of dealing with this translation problem would be to define context-sensitive mappings from source language forms to target language forms in the French-to-English transfer module (Figure 14).

Figure 14: Context-sensitive mappings

In the case of the *présent simple* this would give mappings like

présent simple	⟼	*simple present* / in contexts of type X
présent simple	⟼	*present progressive* / in contexts of type Y
présent simple	⟼	*present perfect* / in contexts of type Z
présent simple	⟼	*present perfect progressive* / in contexts of type W

An alternative way of coping with the discrepancies would be to define mappings between language specific forms and interlingual semantic representations in the monolingual modules. In that case the *présent simple* is mapped onto a semantic representation in the French analysis module:

présent simple ⟼ *Meaning 1* / in contexts of type A
présent simple ⟼ *Meaning 2* / in contexts of type B
...
présent simple ⟼ *Meaning i* / in contexts of type I

In transfer the semantic representations are simply copied and in the English generation module they are mapped onto target language forms:

Meaning 1 ⟼ *simple present*
Meaning 2 ⟼ *present progressive*
...

In this approach the complex mappings are performed in the monolingual modules, whereas the bilingual mappings are trivially simple (Figure 15).

Figure 15: Using meaning as an interlingua in a MT system

Since the number of monolingual modules in a multilingual system is smaller than the number of transfer modules, it is certainly more *ergonomic* to shift the more complex operations to the monolingual modules.

In that case one needs a theory for the semantic analysis of the tense and aspect forms which can support such an interlingual approach, and it is precisely such a theory that I wanted to provide. A fuller account of how the given analysis can be used for MT is given in [Eynde, 1988] and in the Eurotra Reference Manual.

As for this paper I will just give an illustration of how the analysis actually works. As an example I take the translation of the French sentence

(4)   *elle travaille à Porto depuis 1980*

into English. The tense in (4) is the present, and the corresponding semantic representation is {*simul, posterior*}; the aspect form is the simple and this corresponds to {*perfective, durative, terminative*}; there is one temporal modifier, the boundary adverbial *depuis 1980*, which is terminative. Since there is no posterior adverbial in (4), the tense meaning is {*simul*}, and because of the boundary adverbial the aspect meaning is {*terminative*}.

These representations are copied in transfer, and form the input for the English generation module, which maps {*simul*} onto the present —there is no other possibility— and {*terminative*} onto either the perfect or the perfect progressive; the choice between the latter is dependent on the type of the clause: if the clause expresses a state, there is a preference for the perfect, and if it expresses an event or a process, there is a preference for the perfect progressive. Since the tenseless clause *she work in Porto* is of the latter type, the preferred aspect form is the perfect progressive. In this way (4) gets translated into

(28)   *she has been working in Porto since 1980*

Notice that the transition from the French *présent simple* to the English present perfect progressive has been done by means of general form-to-meaning rules.

Apart from its applicability for machine translation the analysis can also be used in question-answering systems and man-machine interfaces. As a matter of fact, a slightly modified version of it has already been incorporated in an NL interface between Portuguese sentences and a temporal database (cf. [Moreira, 1989]).

Simplifying and Correcting the Treatment of Intentionality in Montague Semantics

João Falcão e Cunha

Faculdade de Engenharia da Universidade do Porto

Rua dos Bragas — 4099 Porto CODEX — Portugal

E-mail: jfcunha@fe.up.ctt.pt — Tel: 351-(0)2-382 071

1 Introduction

"To most logicians (like the first author) trained in model-theoretic semantics, natural language was an anathema, impossibly vague and incoherent. To us, the revolutionary idea in Montague's paper *PTQ* (and earlier papers) is the claim that natural language is not impossibly incoherent, as his teacher Tarski had led us to believe, but that large portions of its semantics can be treated by combining known tools from logic, tools like functions of finite type, the λ-calculus, generalized quantifiers, tense and modal logic, and all the rest.

Montague had a certain job that he wanted to do and used whatever tools he had at hand to do it. If the product he built looks a bit like a Rube Goldberg machine, well, at least it works pretty well."

[Barwise and Cooper, 1981]

Two of the principles underlying Montague's treatment of natural language are the principle of compositionality and the principle that formal logic can be used to provide the characterizations of meaning. Although they are used together, it is quite important to recognize that they are different principles. Some schools seem to reject explicit compositionality while still accepting different forms of formal logic. It is common understanding that Montague accepted both compositionality and high-order logic. We accept Montague's view on compositionality and on using formal logic, although we do not accept an unrestricted use of a high-order logic.

According to [Montague, 1970], the importance of syntax is due to its role as a preliminary to semantics. If we accept a separation between syntax and semantics coming from the difference between the study of the forms and of the uses of languages, syntax studies whatever is not dependent on contexts of uses. We would say that for the context of use in which our formalization is being built, syntactic definitions deal with context insensitive objects or *forms*. Whether syntax is or is not context-free, as in Chomsky's hierarchy of grammars is a separate problem.

Computer Science has developed many different formalisms to define formal languages. The construction of computable natural language approximations should use the most interesting of those formalisms. For instance, we can take advantage of the expressive power of attribute-value grammars and the existence of efficient parser generators for such formalisms. Moreover by restricting the syntax to the subset of context-free grammars known as LR, we can guarantee parsing strings in linear time and memory space, i.e. proportional only to the length of the string (for unambiguous grammars). The use of such restriction also guarantees termination, which should be a property proved for implementations of grammars. Attribute-value grammar formalisms, parser generation and computational efficiency are discussed in [Pitt, 1990].

From basic principles we will accept that semantic functions which characterize the use of natural language should be restricted to computable ones. Functions used in the definitions should prove to be monotonic and continuous.

If we accept the importance of syntax, a formal semantics for natural language has to do the job of characterizing contexts of use and the uses of the syntactic forms. To be formal it has to provide both a formal definition for contexts of use and for the semantic function. This requires a formal language were contexts of use are explicit. This is the case, for example, of the constructively typed language we will be using to define the semantics of the intensional language L.

In this article we introduce a simplified version of the intensional interpretation of Natural Language of PTQ. It has been proved [Cunha, 1989] that this intensional interpretation is equivalent to the original presentation of Montague. This version does not use the *cap* ($^\wedge$) and *cup* ($^\vee$) operators, and has a simpler type structure. This presentation only uses one notational system and avoids Montague's original double formalization for intensionality[1] , which is still widely and incorrectly being used.

The role of the meaning postulates in the definition of logical equivalence is analyzed. The cap and cup operators are criticized due to their non intuitive usage as constant function constructor and intensional function destructor respectively. Regarding them as such functors is the only intuitive way to directly understand or 'read' Montague's meaning postulates. Given that meaning postulates are the only source of high-order quantification in Montague Semantics we argue for their elimination or substitution.

Intentionality is closely related with the apparent failure of compositionality and

---

[1]The word *intension* was introduced by [Carnap, 1946] in logical terminology and has been widely used in formal treatments of *intentionality*. In Philosophy, the word 'intentionality' is used when we are dealing with the objects of knowledge, belief and necessity, as opposed to immediate sense objects involved in using the physical senses; see for instance [Malmgren, 1971]. As [Hodges, 1977] says, "Alas for the infelicities of logical terminology". In general remarks we will be using the word 'intentionality', but we will use in the logical tradition 'intension' and 'intensional verbs' (and 'extension' and 'extensional verbs'). Some authors (for instance [Turner, 1988]) use the word 'intensionality' where they should be using 'intentionality'.

therefore with omniscience. In [Cunha, 1990a] it is explained why Montague semantics does not seem to offer a good treatment for the propositional attitudes of *knowledge* or *belief* and for perception sentences. Montague semantics still offers an acceptable treatment for intensional verbs such as seek or try to find and for objective modalities such as *necessity*.

2 The Simplified Intensional Interpretation

The simplification we will propose to Montague Semantics brings the intermediate logical notation used, an Intensional Logic, closer to a simply typed Modal and Temporal Logic. Although we still allow high-order quantification, it is simple to see that it is not necessary in translating *PTQ*'s English. If *NL* is *PTQ*'s English, *IL* is the Intensional Logic of *PTQ*, t_{IL} is the translation function of *PTQ*, u_{IL} is the interpretation function of *PTQ*, then [Cunha, 1989] shows that for the simplified Intensional Logic L introduced below, and with appropriate t_L and u_L we have an isomorphism between the interpretations of *NL* expressions, as shown in Figure 1.

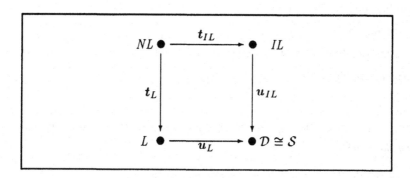

Figure 1: Isomorphic Interpretations

We introduce the language L which will replace *IL* in the intermediate representation for *NL*. Unlike *IL*, it does not have in its syntax the cup-cap operators. Syntactically, it is the language of a Modal and Temporal Logic, with constants of different types and the simply typed operations of lambda abstraction and application. We first introduce its alphabet and syntax. The basic or primitive domains required for its interpretation are the same as the ones for *IL*. We will then define the domains of denotations and the interpretation function. With this semantic function we define the notions of intension and extension as different forms of the same object, the interpretation. We cannot express the meaning postulates in this intermediate language L. We explain why this is intuitively acceptable. We show that meaning postulates are used by Montague as a parallel device to help in the definition of the interpretation, working as constraints on the meaning of the constants of the language. We believe that such constraints should be explicit in the definition of the constants.

2.1 Syntax of L

Definition 2.1 *The set of types of Intensional Logic* L *is defined as follows:*

1. *Basic categories* e *and* t *are types.*
2. *If* α *and* β *are types so is* $\alpha \rightarrow \beta$.

Definition 2.2 *We will define eight different kinds of symbols in the alphabet of the language.*

1. *Connectives:* $\wedge$, $\vee$, $\neg$, $\leftrightarrow$, $\rightarrow$, $=$
2. *Quantifiers:* $\exists$, $\forall$
3. *Modal operators:* $\Diamond$, $\Box$
4. *Temporal operators:* $\mathcal{F}$, $\mathcal{P}$
5. *Punctuation marks:* ., (,)
6. *Abstractor:* λ
7. *Constants of type* α: $c_{\alpha,1}$, $c_{\alpha,2}$, $\ldots$, $c_{\alpha,i}$, $\ldots$
8. *Variables of type* α: $v_{\alpha,1}$, $v_{\alpha,2}$, $\ldots$, $v_{\alpha,i}$, $\ldots$

Definition 2.3 *The set* E_α *of well-formed expressions of type* α *in the language* L *is defined by the rules:*

1. *Every constant* $c_{\alpha,i}$ *and every variable* $v_{\alpha,i}$ *is in* E_α.
2. *If* $e_{\beta \rightarrow \alpha}$ *is of type* $\beta \rightarrow \alpha$ *and* e_β *is of type* β, *then* $e_{\beta \rightarrow \alpha} e_\beta$ *is in* E_α.
3. *If* α *can be analysed as* $\beta \rightarrow \rho$ *then* $\lambda v_\beta . e_\rho$ *is in* E_α.
4. *If* α *is* t, e_t, $e_{t,1}$ *and* $e_{t,2}$ *are any expressions of type* t, *and if* $e_{\pi,1}$ *and* $e_{\pi,2}$ *are any expressions of the same type* π, *then the following expressions are in* E_α:

$$
\begin{array}{ll}
e_{\pi,1} = e_{\pi,2} & \neg e_t \\
\Diamond e_t & \Box e_t \\
\mathcal{F} e_t & \mathcal{P} e_t \\
\exists v_\alpha . e_t & \forall v_\alpha . e_t \\
e_{t,1} \wedge e_{t,2} & e_{t,1} \vee e_{t,2} \\
e_{t,1} \rightarrow e_{t,2} & e_{t,1} \leftrightarrow e_{t,2}
\end{array}
$$

The set of all expressions of L *is* E.

2.2 Semantics of L

Up to this point we have only defined syntactic objects, the well formed strings of symbols or expressions. In Natural Language every phrase may be seen as unambiguously referring to some object, e.g. an entity. However this is not enough for compositionality to hold in a theory of meaning. In different contexts of use expressions will be likely to have different meanings and semantic objects as referents. This enlarged notion of meaning is usually called the intension or sense of an expression. It can take into account the place, time and world, or situation, in which the expression is used. If we let the meaning or denotation of an expression became this sense, instead of a primitive object, we can have a compositional theory of meaning. For our formalized language this tells us that each expression should denote a function from contexts of use to primitive objects, for example entities. So if $\mathcal{E}$ is the domain of primitive possible objects referred to by an expression in L of type e, then we should define its denotation as a function from possible contexts of use $\mathcal{I}$ to $\mathcal{E}$. Below we introduce the domains and functions required to construct the semantics for L. $\mathcal{B}$ is the standard Boolean domain.

Definition 2.4 *The domains $\mathcal{D}_\alpha$ of possible denotations of type α are constructed as follows:*

1. *If $\alpha = e$, $\mathcal{D}_\alpha = \mathcal{I} \to \mathcal{E}$.*

2. *If $\alpha = t$, $\mathcal{D}_\alpha = \mathcal{I} \to \mathcal{B}$.*

3. *For all α such that $\alpha = \rho \to \beta$, $\mathcal{D}_\alpha = \mathcal{D}_\rho \to \mathcal{D}_\beta$.*

The domain of all possible denotations is $\mathcal{D}$.

Definition 2.5 *For each variable and constant of type α we define a variable-assignment function g_α and a constant-interpretation function f_α.*

Definition 2.6 *The semantic interpretation function u_α, which gives the value in domain $\mathcal{D}_\alpha$ of an expression e_α of E_α, given g, $u_\alpha e_\alpha g : \mathcal{D}_\alpha$, is defined recursively for each type α, following the definition 2.3 of language L:*

1. *$u_\alpha c_\alpha g = f_\alpha e_\alpha$ and $u_\alpha v_\alpha g = g_\alpha e_\alpha$*

2. *If $e_{\beta \to \alpha} e_\beta$ is in E_α then, $u_\alpha (e_{\beta \to \alpha} e_\beta) g = u_{\beta \to \alpha} e_{\beta \to \alpha} g (u_\beta e_\beta g)$.*

3. *If α is $\beta \to \rho$ and $\lambda v_\beta . e_\rho$ is in E_α then, $u_\alpha (\lambda v_\beta . e_\rho) g = \lambda x_\beta . u_\rho e_\rho g_{(x_\beta \leftarrow v_\beta)}$.*

4. *If α is t, e_t, $e_{t,1}$ and $e_{t,2}$ are any expressions of type t, and if $e_{\pi,1}$ and $e_{\pi,2}$ are any expressions of the same type π, then the interpretation of the logical expressions is defined in the standard way (see for instance [Cunha, 1989]).*

The function u *is the element which sums all* u_α, $ueg : \mathcal{D}$

Informally, the meaning of an expression with unknown context of use is a function from possible contexts of use to its possible meanings. Usually we refer to this as the *intension* of an expression. The meaning of the expression when a context of use is known, is its *extension* in that particular context. The extension of an 'out-of-context' expression should be undefined, except when the expression is supposed to denote a constant in every context of use.

The semantic function u allows for an elegant formalization of the concepts of intension and extension, as we can see in the following definitons.

Definition 2.7 *The* intension *of an expression* e *is a function* int: $E \to \mathcal{D}$, *which is defined as* int$(e) = ueg$.

Definition 2.8 *The* extension *of an expression* e *on context of use* i *is a function* ext: $(E \times \mathcal{I}) \to \mathcal{O}$, *which is defined as* ext$(e, i) = uegi$.

Conclusion 2.1 *The extension of* e *on context* i *is the same as the intension of* e *evaluated at* i *as* ext$(e, i) = $ int$(e)i$.

Conclusion 2.2 *It follows from the previous definitions that the functions* int *and* ext *are related by the equation* int $=$ **curry** ext, *where* **curry** *is an appropriate currying function.*

2.3 Logical Equivalence and Meaning Postulates

Logical equivalence between sentences is a difficult subject in *PTQ*. According to Montague, a logically possible interpretation is any interpretation u which is logical, i.e. it 'respects' the meaning of the logical constants such as **and**, **or** and **necessity**, and which is possible, i.e. 'respects' a set of expressions, usually called the *meaning postulates*, in the sense that it makes them true in all contexts of use.

Definition 2.9 *Given a set of expressions* m_p, *the meaning postulates of* IL, *a logically possible interpretation is any interpretation which makes all those expressions true in all indices* i.

$$\text{logically-possible } u = (\forall p, i.um_p i = \text{true})$$

As Montague says logical truth, logical consequence and logical equivalence are to be characterized accordingly.

The difficulty we mentioned with logical equivalence is that the meaning postulates are supposed to cover all the distinctions of words or phrases of English which were not directly made in the syntactic or in the semantic definitions. If we exclude the postulates, there is no difference between intensional and extensional verbs. It may seem rather contrived to use meaning postulates to define the use of words, which should be clearly and uniformly made in the definition of the language, in its grammar.

As well, synonymy between words or phrases of English is defined through the inclusion in the set of meaning postulates of expressions which will guarantee equivalent use of words.

Perhaps the most noticeable problem, for a computational treatment, is that quantification on variables ranging over predicates is introduced in PTQ's treatment of English exclusively through the meaning postulates. It is simple to check that there are no such expressions introduced in the translation of English into IL.

3 Intentionality in PTQ

There are two formalizations for intentionality in PTQ. There is the interpretation as *intension* of an expression ζ, and there is as well, the interpretation of its *concept* $^\wedge\zeta$. We argue that the latter is counter-intuitive and it only survived in PTQ because Montague used two distinct functional notations.

In this section we summarize Montague's definitions for intensional and extensional interpretations, and for the cap-cup operators. The use of these operators creates counter-intuitive results as shown by [Dowty *et al.*, 1981]. We claim that the observations in [Gallin, 1975] which were made as well in the previous reference, are not correct, that the cap-cup operators' usage is puzzling and that their definitions are generally counter-intuitive. Then the semantical treatment of some NL compound expressions involving oblique or intensional contexts is traced, from their English definition, through their translation into IL and semantic interpretation. We conclude that Montague's formalization of English, with correct compositional intentionality, was achieved through a complex use of the cap-cup operators and *in spite* of counter-intuitive definitions.

3.1 Montague's Definitions

Montague accepted Frege's functional analysis of natural language. In order to provide a correct formalization it was necessary to formally define Frege's notion of intentionality. In order to do this Montague introduced a language for which the principle of compositionality of extensions holds (cf. [Gallin, 1975]) and he defined for expressions of this language both an extensional and intensional semantics. Then he provided a translation (syntax to syntax) from English phrases into expressions of this language, so securing indirectly an intensional and extensional interpretation for English. In its intermediate language he had introduced two operators $^\wedge$ and $^\vee$, usually referred to as the 'intensional' operators. Intuitively, the cap operator was used in the translation of compound expressions when oblique contexts might require intensional meanings, and the cup operator if the translation of compound expressions did not require intensional meanings. We will reproduce here the notation used by Montague and some of its definitions. We will argue that Montague used an intermediate language with excessive expressive power by introducing the 'intensional' operators. The example in Dowty *et al* shows that their use is counter-intuitive. Gallin shows that Montague's translations of natural language phrases only covers a subset of expressions of *IL*.

In the following section we show how Montague's double notation contributed to keep the double formalization of intentionality unnoticed. It is remarkable how Montague managed to reconcile the semantic definitions of intension and extension with the definitions of the cap-cup operators and the definition of the translation from English, in such a way that the counter-intuitive results to be found in pure *IL* never have to be used. We will utilize definitions 3.1 through 3.4 to reproduce Montague's original definitions.

3.1.1 Extensional and Intensional Meaning for Expressions in *IL*

Definition 3.1 *The extension of an expression* exp *with respect to U (interpretation), i (world-time index) and g (variable-assignment), is denoted by* $exp^{U,g,i}$. *This extension is defined recursively and compositionally on the expressions of the intensional language.*

Definition 3.2 *The intension of an* exp *with respect to U and g, is denoted by* $exp^{U,g}$ *and is defined as the function h with the domain of indices i such that* $hi = exp^{U,g,i}$:

$$exp^{U,g} = h$$
$$hi = exp^{U,g,i}$$

This is the same as defining the intensional interpretation of an expression as:

$$exp^{U,g} = \lambda i. exp^{U,g,i}$$

It is very simple to prove from the previous definitions that the following equation holds:

$$exp^{U,g,i} = exp^{U,g}(i).$$

3.1.2   Intensional Operator

Definition 3.3 *The extension of the intensional operator, $[^\wedge exp]^{U,g,i}$, is defined as the function h with the domain of indices i such that $h(i) = exp^{U,g,i}$.*

This form of the definition is ambiguous because i is used in three different places. But everyone agreed that it was obvious which was the scope intended:

$$[^\wedge exp]^{U,g,i} = h$$
$$hi = exp^{U,g,i}$$

This is the same as defining the intensional interpretation of $^\wedge exp$ as:

$$[^\wedge exp]^{U,g,i} = \lambda j. exp^{U,g,j}.$$

We notice the similarity of this definition for extensional meaning of the intensional operator with the definition of intensional meaning in definition 3.2. Its intension under the obvious interpretation using 3.2 is,

$$[^\wedge exp]^{U,g} = \lambda i.\lambda j.[^\wedge exp]^{U,g,j}.$$

3.1.3   Extensional Operator

Definition 3.4 *The extension of the extensional operator, $[^\vee exp]^{U,g,i}$, is defined as follows:*

$$[^\vee exp]^{U,g,i} = exp^{U,g,i}(i).$$

The intensional meaning under the obvious interpretation is,

$$[^\vee exp]^{U,g} = \lambda i. exp^{U,g,i}(i).$$

This cannot be further reduced as the η reduction rule cannot in general be applied if i is a free variable:

$$[^\vee exp]^{U,g} \neq exp^{U,g,i}.$$

What we have done in section 2.2 was to identify the interpretation U with $\boldsymbol{u}$ and the variable-assignment g with $\boldsymbol{g}$, and we have made use of just one type of functional notation to define the interpretation function. Then the intensional and extensional meaning functions are defined for expressions of IL using the interpretation function.

3.2 Using the Intensional Operators

3.2.1 Dowty's Example

Returning to our notational system, we will present an example where the definitions of intension, extension and the interpretation of the intensional operators have been found to create an intuitively problematic result, the failure of the equivalence between the interpretations of k and $^\wedge{}^\vee k$, where k denotes a constant of Montague's *IL*. It is also counter-intuitive that the intension of $^\vee k$ is not the extension of k.

We will calculate (cf. [Dowty *et al.*, 1981]) the meaning of a constant k of type $s \to e$ and of the related expressions $^\vee k : e$, $^\wedge k : s \to (s \to e)$, $^\vee{}^\wedge k : s \to e$ and $^\wedge{}^\vee k : s \to e$. We will use the standard definitions for the meaning of the cap-cup operators. The interpretation u is constructed on a finite set of entities $E = \{a, b, c, d\}$, and a finite set of points of reference $\mathcal{I} = \{1, 2, 3, 4\}$. Let f, the interpretation function for constants of the language, be given with the value for constant k as shown below in a convenient graphic representation:

$$
fk =
\begin{bmatrix}
1 & \begin{bmatrix} 1 & a \\ 2 & a \\ 3 & a \\ 4 & a \end{bmatrix} \\
2 & \begin{bmatrix} 1 & a \\ 2 & b \\ 3 & c \\ 4 & d \end{bmatrix} \\
3 & \begin{bmatrix} 1 & c \\ 2 & b \\ 3 & d \\ 4 & a \end{bmatrix} \\
4 & \begin{bmatrix} 1 & c \\ 2 & d \\ 3 & a \\ 4 & b \end{bmatrix}
\end{bmatrix}
=
\begin{bmatrix}
1 & A \\
2 & B \\
3 & C \\
4 & D
\end{bmatrix}
$$

Meaning of k. The intension of the constant expression k is fk as shown above.

$$int(k) = fk.$$

Meaning of $^\vee k$. The intension of the expression $^\vee k$ is:

$$int(^\vee k) = \lambda i.u(^\vee k)gi = \lambda i.ukgii = \lambda i.fkii.$$

$$int(^\vee k) = \begin{bmatrix} 1 & a \\ 2 & b \\ 3 & d \\ 4 & b \end{bmatrix}$$

Conclusion 3.1 $\neg(\forall i.\text{ext}(k, i) = \text{int}(^\vee k))$

Meaning of $^\wedge k$. The intension of the expression $^\wedge k$ is:

$$int(^\wedge k) = \lambda i.u(^\wedge k)gi = \lambda i.\lambda j.ukgj = \lambda i.fk$$

$$int(^\wedge k) = \begin{bmatrix} 1 & \begin{bmatrix} 1 & A \\ 2 & B \\ 3 & C \\ 4 & D \end{bmatrix} \\ 2 & \begin{bmatrix} 1 & A \\ 2 & B \\ 3 & C' \\ 4 & D \end{bmatrix} \\ 3 & \begin{bmatrix} 1 & A \\ 2 & B \\ 3 & C \\ 4 & D \end{bmatrix} \\ 4 & \begin{bmatrix} 1 & A \\ 2 & B \\ 3 & C \\ 4 & D \end{bmatrix} \end{bmatrix}$$

Conclusion 3.2 $\forall i.\text{ext}(^\wedge k, i) = \text{int}(k)$

Meaning of $^\wedge{}^\vee k$. The intension of the expression $^\wedge{}^\vee k$ is:

$$int(\,^{\wedge\vee}k\,) = \begin{bmatrix} 1 & \begin{bmatrix} 1 & a \\ 2 & b \\ 3 & d \\ 4 & b \end{bmatrix} \\ 2 & \begin{bmatrix} 1 & a \\ 2 & b \\ 3 & d \\ 4 & b \end{bmatrix} \\ 3 & \begin{bmatrix} 1 & a \\ 2 & b \\ 3 & d \\ 4 & b \end{bmatrix} \\ 4 & \begin{bmatrix} 1 & a \\ 2 & b \\ 3 & d \\ 4 & b \end{bmatrix} \end{bmatrix}$$

Conclusion 3.3 $int(\,^{\wedge\vee}k) \neq int(k)$

Meaning of $\,^{\vee\wedge}k$. The intension of the expression $\,^{\vee\wedge}k$ is:

$$int(\,^{\vee\wedge}k\,) = \begin{bmatrix} 1 & A \\ 2 & B \\ 3 & C \\ 4 & D \end{bmatrix}$$

Conclusion 3.4 $int(\,^{\vee\wedge}k) = int(k)$

3.2.2 Dowty's Conclusion

There is no explanation in [Dowty $et\ al.$, 1981] why the equivalence beetween $int(\,^{\wedge\vee}k)$ and $int(k)$ does not hold. It is only observed that there are two reasons to ignore the failure of the equivalence. The first one is that constants of type $s \to \alpha$ are never used in the interpretation of English. The second reason is that expressions of the form $\,^{\wedge\vee}\alpha$ will never be used in translating Montague's English.

3.2.3 Gallin's Observation Criticized

The suggestion made in [Gallin, 1975] was that $^{\wedge}$ works as a kind of hidden functional abstractor on indices or contexts of use. Although indices do not appear in IL, the application of $^\wedge$ to an expression α will result in another expression which intension denotes a constant function on domain indices that computes, for any index, the value of the intension of α, which is independent of any index. This interpretation of the $^\wedge$ operator is extremely counter-intuitive. The result of applying $^\wedge$ to an expression α just creates another expression whose intension denotes a constant function on indices. Then the operator $^\wedge$ is just a constant function constructor.

On the other hand Gallin says that $^\vee$ acts as a kind of hidden 'functional application' operation on indices. What in fact it does, except in the particular case where α denotes a constant function on indices, is to 'destroy' the information contained on the function of type $\mathcal{I} \to \mathcal{I} \to \mathcal{D}$ by creating a completely new function of type $\mathcal{I} \to \mathcal{D}$.

The intensional denotation of $^\vee\alpha$ has to be a function on indices. For each index, this expression has as value the value of the intensional denotation of α (of type $\mathcal{I} \to \mathcal{I} \to \mathcal{D}$) evaluated at that index *and again* evaluated at that index.

This is way we think that this is an extremely confusing view of that operator's use, and we say that it 'destroys' information.

If all expressions are 'protected' by the $^\wedge$ operator, there are no problems in using the $^\vee$ operator. This is the explanation for the fact that $^\vee{}^\wedge\alpha$ is always equivalent to α. It also explains why the other equivalence is not valid except when α denotes a constant function on indices, and not just a primitive constant of IL. It is straightforward to prove that if β denotes a constant function on indices, e.g. $\beta = {}^\wedge\alpha$ or if for all indices i, $\boldsymbol{u}\beta i$ is a constant, then the other equivalence always holds, $^\wedge{}^\vee\beta = \beta$.

It is not so strange that these operators are so puzzling when used in the treatment of intentionality.

3.3   The Double Formalization of Intentionality in PTQ

3.3.1   Failure of Compositionality in NL

Montague recognized that the naive composition of extensions in not sufficient to model adequately the intensional aspects of Natural Languages. In general if F_n is a syntactic function or structural operation and α, β and γ are natural language phrases, the second equality does not hold in general, because there is no such function S_n:

$$\alpha = F_n(\beta, \gamma)$$
$$^*ext(\alpha) = S_n(ext(\beta), ext(\gamma))$$

For example if the syntactic operation F_n corresponds to simple concatenation or F_6 in PTQ, and S_n corresponds to functional application we would write:

$$\alpha ::= \beta\gamma$$
$$^*ext(\alpha) = ext(\beta)(ext(\gamma))$$

The classical examples involve replacement of co-extensional phrases in compound expressions involving necessity, **Necessarily the morning star is the evening star**, and compound expressions involving time, in a context where Jones is a US senator, **colleague of Jones** is co-extensional with **US senator** but we do not have that **former colleague of Jones** means the same as **former US senator**.

3.3.2 Compositionality in *IL*

According to [Gallin, 1975], Frege did not abandon the functionality principle for extensions, but rather held that the extension of an expression depends on the syntactic context in which it occurs. In principle one could eliminate the difficulties by introducing, for each expression ζ, a new expression $^\wedge\zeta$, called the concept of ζ, whose extension is the intension of ζ. For this language then we would have that:

$$
\begin{aligned}
\alpha &= F_n(\beta, \gamma) \\
ext(\alpha) &= S_n(ext(\ ^\wedge\beta), ext(\ ^\wedge\gamma))
\end{aligned}
$$

Montague's *IL* is such a language. In Montague's notation we would write:

$$
\begin{aligned}
\alpha &= F_n(\beta, \gamma) \\
\alpha^{U,g,i} &= S_n((^\wedge\beta)^{U,g,i}, (^\wedge\gamma)^{U,g,i})
\end{aligned}
$$

or

$$
\alpha^{U,g,i} = S_n(\beta^{U,g}, \gamma^{U,g})
$$

For rule 4 in the definition of *IL* in *PTQ* we would write:

$$
\begin{aligned}
\alpha &::= \beta(\gamma) \\
\alpha^{U,g,i} &= \beta^{U,g,i}(\gamma^{U,g,i})
\end{aligned}
$$

However this notation does not clearly expose the proposal, which Gallin attributes to Carnap, that the extension of an expression is really a function on two variables, the expression and the state of affairs or context of use. For closed expressions, which contain no free variables, we should write in our notation:

$$
ext(\alpha, i) = S_n(ext(\beta, i), ext(\gamma, i))
$$

For rules 4, 9 and 10 we would have:

$$\alpha \quad ::= \quad \beta(\gamma)$$
$$ext(\alpha, i) \quad = \quad ext(\beta, i)(ext(\gamma, i))$$

$$\alpha \quad ::= \quad {}^{\wedge}\gamma$$
$$ext(\alpha, i) \quad = \quad \lambda j.ext(\gamma, j)$$

$$\alpha \quad ::= \quad {}^{\vee}\gamma$$
$$ext(\alpha, i) \quad = \quad ext(\gamma, i)(i)$$

We must stress that these definitions are for expressions of IL. This is supposed to be an extensional language, i.e. such that the extension of any expression at any index is either given or compositionally evaluated. This compositionality tells us that each expression of the language has one object standing for meaning.

As the equations above show, the use of the cap operator corresponds to constructing a constant function on indices, which value for each index i is itself a function, $\lambda j.ext(\gamma, j)$, the intensional meaning of γ. As we have shown, this operator just constructs a constant function on indices. The cup operator is usually just destroying the information content of the object γ to which it is being applied, except for the case when such γ *represents a constant function on indices*. In IL, applying the cup operator to any other constant corresponds to lose information on the meaning of such constant. But as [Dowty *et al.*, 1981] also shows, that never happens in Montague Semantics. Before showing why, we observe that such result is telling us that Montague is not using all the expressive power of IL when translating English.

3.3.3 Translation from NL into IL

After defining IL, Montague translates English phrases into IL expressions using a translation function t. The meaning of English is then defined with one of the folowing two equations:

$$meaning\ \alpha\ i \quad = \quad ext(t(\alpha), i)$$
$$meaning\ \alpha \quad = \quad \lambda i.ext(t(\alpha), i)$$

In particular for all compound expressions α, for which oblique contexts could affect compositionality, Montague made his system to look as follows.

$$\alpha \quad ::= \quad \beta(\gamma)$$
$$t(\alpha) \quad = \quad t(\beta)({}^{\wedge}t(\gamma))$$

$$meaning\ \alpha\ i\ =\ ext(t(\alpha),i)$$
$$=\ ext(t(\beta)(\ ^{\wedge}t(\gamma)),i)$$
$$=\ ext(t(\beta),i)[ext(\ ^{\wedge}t(\gamma),i)]$$
$$=\ ext(t(\beta),i)[\lambda j.ext(t(\gamma),j)]$$
$$meaning\ \alpha\ =\ \lambda i.ext(t(\beta),i)[\lambda j.ext(t(\gamma),j)]$$

3.3.4 Compositionality Restored in NL

The last equations became easier to write if we use intension, int, instead of extension ext, where as we have seen in conclusion 2.1, $int(e)i = ext(e,i)$:

$$meaning\ \alpha\ =\ \lambda i.([int(t(\beta))i][\lambda j.int(t(\gamma))j])$$
$$=\ \lambda i.([int(t(\beta))i][int(t(\gamma))])$$

It is simple to prove that by applying a curry function to the right hand side corresponds (up to isomorphism) to restoring compositionality of intensions for natural language. Assume both:

$$meaning\ \alpha\ :\ \mathcal{I} \to \mathcal{X}$$
$$int(t(\gamma))\ :\ \mathcal{Y}$$

Then it is simple to show that we will have:

$$int(t(\beta)) : \mathcal{I} \to (\mathcal{Y} \to \mathcal{X})$$

But we also have that:

$$\mathcal{I} \to (\mathcal{Y} \to \mathcal{X}) \cong \mathcal{Y} \to (\mathcal{I} \to \mathcal{X}).$$

Therefore we should be able to conclude that $meaning\ \alpha$ is isomorphic to the meaning of $\lambda i.int^c(t(\beta))[int(t(g))]i$, where int^c is an appropriate curried form of int. With meanings seen as 'curried' intensions if necessary, we would conclude that:

$$meaning\ \alpha = meaning\ \beta\ (meaning\ \gamma)$$

At this stage we believe that Montague could have directly achieved this result if he had started by using the following definitions:

$$\alpha_{IL} = f_n(\beta_{IL}, \gamma_{IL})$$
$$\alpha_{IL}^{U,g} = s_n(\beta_{IL}^{U,g}, \gamma_{IL}^{U,g})$$

or

$$\alpha_{IL} ::= \beta_{IL}(\gamma_{IL})$$
$$int(\alpha_{IL}, i) = int(\beta_{IL})(int(\gamma_{IL}))$$
$$t(\alpha) = t(\beta)(t(\gamma))$$

and with,

$$meaning\ \alpha = int(t(\beta))(int(t(\gamma)))$$

A very similar thing happens with the treatment of *necessity* but at a syncategorematic level. At this stage we are almost tempted to think that Montague in fact did not really use the cap-cup operators for his semantics of English. If he had written clause 4 in the definition of the interpretation of IL using only one kind of notation, he surely would have realized that that definition together with his definition of the translation would be achieving the equivalent of composing intensions directly in English or in IL. In [Cunha, 1989] we have given a formal proof that we can drop the operators and still have for any English expression the same meaning induced in PTQ by the use of intensional language L.

3.4 Excessive Expressiveness of IL

The observations in [Dowty *et al.*, 1981] which were used to justify the acceptance of the use of the cap-cup operators are equivalent to saying that IL has a subset of expressions which is not required to formalize Montague's English. In fact it has been shown ([Cunha, 1989]) that we do not need the cap-cup operators in order to achieve an equivalent interpretation for Montague's English. This result may seem puzzling, given that we are used to think that in the treatment of intensional verbs we need the 'expressive power' of the cap-cup operators.

It can be shown that the meaning postulates related with the distinction between intensional and extensional verbs are just constraining the constant-interpretation function of those verbs (as constants in the English lexicon or their translations as constants of IL) to be extensional on the subject or object argument. This same constraint can be written using a normal extensional logic without the cap-cup operators, and directly on the definition of the constant-interpretation function.

Dowty's result also reminds us that it is not sufficient to show that IL is a high-order logic to show that Montague's English is equivalent to a high-order logic. IL can be a high-order logic and still we may be using in translating English only its first-order subset. To show that Montague's English is equivalent to a logic where we quantify on predicates we would need to show that in its translation we are using that possibility of *IL*, and exactly where are expressions of *IL* being introduced which are not first-order.

4 Reading the Meaning Postulates

As we remarked earlier, accepting the meaning postulates of *PTQ* is equivalent to constrain the constant-interpretation function. When we replace *IL* by *L* we are unable to express the restrictions directly in the new intermediate intensional language *L* which translates English.

As we have seen, we should think of the cap-cup operators in the following way. The cap operator constructs a constant function on indices, and the cup operator 'destroys' a function except in the case when it is applied to a variable x, in which case it 'means' the variable assignment itself,

$$u(^\wedge f)g = \lambda i.ufg \qquad \text{and we can prove that:} \qquad \forall i.u(^\wedge f)gi = ufg.$$
$$u(^\vee x)g = gx \qquad \text{and we can prove that:} \qquad \forall i.u(^\vee x)gi = gxi.$$

It is clear to us, from what we have seen, that the operators are used in the meaning postulates of *IL* to talk about functions, constant functions, or about elements of the semantic domains. In this new intensional language we cannot speak about constant functions or constant meanings, so we will need to express the postulates directly as our intuitions indicate, as constraints on the constant-interpretation function. We should be using an extensional language which allows us to speak about indices, the language of our semantic domains.

We say that this is closer to our intuitions because it corresponds to translating directly our English description (and Montague's description) of what is, let us say, a proper noun or a common noun. We claim that Montague's meaning postulates can only be understood after mastering the use of the cap-cup operators to speak about interpretation functions. We will describe what we have just said using as example meaning postulates 1, 2 and 3 of *PTQ*. For the others a similar but rather lengthy proof can be given of what we have just said. We do not think however that meaning postulates are the correct way to go about restricting possible interpretations.

4.0.1 Examples

Meaning Postulate 1

$$\exists u_e.\Box[u_e = c_e]$$

"The Truth of 1 guarantees that proper nouns will be 'logically' determinate according to the interpretations under consideration, that is, will have extensions invariant with respect to possible worlds and moments of time."

[Montague, 1970] (PTQ).

Our constraint corresponds to an almost direct translation of Montague's English sentence, saying that fc is a constant function on indices,

$$\exists u.\forall i.fci = u \qquad \text{where} \qquad u : \mathcal{E}$$

Meaning Postulate 2

$$\forall x_{s\to e}.\Box[\text{horse'}(x) \to \exists u_e.x = {}^\wedge u]$$

"In view of 2 'ordinary' common nouns (for example **horse**) will denote sets of constant individual concepts (for example the set of constant functions on worlds and moments of time having horses as their values; from an intuitive viewpoint, this is no different from the set of horses). It would be unacceptable to impose this condition on such 'extraordinary' common nouns as **price** and **temperature**."

[Montague, 1970] (PTQ).

Our constraint says that if $fcxi$ (with for instance $c = $ horse') is true on indices i, for individual concepts x then those individual concepts are constant functions on indices j,

$$\forall x.\forall i.[f\text{horse'}xi \to \exists u.\forall j.xj = u] \qquad \text{where} \qquad x : \mathcal{I} \to \mathcal{E}$$

Meaning Postulate 3

$$\exists m_{s\to e\to t}.\forall x_{s\to e}.\Box[\text{walk'}(x) \leftrightarrow {}^\vee m({}^\vee x)]$$

"The truth of 3 is the natural requirement of extensionality for intransitive verbs."

[Montague, 1970] (PTQ).

We would say that,

$$\exists m.\forall x.\forall i.[f\text{walk'}xi \leftrightarrow mi(xi)] \qquad \text{where} \qquad m : \mathcal{I} \to \mathcal{E} \to \mathcal{B}$$

The other meaning postulates correspond basically to express the constraints on f using the cap-cup operators, with box meaning truth in all indices. Once we understand how the operators are used, basically, to speak about functions and in particular constant functions, the constraints on the interpretations (on the constant-interpretation) can be re-phrased using *IL* and meaning postulates, but not before that. It is also clearer that we would need a lot more meaning postulates to constraint f for a 'possible interpretation'. We would need to restrict the interpretations not only to impose 'equality' or synonymy but also 'inequality' or antonymy. We would need for instance to guarantee that the interpretations of **fish** is not the same as of **woman**, and the one of **man** is not the same as of **horse**.

4.0.2 Surviving without Meaning Postulates

Some of the meaning postulates can be avoided if, as [Dowty, 1979b] (pp. 197) observes, we use a direct complex translation from *NL* into *IL*. However we do not think that eliminating a few meaning postulates will be enough. We could ask ourselves what happens if we decide to change the use of **necessarily** from *true in any world* to *true in accessible worlds*. Should we assert as meaning postulates the same expressions Montague used, or keep restrictions on the constant-interpretation function?

As we have observed, there is no sentence of Montague's English which translates into any meaning postulate. If English is a formal language, and if Montague Grammar is to be a general theory of language we cannot accept meaning postulates which cannot be stated in English. Otherwise the program is also telling us that there are 'truths' which cannot be expressed in that universal language.

The last remark forces us to reject the possibility of using meaning postulates to constrain possible interpretations, as it leads into a contradiction in the objectives of Montague Grammar as a Universal Grammar.

The solution to this problem still accepts both compositionality and a formal reduction of Semantics. Syntax should still be a prelude to Semantics, with the difference that in the latter we try to take into account all the information about *use* that is known. Such information must be made explicit in the semantic definitions, and not separately in meaning postulates.

Intuitively, we want to say that if we have learnt that there is a difference between say 'extraordinary' and 'ordinary' common nouns or between intensional and extensional verbs, that classification not only can but must be explicit in my syntactic or semantic rules. Once the distinction is made, the semantic interpretation can be directly constructed to take account of the difference in use. Once again the main distinction we see between syntax and semantics is that the former is not context of use sensitive while the latter is, even having to accept this as an imprecise distinction.

5 Conclusions

The use of denotational semantics brings into Montague semantics an unified notational description. This helps to expose the counter-intuitive usage of the cap-cup operators, and provides insights on how they are used in the meaning postulates. We observe as well that meaning postulates introduce high-order quantification in *PTQ*. We conclude that those operators have undesirable properties and that their use in the formalization of intentionality is unnecessary and counter-intuitive.

The main conclusion of this chapter is that we should use neither the cap-cup operators nor meaning postulates in a treatment of intentionality.

Compositionality and Omniscience in Situation Semantics

João Falcão e Cunha

Faculdade de Engenharia da Universidade do Porto

Rua dos Bragas — 4099 Porto CODEX — Portugal

E-mail: jfcunha@fe.up.ctt.pt — Tel: 351-(0)2-382 071

1 Introduction

> What I suggest is that *it is always undesirable to make an effort to increase precision for its own sake—especially linguistic precision—since this usually leads to loss of clarity* [...] , *one should never try to be more precise than the problem situation demands.*
>
> [Popper, 1974], pp. 24.

Situation Semantics was developed to become a viable alternative to a propositional possible-worlds semantics for natural language, such as Montague's. Barwise expresses the view that possible-worlds semantics rests on dubious metaphysical and epistemological grounds, and refers to logical omniscience as a major defect which forces him to develop Situation Semantics ([Barwise, 1981]). This semantics is to be regarded as a new model-theoretic approach to the analysis of natural language. In particular, Barwise uses a puzzle of logical equivalence involving perception verbs to show that in the propositional possible-worlds account we cannot get the right logical laws for perception, as well as for belief, doubt and knowledge, because of logical omniscience. The conclusion is that possible-worlds semantics offers an unacceptable framework for a mathematical semantics of natural language.

1.1 Overview

The puzzle of perception in [Barwise, 1981] was used to criticize Montague Semantics (*MS*), and to criticize model-theoretic semantics based on possible-worlds for its incapacity to provide a suitable formalization for propositional attitudes and for perception sentences.

Given Barwise's analysis, based on [Hintikka, 1975], there is a proposal for a new Semantics, one based on situations instead of possible-worlds. This semantics was originally presented in [Barwise and Perry, 1983] and is the subject of [Cooper, 1990]. It has many attractive aspects, of which we find extremely important its unstated requirement of not quantifying the overall interpretation function of natural language. This requirement, we believe, is the ultimate reason why its treatment may not suffer from omniscience.

We begin this lecture by introducing Barwise's puzzle. In order to highlight Situation Semantics' similarities to *MS*, we introduce *Determiner Free Aliass* or *DFA*, Barwise and Perry's subset of English, and illustrate how it is interpreted in 'Yet Another Situation Semantics', which may be seen as a theory founded on a combination of Property and Domain Theory. We stress the differences between the notions of boolean interpretation and interpretation, and between weak and strong equivalence.

DFA is then extended to cover sentence embedding, for the cases of propositional attitudes and perception sentences. We will see under which conditions omniscience is not observed and offer some ideas on how such conditions could change the treatment presented in [Cunha, 1990b] in terms of intensional logic.

2 A Puzzle of Perception

Barwise ([Barwise, 1981]) uses a puzzle as an example of the deficiencies with possible-worlds semantics. This puzzle raises questions about the technical use of worlds in the semantics of classical modal logic when formalizing the language of perception. The problems that Barwise finds leads him into Situation Semantics. As we believe in the general approach of compositional semantics and model-theory for modal logic as being particularly intuitive, we think that it should be able to explain Barwise's solutions and incorporate them. We start by summarizing the puzzle and the conclusions. Then we investigate the expressive power of the formal language used, first as a classical logic with extensional boolean meanings and then with intensional meanings on worlds. Finally we discuss the notion of logical equivalence and whether the puzzle creates a good case against the use of possible world semantics.

Can a man's death be attributed to a breakdown in the laws of modal logic? Brown is accused of murdering his mortal enemy Fred Smith. At Brown's trial, Smith's wife, Mary, testifies as follows: "Brown and I happened to enter the room at the same time, by different doors. Fred, facing my door, saw me enter. I saw Brown enter, but Fred did not see Brown enter." Brown who is pleading self-defence, needs to refute the claim that Fred did not see him enter the room. So he calls in an expert witness, a famous modal logician K who "proves" that, by the very laws of logic, the situation could not possibly be as Mary Smith described! How?

[Barwise, 1981], pp 381.

The solution given by the expert witness uses the following translations into a formal logic:

m :   Mary Smith.
f :   Fred Smith.
b :   Brown.
$F(x)$: x entering by the door more or less in front of Fred.
$B(x)$: x entering by the other door.

The testimony of Mary would then be formalized as:

(1) m saw $B(b)$.
(2) f saw $F(m)$.
(3)   not $(f$ saw $B(b))$.

It is assumed that the following principles (A) to (E) are accepted for a logic of perception.

(A)   if a sees ϕ then ϕ.
(B)   if ϕ then not $(f$ sees not $\phi)$.
(C)   if f sees $(\phi$ or $\psi)$ then f sees ϕ or f sees ψ.
(D)   if f sees $(\phi$ and $\psi)$ then f sees ϕ and f sees ψ.

According to Barwise, the modal logician must also accept the following principle (E), for ϕ and ψ *logically equivalent*.

(E)   if f sees ϕ then f sees ψ.

It is also accepted that[1]:

(4) $F(m)$ is *logically equivalent* to $(F(m)$ and $B(b))$ or $(F(m)$ and not $B(b))$.

Then the expert witness is able to deduce from Mary's testimony that f **saw** $B(b)$ and therefore arrived at a contradiction, that f **saw** $B(b)$ and not $(f$ **saw** $B(b))$. From (1) and (A) deduce $B(b)$. From $B(b)$ and (B) deduce not $(f$ saw not $B(b))$. Whence, from (4), (C) and (D) we derive f saw $B(b)$, which contradicts Mary's testimony.

The conclusion Barwise takes is that "the old problem of logical omniscience" is responsible for the puzzle. According to Barwise, the modal logician is committed to the claim that if you know, believe or see ϕ, you must also know, believe or see any ψ logically equivalent to ϕ. Barwise cannot accept this view, particularly for perception verbs, and he claims this to be the reason for his rejection of possible-worlds semantics and modal logic in the treatment of attitudes and perception. As we have said, technical support but mainly the philosophical support for Barwise's decision is given in [Hintikka, 1975].

---

[1] We could reject this particular equivalence, as arising from strict implication. The use of a system which avoids the so-called 'paradoxes of strict implication' could stop this particular equivalence (see for instance in [Hughes and Cresswell, 1968] system E). However, the argument rests on any logical equivalence, and any formal system should provide some kind of equivalence.

3 Determiner-Free Aliass

The following definition of the syntactic system for *Determiner-Free Aliass* or *DFA* follows closely the presentation in [Barwise and Perry, 1983], from now on referred to as *S&A*. However, our style is much closer to *PTQ*. We give a set of syntactic categories and basic expressions for each syntactic category. Classically, the basic expressions constitute the lexicon of the language, although, as we will see, in *S&A* there are basic expressions which are not in the lexicon. The non-basic expressions of the language, phrases and sentences, are then defined recursively.

Definition 3.1 *The set* **CAT** *of syntactic categories of Barwise and Perry's Formal English,* DFA, *is defined as follows:*

1. Basic syntactic categories is the set $\{V, N, W, I, R^1, R^2, NAM\}$.
2. Syntactic categories is the set **CAT** $=\{RS, IT, TM, LRP, PP, NP, S\}$.

Definition 3.2 *The following names will be used for the syntactic categories defined before:*

V	or	variables.
N	or	present tense markers.
W	or	past tense markers.
I	or	indeterminates.
R^1	or	unary relation symbols.
R^2	or	binary relation symbols.
NAM	or	names.
RS	or	relation symbols.
IT	or	individual terms.
TM	or	tense markers.
LRP	or	located relation phrases.
PP	or	property phrases (common noun phrases and verb phrases).
NP	or	noun phrases.
S	or	sentences.

Definition 3.3 *The sets* $\mathbf{B}_a$ *of basic expressions* b_a *of category a are given. For instance the set* $\mathbf{B}_v$ *is the set of basic expressions of the syntactic category of variables.*

$$
\begin{aligned}
\mathbf{B}_V &= \{h_1, h_2, h_3, \ldots\}. \\
\mathbf{B}_N &= \{n_1, n_2, n_3, \ldots\}. \\
\mathbf{B}_W &= \{w_1, w_2, w_3, \ldots\}. \\
\mathbf{B}_I &= \{sbj, obj, loc, bol\}. \\
\mathbf{B}_{R^1} &= \{\text{running, walking, barking, } r^1, s^1, \ldots\}. \\
\mathbf{B}_{R^2} &= \{\text{eating, touching, biting, } r^2, s^2, \ldots\}. \\
\mathbf{B}_{NAM} &= \{\text{John, Mary, Bill, Jackie, } \ldots\}. \\
\mathbf{B}_{RS} &= \mathbf{B}_{R^1} + \mathbf{B}_{R^2}. \\
\mathbf{B}_{IT} &= \{\text{I}\} + \mathbf{B}_{NAM} + \mathbf{B}_V. \\
\mathbf{B}_{TM} &= \mathbf{B}_N + \mathbf{B}_W.
\end{aligned}
$$

The sets of *basic expressions* of other categories are empty. By definition a *basic expressions b* is a member of **B**.

The elements in the sets $\mathbf{B}_{RS}$, $\mathbf{B}_{IT}$ and $\mathbf{B}_{TM}$ are called by Barwise and Perry the *lexicon* of the language *DFA*.

Definition 3.4 *The sets* $\mathbf{P}_a$ *of* phrases p_a *of category a are introduced by the rules:*

Basic rule:

1. For all *syntactic categories* a, any member of $\mathbf{B}_a$ is in $\mathbf{P}_a$.

Sentence rules:

2.1. If $\alpha \in \mathbf{P}_{NP}$ and $\beta \in \mathbf{P}_{PP}$ then $F_1(\alpha, \beta) \in \mathbf{P}_S$, where:
$$F_1(\alpha, \beta) = (\alpha\beta).$$

2.2. If $\phi, \psi \in \mathbf{P}_S$ then $F_2(\phi, \psi) \in \mathbf{P}_S$, where:
$$F_2(\phi, \psi) = (\phi \text{ and } \psi).$$

2.3. If $\phi, \psi \in \mathbf{P}_S$ then $F_3(\phi, \psi) \in \mathbf{P}_S$, where:
$$F_3(\phi, \psi) = (\phi \text{or} \psi).$$

Property phrase rules:

3.1. If $\alpha \in \mathbf{P}_{LRP}$ then $F_4(\alpha) \in \mathbf{P}_{PP}$, where:
$$F_4(\alpha) = (\alpha).$$

3.2. If $\alpha \in \mathbf{P}_{LRP}$ and $\beta \in \mathbf{P}_{NP}$ then $F_1(\alpha, \beta) \in \mathbf{P}_{PP}$.

3.3. If $\alpha \in \mathbf{P}_{PP}$ and $\beta \in \mathbf{P}_{PP}$ then $F_2(\alpha, \beta) \in \mathbf{P}_{PP}$.

Noun phrase rules:

4.1. If $\alpha \in \mathbf{P}_{IT}$ then $F_4(\alpha) \in \mathbf{P}_{NP}$.

4.2. If $\alpha \in \mathbf{P}_{NP}$ and $\beta_i \in \mathbf{P}_V$ then $F_5(\alpha, \beta_i) \in \mathbf{P}_{PP}$, where:
$$F_5(\alpha, \beta_i) = (\alpha_i).$$

Located relation phrase rule:

5. If $\alpha \in \mathbf{P}_{RS}$ and $\beta \in \mathbf{P}_{TM}$ then $F_6(\alpha, \beta) \in \mathbf{P}_{LRP}$ and $F_7(\alpha, \beta) \in \mathbf{P}_{LRP}$, where:
   $F_6(\alpha, \beta) = (\alpha_\beta)$,
   $F_7(\alpha, \beta) = (\mathbf{not}\ \alpha_\beta)$.

A *meaningful* or *well-formed expression* p of *DFA* is a member of **P**.

For instance the following is a sentence, an element of $\mathbf{P}_S$, of the language *DFA*.

(Jackie biting w_1 Mary) and (h_1 walking w_1)

This sentence in turn directly corresponds to a more natural language sentence like **Jackie was biting Mary and she was walking**, with w_1 being a past tense marker and h_1 a variable standing for **she**.

4   Interpretation of *NL*

A very Montagovian approach is taken to achieve this objective. We provided a syntactic definition for *NL*, and then we introduced a theory of situations *SSL*, as for instance in [Cunha, 1989], which is used to express a compositional semantics for the language as in figure 1.

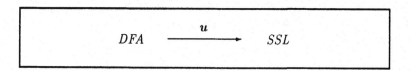

Figure 1: Interpretation of *DFA*

And according to Situation Semantics, if $\alpha \in \mathbf{P}_S$, i.e. α is a sentence of the language, then:

$$u\alpha\ :\ \text{SIT} \to \text{SIT} \to \mathcal{B}$$

$$u\alpha ue\ :\ \mathcal{B}$$

The domain **SIT** is the domain of situations, u is the situation where the sentence is uttered (a discourse situation plus a connection situation), and e is the situation being referred to by the utterance of the sentence. The domain **SIT** $\to$ **SIT** $\to \mathcal{B}$ is a domain of constraints, as in Situation Semantics the meaning of a sentence is said to be a *constraint on an utterance of a sentence*.

Definition 4.1 *Two sentences* α *and* β *are* semantically equivalent *if they have the same interpretation for any uttering and referring situations, i.e. if and only if* $\mathbf{u}\alpha u e = \mathbf{u}\beta u e$.

4.1 Weak and Strong Equivalence

The notions of equivalence are defined in *S&A* only for statements. The reasons for this will be explained later. Intuitively a statement is the utterance of a sentence. The interpretation of a statement in *S&A* is the collection of the referred situations by the sentence in the uttering situation. Given the interpretation of the language, the interpretation of a statement is determined. Strong equivalence is then defined between statements, not sentences, and it does not use quantification over possible interpretations, as does the notion of *logically equivalent* sentences in *PTQ*. The interpretation works very much like a given constant which determines the meaning of the expressions in the language.

Definition 4.2 *The* domain of *statements* $\Phi = (\alpha, u)$ *is defined as* **STAT** $= \mathbf{P}_S \times \mathbf{SIT}$.

Definition 4.3 *The* interpretation $\mathbf{u}$ *of a statement* $\Phi = (\alpha, u)$ *is defined as follows using the semantic interpretation* $\mathbf{u}^2$.

$$\mathbf{u} \quad : \quad \mathbf{STAT} \rightarrow \mathbf{SIT} \rightarrow \mathcal{B}$$
$$\mathbf{u}\Phi e \quad = \quad \mathbf{u}\alpha u e$$

Definition 4.4 *Two statements* Φ *and* Ψ *are* strongly equivalent *if they have the same interpretation. By definition we write* $\Phi \equiv \Psi$ *iff* $\mathbf{u}\Phi = \mathbf{u}\Psi$.

In order to define the notion of weak equivalence, *S&A* defines the boolean meaning of a statement. This definition uses the notion of a *structure of situations*. According to Barwise and Perry this substitutes the traditional definition of a model-theoretic structure.

Definition 4.5 *The* boolean value b *of a statement* Φ *given a* structure of situations m *is defined as follows.*

$$b \quad : \quad \mathbf{STAT} \rightarrow \mathbf{S}_{\mathbf{SIT}} \rightarrow \mathcal{B}$$
$$b\Phi m \quad = \quad \exists e.me \wedge \mathbf{u}\Phi e \wedge \text{actual } e$$

---

[2]We use the same letter for both functions, but from the type of the argument it is clear which one is being used.

We would need to define as well the domain S_{SIT} and the function of **actual**, in a similar way to what is done in *S&A*.

Definition 4.6 *Two statements* Φ *and* Ψ *are* weakly equivalent *if they are true in the same structures of situations. By definition, we will write* $\Phi \leftrightarrow \Psi$ *iff* $b\Phi m = b\Psi m$.

The definition of boolean value (boolean meaning) as we can see, is not syntactically compositional, in the sense that it does not depend on the boolean value of the immediate constituents of the sentence, part of the statement. Intuitively, the utterance of an indicative sentence, a statement, is true in some model m (structure of situations) when we can find in that model a referred situation e which satisfies the constraint the statement imposes ($u\Phi e$) and e is judged to be *actual*. This definition uses a verificationist theory of meaning for boolean value. In some situations an alternative definition based on a falsifiability theory might be better suited.

5 About Omniscience

5.1 Compositional Semantics

The treatments of natural language we have been using, inspired by Montague and in Barwise and Perry, share the property that the meaning of expressions is mathematically defined with a compositional semantics. However the different concepts of what meaning is, are reflected on the form of the semantical objects. Montague takes the Tarskian view that "the basic aim of semantics is to characterize the notion of a true sentence and of entailment" while for Barwise and Perry, as we have seen, the aim is to characterize "constraints on utterances of sentences".

5.2 Omniscience

In *MS* the concept of logical equivalence is defined between sentences. As Hintikka ([Hintikka, 1975]) has originally shown, its extension to propositional attitudes, like belief or knowledge, and the acceptance of inference rules or logical equivalences introducing new information indirectly brings logical omniscience into the semantical treatment. In Barwise and Perry semantics, (*B&PS*), semantic equivalence concepts are defined directly only for statements, the utterances of sentences. Because the boolean value of statements is not compositionally defined, as we will show, no logical omniscience as such (logical as boolean) is ever observed. However, given that both treatments respect semantic compositionality, and because both treatments allow syntactic embedding of sentences, we would expect that in general both would suffer from some form or another of omniscience. As we will see, it may or may not be present in a particular formalization of *B&PS*, depending on the properties of the semantic interpretation function. If it is not explicitly excluded, or if we do not prove it free of omniscience, we cannot be certain. Since Hintikka's paper there have been several other attempts to deal with omniscience, in particular the kind originating from the propositional attitudes of belief and knowledge. Several formal systems based on non-normal modal logics[3] have been introduced with partial success. As was referred to in [Dieu, 1989], in all these approaches the attempt to avoid omniscience has resulted in having the syntactic and semantic levels so mixed up that it is usually difficult to find the correct balance to provide an intuitively acceptable formalization. But possibly worst, as [Dieu, 1989] claims, is that they still suffer from omniscience at the reasoning level.

Having discovered potential omniscience in the approach of Situation Semantics, we believe that we need a more fundamental discussion about its causes. On this respect we think that Barwise should have taken further his doubts on logical equivalence[4]. After reading [Hintikka, 1975] we also believe that more than ever the notions of *formality* and *logic* must be well understood if we want to make computational sense out of the discussions on omniscience.

For sentences involving perception we need formal logics of the kind used for instance for belief, i.e. of the non-normal kind referred to above. As we have seen, even if for propositional attitudes it was possible to live with omniscience, that is completely unacceptable for perception. This is the main reason why we mainly use perception sentences to discuss omniscience, and Barwise and Hintikka's views on the subject.

5.3   Formal Semantics, Synonymy and Omniscience

Intuitively, sentences in a natural language can have the same meaning or can be used in the same way, even when the constituent words are different or ordered differently. This happens for instance when we change a word for a synonym[5] in a sentence. We also hope

---

[3]For non-normal modal logics see [Hughes and Cresswell, 1968], for instance the modal systems $S1$, $S2$ and $S3$, which do not have the rule of necessitation.

[4]"[...] After all, logical equivalence *is* logical equivalence, isnt́ it ? But is it ?"([Barwise, 1981], pp. 388).

[5]**Synonym. 1.** Strictly, a word having the same sense as another (in the same language); but more usu., either of any two or more words (in the same language) having the same general sense, but possessing each of them meanings which are not shared by the other or others, or having different shades of meaning appropriate to different contexts [...]. **2.** By extension: A name or expression which involves or implies a meaning properly or literally expressed by some other [...]. *The Shorter OED on Historical Principles*, Third Edition 1944, Vol II, ©OUP 1973, (1986 reprint), pps. 1279-2672. Formally, the notion of strict synonymity is treated as equality of meaning; for instance as logical equivalence for sentences. The notion of non-strict synonymity seems to be captured for instance in *S&A*'s notion of strong equivalence for statements, *utterances of sentences*. We believe it could be extended to utterances of words. In this case we would require that the interpretation of synonyms must be somehow different with different contexts, apart from words which are, or are imposed to be, strict synonyms. The interpretation u

that syntactically different sentences can be used to express the same idea, because they have the same meaning. We also expect that different expressions can be used together consistently or without contradictions. When providing a formal semantics for a language it is expected that notions of equivalence are defined to formalize those intuitive relations. Equivalence notions are also used as the basis to provide formal inference mechanisms. As Barwise and Perry say, "with the right semantics, the inferences take care of themselves" (*S&A*, pp. 183). In *MS* two sentences can have the same extension and have therefore the same extensional meaning or truth value, for a given context of use or index and logical interpretation. They can as well have the same meaning in any context of use and under a fixed logical interpretation. Finally they can be logically equivalent, if under any logically possible interpretation[6] and in any context of use they have the same extensional meaning. This is the definition for logically equivalent sentences used in *PTQ* and also used in [Gallin, 1975] to provide an axiomatization for a version of *IL*. In *B&PS* two sentences have the same meaning if their interpretation builds the same constraint on situations. But in *B&PS* there are other definitions that correspond to equality of meaning, that of statements, and which are supposed to model inference as being situated. Two statements are weakly equivalent, given a structure of situations, if they have the same boolean value and two statements are strongly equivalent if they have the same interpretation. A statement is defined as a sentence together with its context of use called the uttering situation.

5.4 Compositionality and Semantic Omniscience

The language *DFA* which we defined in the previous sections of this chapter does not treat attitude or perception sentences. In order to do so we would have to extend its syntax and semantics. We assume that this is possible. We also observe that Situation Semantics is guided by compositionality as in pp. 130 of *S&A*. We also note that attitude and perception sentences, either epistemically active or neutral, embed other sentences. "Epistemically neutral reports embed sentences, just as other attitudes do" (*S&A*, pp. 180).

If we accept that sentences embed other sentences, our syntactic definition of the language will include a rule of the following form, where the domain $\mathbf{P}_S$ is the domain of syntactically defined sentences of the language, and $\mathbf{P}_X$ corresponds to some sentence taking syntactic category:

If $\alpha \in \mathbf{P}_X$ and $\beta \in \mathbf{P}_S$ then $\gamma = F_x(\alpha, \beta) \in \mathbf{P}_S$, where
$F_x(\alpha, \beta) = \alpha\beta$.

---

of the language for two different words is equal, exactly when (iff) they strictly are synonyms (when those two words have always the same meaning). If I allow strict synonymity between expressions in my formalization then, as we will see, I will have to accept all the consequences of that decision. In *S&A* the notion of synonymy is never explicitly referred to.

[6] An interpretation is logical if it respects an accepted constant meaning for the logical symbols.

If we accept compositionality of meaning, whatever the meaning objects may be, our semantic definition will include a rule of the following form, where u is the interpretation function being defined and S_x is the semantic composition function.

$$u\gamma = S_x(u\alpha, u\beta).$$

It is clear that if in our semantic definition of u we have two sentences β_1 and β_2 for which $u\beta_1 = u\beta_2$ then we will have semantic omniscience[7].

So we conclude that any such compositional treatment with sentence embedding in general is bound to suffer from omniscience. The same argument is valid for syntactic expressions other than sentence. It may look like that the argument could be rejected on the grounds that equality between functions cannot be decided in general. This argument applies to both *MS* and *B&PS*, but it is obvious that we are not after the general case as the existence of some rule for which we can prove the equality is sufficient to show omniscience.

5.5   Example with Sentences

The syntactic system of *MS* defines a category of expressions called sentences. The treatment of propositional attitudes and perception verbs is included when we allow a syntactic rule which combines a sentence as the object of such verb. Let us call this rule syntactic rule $n1$ and let F_{n1} be the syntactic function that composes a Term-Perception Verb phrase, an element of $\mathbf{P}_{TPV}$, such as **John believes that**, with a sentence:

$$SENT_{1.1} \quad = \quad \textbf{John believes that Natassia was kissing Peter.}$$
$$SENT_1 \quad = \quad \textbf{Natassia was kissing Peter.}$$

Syntactic Rule $n1$:

If $\alpha \in \mathbf{P}_{TPV}$ and $\beta \in \mathbf{P}_S$ then $F_{n1}(\alpha, \beta) \in \mathbf{P}_S$, where:
$$F_{n1}(\alpha, \beta) = \alpha\beta.$$

For instance:

$$SENT_{1.1} = F_{n1}(\textbf{John believes that}, SENT_1)$$

Given that *MS* defines a compositional logical interpretation u, the interpretation of $SENT_{1.1}$ could be as follows, where S_{n1} is the semantic function corresponding to the syntactic rule $n1$,

Semantic Rule $n1$:

$$u\gamma \quad = \quad S_{n1}(u\alpha, u\beta)$$

---

[7]In fact we need in general a less strong property on u, for example that $u\beta_1$ *implies* $u\beta_2$, where the type of *implies* depends on the type of the interpretation.

For instance:

$$uSENT_{1.1} = S_{n1}(u\text{John believes that}, uSENT_1).$$

A similar thing happens in *B&PS* for the syntactic and semantic definition for such expressions. The difference has to do with the types of the interpretation functions,

MS: $uSENT = \mathcal{I} \rightarrow \mathcal{B}.$
B&PS: $uSENT = \text{SIT} \rightarrow \text{SIT} \rightarrow \mathcal{B}.$

In *MS*, if we replace **Natassia was kissing Peter** by another logically equivalent sentence $SENT_2$, i.e. one which has the same truth value in any index, John has to believe $SENT_2$ also. In *B&PS*, if we replace **Natassia was kissing Peter** by another semantically equivalent sentence like $SENT_2$, i.e. one that *constrains situations* in the same way, John also has to believe $SENT_2$. Because the compositional interpretations are defined in different ways, the sentences which in each case have to be believed are different, but unless we restrict the interpretations, the omniscience is possibly present.

5.6 Example with Statements

This second example is an attempt to clarify what happens when we use statements instead of sentences. *S&A* claims that inference is based on statements, the utterance of indicative sentences (pp. 139 and followings of *S&A*). We will see how this affects omniscience.

As we have seen the boolean value of a statement is not defined compositionally. Therefore inferences arising from boolean equality or weak equivalence do not fall under the previous discussion, and so we may say that there is no logical omniscience if logical is identified with boolean. Strong equivalence however is compositionally defined, and therefore it seems to fall under the same conclusion.

Let us analyse the previous example, with $u_{1.1}$ being a situation which characterizes the utterance of $SENT_{1.1}$.

$SENT_{1.1}$ = **John believes that Natassia was kissing Peter.**
$SENT_1$ = **Natassia was kissing Peter.**
$STAT_{1.1}$ = **(John believes that Natassia was kissing Peter,** $u_{1.1}$**).**

In the grammar we will have as before,

$$SENT_{1.1} = F_{n1}(\text{John believes that}, SENT_1).$$
$$uSENT_{1.1} = S_{n1}(u \text{ John believes that}, uSENT_1)$$

And the interpretation of this statement is:

$$\boldsymbol{u}STAT_{1.1} = \boldsymbol{u}SENT_{1.1}u_{1.1}$$

Now suppose we have also:

$SENT_2 =$ **Natassia was kissing Peter and John was walking or John was not walking**

This sentence in MS is logically equivalent to **Natassia was kissing Peter**. The question we ask in $B\&PS$ is what is the interpretation of the statement which results from uttering in the same situation the sentence $SENT_{1.2}$, i.e. $STAT_{1.2}$.

$$SENT_{1.2} = \text{John believes that} SENT_2.$$
$$STAT_{1.2} = (SENT_2, u_{1.1}).$$

$$\boldsymbol{u}SENT_{1.1} = S_{n1}(\boldsymbol{u} \text{ John believes that}, uSENT_1).$$
$$\boldsymbol{u}SENT_{1.2} = S_{n1}(\boldsymbol{u} \text{ John believes that}, uSENT_2).$$

$$\boldsymbol{u}STAT_{1.1} = \boldsymbol{u}SENT_{1.1}u_{1.1}.$$
$$= S_{n1}(\boldsymbol{u} \text{ John believes that}, \boldsymbol{u}SENT_1)u_{1.1}.$$

$$\boldsymbol{u}STAT_{1.2} = \boldsymbol{u}SENT_{1.2}u_{1.1}.$$
$$= S_{n1}(\boldsymbol{u} \text{ John believes that}, \boldsymbol{u}SENT_2)u_{1.1}.$$

So if we want to avoid any two statements being strongly equivalent, we need to prove that for our definition of the interpretation $\boldsymbol{u}SENT_1$ and $\boldsymbol{u}SENT_2$ are different functions in general, i.e. are different constraints on situations in order for the meaning of the embedding sentence to be able to be also different. In this case $\boldsymbol{u}SENT_1$ should be different from $\boldsymbol{u}SENT_2$. The main conclusion is very simple: if we want to avoid omniscience in general, we must not quantify $\boldsymbol{u}$, exactly as Barwise does, in the definition of equivalence. In the limit where our system involves attitudes, perception and other more explicitly syntactical sentence-taking phrases, we need to be sure that for any two syntactically different sentences there will be a different semantic value.

6 Logics of Perception

Our main objective is to expose some problems with Hintikka's treatment of knowledge and belief, of sentences involving the phrases **knows that** and **believes that**, through the study of the less epistemically connotated perception sentences involving the phrase **sees that**. For a question of simplification of notation we will use the following abbreviations:

$K_a p$ for a **knows that** p.
$B_a p$ for a **believes that** p.
$S_a p$ for a **sees that** p.

6.1   Other Propositional Words and Phrases

One of the characteristics of these phrases K_a, B_a, S_a and also of a phrase like **It is necessary that** is that they are not truth functional on the extensional meaning of the proposition following them. We will call such phrases propositional phrases. We list in some partial order of decreasing 'logical power', sentences with propositional phrases.

It is necessary that p : *It is necessary that 1+1=2. It is necessary that 7,536,429 + 8,897,698 = 16,434,127.*

a knows that p : *Natassia knows that the morning star is the evening star.*

a believes that p : *Natassia believes that the morning star is the evening star.*

a sees that p : *Charles sees that Robert is kissing Natassia.*

It is obvious that p : *It is obvious that 1+1 = 2. It is obvious that 7,536,429 + 8,897,698 = 16,434,127.*

6.2   Hintikka's Treatment of Propositional Attitudes

Given the success of Kripke's possible worlds semantics for modal logics involving the formalization of necessity and possibility, Hintikka decided to take the same approach into the treatment of propositional attitudes ([Hintikka, 1967]). For instance, there is a *knowledge* operator, for which he introduces an accessibility relation on epistemically possible worlds, the *epistemic a-alternative relation*:

$$u K_a p w \quad iff \quad \forall w'. epist\text{-}alt(a, w, w') \rightarrow u p w'$$

In principle this will allow the operator K_a to be intensionally truth-functional. Given that we want such semantics for S_a we may think of doing the same thing. We could justify this step on a basic identification of seeing with **knowing**. For instance Martin-Löf ([Martin-Löf, 1983]) makes detailed observations on how often we use **I see that** instead of saying **I know that**. This is basically the main justification we have to write the following formula, where *vis-alt* can be read, paraphrasing Hintikka, as the *visual a-alternatives* relation:

$$u S_a p w \quad iff \quad \forall w'. vis\text{-}alt(a, w, w') \rightarrow u p w'$$

We believe it is much easier to discuss perception than knowledge. It may be simpler to ask the question whether this later definition makes any sense, and then relate the conclusions to Hintikka's formalization of knowledge. As we have seen omniscience is definitely not acceptable in a logic of perception.

6.3 Axiomatization

The main technical problem with the definition above is that it is equivalent to accept a form of the rule of necessitation. We think of a formal system, for instance as in [Hughes and Cresswell, 1968], presented by a set of axioms AX and rules of inference RI where the turnstile $\vdash$ expresses formal inference. Then, with a logical notion of validity as truth in all possible-worlds, we would have that if we deduce p we need to deduce $S_a p$ as well. If $\vdash p$ means that $\forall w.upw = true$, then from the definition above we also must have that $\forall w.uS_a pw = true$ or that $\vdash S_a p$. Therefore we conclude that the following inference rule, similar in form to necessitation, is inescapable: $p \vdash S_a p$.

It is at this point that we will start diverging from Hintikka and in some respect from Barwise. We do not take this as a failure of possible worlds semantics, neither of modal logic, but as a problem with the understanding of formality, logic and validity. We know that modal logic is able to cope with this situation. It is well known that we can have modal formal systems for which the rule of necessitation is not valid, for instance the modal systems $S1$, $S2$ and $S3$ described in [Hughes and Cresswell, 1968]. It is also presented in that reference a Kripkian style semantics for $S2$ and $S3$, but it seems that there is no satisfactory semantics for $S1$. More recently, in [Dieu, 1989], we can find a review of a few formal systems for belief in which satisfactory inference mechanisms can be built. We think that those systems have unsatisfactory semantics, and we find counter-intuitive the use of notions of *non-normal* or *impossible possible-worlds*.

The main formal difference between such systems and a logic for perception would rest on the choice of axioms and rules of inference. If we take a propositional version of Barwise and Perry formalization of visual perception[8] , we would require the following axioms together with the normal propositional calculus:

a1: $S_a p \rightarrow p$:
a2: S_a not $p \rightarrow$ not $S_a p$.
a3: $p \rightarrow$ not S_a not p.
a4: $S_a(p$ and $q) \rightarrow S_a p$ and $S_a q$.
a5: $S_a(p$ or $q) \rightarrow S_a p$ or $S_a q$.

And for instance we do not want any of the following rules and axioms:

* $p \vdash S_a p$.
* $p \rightarrow q \vdash S_a p \rightarrow S_a q$.
* $\vdash (S_a p$ and $S_a(p \rightarrow q)) \rightarrow S_a q$.

---

[8]Primary S_a perception reports.

We are not assuming this to be a complete presentation of the formal logic of *seeing* but we believe it shows that building such a logic is quite feasible.

6.4 Semantics

It is not possible to provide a semantics for perception before discussing in general the problem of meaning and validity for propositional phrases, in particular for perception sentences.

However before entering such discussion in the next section, we believe that we need to follow our intuitions of what is that we *see*. We think that we need in the model a set of agents *ag* who can see, and for each agent the equivalent of a visual *information system* which models the states of its visual input. A boolean interpretation for sentences involving seeing would then be given by an agent dependent function that would have as arguments the information system and the proposition for which the question of being seen was asked. One of the characteristics of those functions is that they must be strictly computable, i.e. its implementation must be a program which terminates. If we are interested in declarative sentences $S_a p$, that function needs to have a three value result domain, respectively for the cases when the visual database contains p, contains **not** p, and the case where it contains neither **not** p nor p.

6.5 Formal Representations and Meaning

The following example is presented in [Hodges, 1977] to justify the necessity of an alternative to intensions, as the meaning objects which would satisfy compositionality:

> "For example the two following sentences are necessary truths, and hence they have the same intension (44.2):
>
> 1+1=2.
> 7,536,429+8,897,698=16,434,127.
>
> Nevertheless one of the following sentences is true and the other is false (44.3):
> It is obvious that 1+1=2.
> It is obvious that 7,536,429+8,897,698=16,434,127.
>
> We see at once that some other feature of the sentences (44.2) besides their intension must be weaving an influence."

[Hodges, 1977], pp. 252.

The formalization of mathematics, for instance integer arithmetic, is concerned with creating a formal system for the automatic, or objective, process of problem-solving in integer arithmetic. We would assume that typographical or psychological characteristics are excluded from such formalization, for instance questions involving the font we use to express the arithmetic operators and whether they are known to the readers. We believe therefore that it is not satisfactory to conclude that the example above is a good reason to replace intensions.

The real problem is that the mathematical and logical formalization we start with is an objective formalization for mathematics, and the notion of logical equivalence is objectively formalized in such way that it is acceptable as corresponding to our intuitions of mathematical equivalence.

Hintikka's extensions to knowledge and belief of the formalization of mathematical or logical necessity has, we believe, the same fundamental problem Hodges is facing above, which in the end does not eliminate omniscience. We believe that this becames very clear in [Hintikka, 1975]. There we find two uses of logic. The first one has to do with the definitions of truth-functional classical logical symbols in formal languages, such as mathematical equality and boolean connectives and objective necessity. Given a language with boolean interpretable primitives, truth functional logical connectives and expressions made out of them, such as first order logic, the semantics is given using an interpretation, which is logical if the standard truth functional boolean, logical and objective operations are respected. We have defined the concepts of equivalent sentences and the concept of logically equivalent sentences. The first concept is relative to *some* logical interpretation, the second to *any* logical interpretation. When the logic is extended with modal operators and temporal operators, which are not truth-functional, notions of intensions on logically-possible or objective world and time, accessibility and ordering have to be introduced to preserve truth functionality and to achieve a proper notion of equivalence and logical equivalence[9] . The theorems of such logics depend on the formal axiomatization and inference rules used, which defines the logically equivalent sentences.

The extension of formalization to other non-truth-functional operators, such as the ones necessary to formalize our use of verbs like believe or see requires a proper formalization process, which is intuitively valid *a priori*. Such formal deductive systems would need to square with our intuitive judgements of what can be absolutely taken as *believing-ly* or *seeing-ly equivalent* and never the opposite. The semantics of such formalization would be restricted to possible *believing-ly* or *seeing-ly* interpretations. And here comes the second sense of logic in Hintikka's work, his belief that the use of *logically equivalent* must incorporate *believing-ly* or *seeing-ly equivalents*. Carrying on with this process for all non truth functional words in the language would provide a notion of absolute logical equivalence.

Hintikka wants an intuitively valid formalization of knowledge and belief but at the same time he wants to keep the formal framework of objective or mathematical logic, in which the following inference rules are accepted:

---

[9]For instance we would not dream of rejecting intensions when extending the formal semantics of necessity to an objective formal semantics of time.

$$p \rightarrow q \quad \vdash K_a p \rightarrow K_a q.$$
$$p \rightarrow q \quad \vdash B_a p \rightarrow B_a q.$$

His main reason to keep these rules is attributed explicitly to his rejection of the "positivistic doctrine of the non-informative (tautological) character of logical truths". We believe that this is exactly Martin-Löf's ([Martin-Löf, 1983]) claim on formality, and in particular on knowledge.

> "There is absolutely no question of a judgement being evident in itself, independently of us and of our cognitive activity. That would be just as absurd as to speak of a judgement as being known, not by somebody, you or me, but in itself. To be evident is to be evident *to* somebody, as inevitably as to be known is to be known *by* somebody.
>
> The notion of formal proof [...] has been arrived at by formalistically interpreting what you mean by an immediate inference, by forgetting about the difference between a judgement and a proposition, and, finally, by interpreting the notion of proposition formalistically, that is by replacing it by the notion of formula."

> [Martin-Löf, 1983], pp. 21, 30.

However, such a *positivistic doctrine* of formality does not stop us from formalizing knowledge, belief perception and other propositional aspects of language. Its formal semantics just needs to be intuitively valid, in the sense for instance that it takes into account, if necessary, the correct level of for instance typographical or psychological characteristics. But it is obvious that the necessary consideration of typographical characteristics, for instance in sentences like **There are five e's on this sentence** or in Quine's sentences with quotation marks, requires that the intensional interpretation should have in those cases an explicit typographical or 'syntactical' semantics[10].

We conclude that in general for a real semantic interpretation (as u) we must always be able to totally distinguish between syntactically or typographically different sentences. The great advantage of Situation Semantics on the subject of omniscience, as we have said, is that we may be able for some language, and if we want, make sure that there is no strict synonymity, while being able to have local or situated reasoning, based on local notions of equivalence.

> "[...] Thus deductive inference is, like truth, *objective*, and even *absolute*. Objectivity does not mean, of course, that we can always ascertain whether or not a

---

[10] We would like to make it clear that we are not proposing a system were we would end up with no capability to find equivalences between expressions of different syntactic form. We are just claiming that at the global level, of a real or total or complete interpretation we must take into account that there are no two objects with different forms which are totally equal, i.e. there are no strict synonyms.

given statement is true. Nor can we always ascertain whether a given inference is valid. If we agree to use the term "true" only in the objective sense, then there are many statements which we can *prove* to be true; yet *we cannot have a general criterion of truth*. If we had such criterion, we would be omniscient, at least potentially, which we are not. According to the work of Gödel and Tarski, we cannot even have a general criterion of truth for arithmetical statements, although we can of course describe infinite sets of arithmetical statements which are true. In the same way, we may agree to use the term "valid inference" in the objective sense, in which case we can prove of many inferences that they are valid (that is, they unfailingly transmit truth); yet we have no general criterion of validity—not even if we confine ourselves to purely arithmetical statements."

[Popper, 1974], pp. 143.

7 Conclusions

We have defined the syntax and semantics for the language *Determiner-Free Aliass* of Barwise and Perry using a compositional definition in the same style of *MS*. The interpretation of a sentence is defined as a constraint on situations and required to be computationally expressed. A situation is a finite collection of facts about the world. The notion of statement, the utterance of an indicative sentence, is defined as a pair of an uttering situation and a sentence. The notion of equality of meaning for statements is modeled or formalized with the concept of strong equivalence between statements. We showed that in general such semantics can suffer from the problem of omniscience. However, if we restrict ourselves to real and computable interpretations, where we avoid strict synonymity and quantification of the interpretation on the definition of equivalence, we may avoid that problem. We believe that this solution could be used both for Situation Semantics and for possible-worlds semantics, or alternatively that this would be used as a distinguishing characteristic for the former semantics. We also commented on Hintikka's formal semantics for propositional attitudes, and we noticed that his attempt to make the use of knowledge mathematically objective, always creates omniscience.

Some Remarks on First-Order Intensional Logic

João Falcão e Cunha

Faculdade de Engenharia da Universidade do Porto

Rua dos Bragas — 4099 Porto CODEX — Portugal

E-mail: jfcunha@fe.up.ctt.pt — Tel: 351-(0)2-382 071

1 Introduction

"I can see no other escape from this dilemma (lest our true aim be lost for ever) than that some of us should venture to embark on a synthesis of facts and theories, albeit with second-hand and incomplete knowledge of some of them—and at the risk of making fools of ourselves."

[Schrödinger, 1967], pp. 1.

Several comprehensive logical systems or theories have been proposed as frameworks for the study of natural language, with special emphasis on the study of its semantics. Montague Semantics and more recently Situation Semantics have been widely used amongst Computational Linguists as such systems. However the spread, both in width and depth of the multiple branches of knowledge on those areas requires as well that the main overall simplifications and developments of those areas are presented in synthesis.

The simplified version of Montague Semantics presented in [Cunha, 1989] uses a first-order semantics, in the sense that we only have in the object language quantification of variables ranging over primitive domains. This is also a characteristic of the Intensional Logic proposed by [Moennich and Bealer, 1988] and of the Belief Logics used by [Konolige, 1986]. All these Intensional logics include variants of modal treatments for propositional attitudes and perception sentences.

The original Montague Semantics depends on Intensional Logic *IL* which is a high-order logic. While such logics have been studied and their use supported or criticized for different reasons, their difficulties with mechanized deduction seem to offer a practical argument against their use in modelling our ability to reason and communicate in natural language.

The original presentation of Situation Semantics fundaments its semantics on Aczel's notion of *Hyperset* ([Aczel, 1980]). The use of hypersets was justified to avoid the paradoxes in Set Theory, on which Montague semantics depends. It is also justified to model special and possibly acceptable phenomena of circularity in natural language such as the "Liar Paradox" ([Barwise and Etchemendy, 1987]). However some authors ([Moennich and Bealer, 1988] pp. 194-197) argue against the use of Hypersets.

We will try to summarize the argument in favour of first-order intensional logic which coincides with the general argument of [Moennich and Bealer, 1988]. We will defend the use of an Intensional Logic such as the one presented in [Cunha, 1990b] interpreted with Domain Theory, in a way similar to what Turner ([Turner, 1983]) did. Our approach differs from Montague and Turner in at least two other aspects:

- We will not be using meaning postulates, which violate modularity[1], and are the only source of high-order quantification in Montague Semantics. Instead, we propose to constrain directly the interpretation or translation function of natural language [Cunha and Pitt, 1990].

- Instead of using hypersets, as Situation Semantics does, we propose to use Domains, which theory stresses computability aspects, in our case of natural language semantics.

In the definition of a formal semantics for natural language we are usually not worried about the justification of whether our ability to communicate in Natural Language can be captured or formalized through computable algorithms or whether it cannot. We implicitly accept the justification given by Church's Thesis (see for instance [Cutland, 1980]), according to which any effectively computable algorithm is equivalent to a program in some precise language. However we acknowledge that this thesis is balanced by Popper's Thesis ([Popper, 1935]) according to which it is impossible to develop an Inductive Logic or it is impossible to have a logical rule which would allow an algorithmic inference to be made from a set of finite observations to an irrefutable explanatory theory.

2 The Choice of Logic

We will not attempt to give a precise definition of the various logics we will be referring to. We do this intentionally, because we believe it is well understood what is for instance First-Order Logic (FOL) and what are High-Order Logics (HOL's). According to our understanding the main difference between these two kinds of logics is the *order* of quantification used and not the complexity of types of expressions used. Let $\mathcal{E}$ be a primitive and arbitrary non-empty set of things. FOL only allows quantification over objects of $\mathcal{E}$ and never over arbitrary sets of other things such as $\mathcal{E} \rightarrow \mathcal{E}$. While the quantification used in a logical system is over sets of primitive elements there will be only first-order quantification. So if among the primitive domains there is one of primitive *properties* or

---

[1] As [Pitt, 1990] observes, meaning postulates corrupt modularity because although they operate on translations (semantic objects) they refer to information specified in the syntactic component.

propositions it seems that we may be able to quantify over them using only first-order logic.

We assume that the reader may be able to ascertain for a particular formal system which kind of logic it captures.

2.1 The Case for First-Order Logic

As it is well-known, anything that can be done (read *algorithmically computed*), can be done using *FOL*. However this argument can be applied to any Turing-equivalent language or formal system.

The main reasons for supporting the use of *FOL* have therefore to be found somewhere else, with what are usually called pragmatic reasons. The main reasons to use *FOL* in the treatment of natural language are the following ones which are closely related:

- Efficient Reasoning: There is more knowledge about algorithms for theorem proving in *FOL* than in any other logic. For instance, the resolution and unification algorithms introduced by Robinson have been widely used and since then considerably improved (see for instance [Fitting, 1989a]).

- Logic Programming: first-order logical programming environments offer richer and more developed implementations of reasoning algorithms and better engineering support facilities than environments for any other logics.

- Logic Grammars: first-order logic programming based analysis and synthesis of natural language has several advantages over other formal approaches and offers several well-developed tools for building logic grammars ([Pereira and Warren, 1978]).

2.2 The Case against First-Order Logic

The main problems of using *FOL* in the treatment of natural language are well illustrated if, for instance, we try to represent in such logic sentences of English with temporal aspects, such as the ones in *PTQ*.

Montague has a very simple representation of some temporal aspects involved in natural language sentences. In *PTQ* the logical formulae that represent time-dependent concepts are *very similar* to the original *NL* expressions.

If we want to translate sentences involving temporal aspects into *FOL* we will have to introduce an extra variable for time and make all the predicates time dependent.

For instance, consider the following sentence, adapted from the work of Dov Gabbay ([Gabbay, 1985]):

> **Since Beleza became Minister the Escudo has steadily been going up and in fact it will continue to go up for as long as he is Minister.**

This sentence is quite clear to us and is understood immediately without much effort. Let us write it in *FOL* with time parameters. If we have:

$$
\begin{aligned}
Min(x,t) &= \quad x \text{ is Minister at time } t. \\
VEsc(x,t) &= \quad \text{the value of 1 Escudo at time } t \text{ is } x. \\
n &= \quad now. \\
b &= \quad \textbf{Beleza}.
\end{aligned}
$$

The representation of the sentence becames:

$$
\begin{aligned}
&\exists t < n.[Min(b,t) \land \exists s < t. \forall u.((s < u < t) \rightarrow Min(b,u)) \land \\
&\quad \forall u.((t < u < n) \rightarrow Min(b,u)) \land \\
&\quad \forall u,v,x,y.((t \leq u < v \leq n) \land VEsc(x,u) \land VEsc(y,v) \rightarrow x > y)] \land \\
&Min(b,n) \land \\
&\forall s > n.[\forall t \leq s.Min(b,t) \rightarrow \\
&\quad \forall u,v,x,y.((n \leq u < v \leq s) \land VEsc(x,u) \land VEsc(y,v) \rightarrow x < y)].
\end{aligned}
$$

The above sentence of *FOL* is not readable[2]. Moreover its preparation for resolution theorem provers requires two operations:

- Skolemization and rewriting in disjunctive form.

- Formalization of the temporal aspects in *FOL* which includes the axiomatization of the flow of time.

The Computational Linguistics' literature refers to other problems with *FOL* in the representation of *NL* expressions.

For instance, as the reader can verify, *NL* sentences with adjectives or adverbs will translate into *FOL* sentences but their syntactic structures will be quite different.

According to [Barwise, 1985] (pp. 7), *FOL* is also unsuitable for the treatment of anaphora. In fact many *NL* quantifiers seem to bind pronouns that come before, or even in later sentences. Other types of multiply-quantified natural language sentences, for instance "donkey sentences", cannot easily be translated into *FOL*.

Moreover [Barwise and Cooper, 1981] (pp.160) claim that many *NL* quantifiers such as **more than half** or **most** are not definable using first-order ∀ and ∃ (see as well [Peres, this volume]).

---

[2]In fact it has one simple error.

2.3   The Case for High-Order Logic

Montague's work on the Intensional Logic *IL* can be regarded as the case for the use of *HOL*. It specifies a compositional mapping between *NL*-syntactic structures and the syntactic structures of an *HOL*, covering many complex phenomena of *NL* in a unified logical framework. For instance, *PTQ* includes the treatment of complex forms of quantification, tense and modality and of phrases with adverbs and adjectives.

2.4   The Case against High-Order Logic

The main problem with *HOL* is that there are no efficient reasoning algorithms known for it. It also offers expressive power in excess of what we need or of what we can easily use and understand. For instance, the most comprehensive work on Montague's *Intensional Logic*, partly done under his supervision by Gallin ([Gallin, 1975]), does not even cover *IL*'s tense aspects.

2.5   The Case for First-Order Intensional Logic

From the previous brief critical analysis we conclude that what is necesssary is a logic more expressive than *FOL* but not an *HOL*. In fact there seems to be a growing interest in the use of extensions to *FOL* which do not result in *HOL*, and which is sometimes referred to as First-Order Intensional Logic and which we will call *FOIL*.

Although having different notational apparatus and different semantical foundations many schools of Philosophical Logic seem to me to agree on this. In recent years there has been a number of theories originating from those schools which claim to offer paradox-free and comprehensive frameworks for the study of natural language semantics. The most well-known of those theories have the following names:

- Property Theory.
- Situation Theory.
- Type Theory.

In section 3.2 we will try to outline some of the major differences between their similar although different approaches. The common ground for all these theories is somehow difficult to find, given their different philosophical bases and their different notational conventions. However given their common mathematical foundations it should be possible to conduct a comparative study[3].

For a formal presentation of *FOIL* the reader can see [Moennich and Bealer, 1988].

---

[3] In fact I believe that we are getting to a situation in semantical analysis of natural language similar to the one just before Montague's seminal works, with most of the people working on different schools finding it difficult to communicate between each other.

As a consequence of research on these fundamental areas, there has been a growing interest in this kind of logics from applied *Artificial Intelligence*. For instance, the work of Konolige ([Konolige, 1986]) on belief logics demonstrates an area of application of *FOIL* theory.

There has been at the same time a criticism of the expressive power of modal logics which is contributing to advance the possibilities of theorem proving on *FOIL* (see for instance [Fitting, 1989b]).

2.6 The Cases for and against Computational Logic

So far we have briefly discussed the different sorts of logic that can be used in the treatment of *NL*. There are two problems we did not address. The first one has to do with the reasons why we should be using formal systems which seem to us to behave in logical ways (formal logics), instead of other types of formal systems which do not resemble so closely what we would call *logical*. The second problem has to do with the reasons why formal systems such as logics are sufficient or appropriate to model our abilities to communicate and reason in our native languages.

We believe that this is not the proper place to discuss this later problem, which as we have stated in the introduction has to do with Church's Thesis as well as with Popper's Thesis.

As far as the first problem is concerned, it has been the subject of Logic, since at least Aristotle (see [Lear, 1980]), the study of the laws of reasoning, and the definition of formal systems for its mechanization[4]. Kant, for instance, says that *"Logic is a science of the necessary laws of thought, without which no employment of the understanding and the reason takes place"* ([Kant, 1800], pp. 3). Therefore we will accept that no communication in natural language should be modelled by a formal system which does not incorporate the laws of logic in a very explicit way, according to what is usually understood as such. Beyond historical reasons, this requirement of explicitness has the advantage that we may know how our models are constructed.

3 Semantics and Omniscience

It is usually accepted that the study of Logic is more than the construction of its formal systems or formal logics. We can define a formal logic by specifying its syntax and semantics. While syntactic definitions can be made with few foundational problems, the definition of semantics has faced several problems, of which we would emphasize the following:

---

[4]Aristotle's *Syllogistic* and Frege's *Begriffsschrift* for instance.

- Compositionality, or better its apparent failure. In the treatment of *NL* we need an intensional semantics to achieve compositionality of meaning. This can be done for instance in the lines proposed in [Cunha, 1990b].

- The paradoxes of Set Theory. We need to base our semantics in a theory which does not suffer from them. We can choose, for instance, from the following theories: Domain, Type, Property, Situation, Hyperset or other constructive set theory.

- Omniscience. This is an undesired effect of compositionality which, as we can see in [Cunha, 1990a], arises when we want to provide objective modelling of subjective aspects of language use, such as happens with most of the uses of expressions involving propositional attitudes or perception.

It can be shown ([Moennich and Bealer, 1988]) that in order to solve these problems a Set Theory would need to satisfy the following condition: if b is an element of some set S then we would need to have that $b \in \ldots \in b$. But this is not a *possible* Set Theory. One alternative would be to abandon the standard conception of set and adopt instead a nonstandard one that permits non-well-founded "sets", that is "sets" displaying the previous pattern $b \in \ldots \in b$. However there are three considerations which weight heavily against this alternative.

- Non-well-founded "sets" are ontologically primitive and are virtually on a par with individuals. They do not have their being in ontologically prior entities.

- Non-well-founded "sets" are not strictly and literally sets at all; rather they belong to an entirely new primitive ontological category above and beyond sets. The usual Quinean argument is that sets are epistemologically superior because they can be individuated simply by considering their elements.

- The standard view on sets — according to which, sets have their being in their instances — provides an intuitive diagnosis and resolution of the set-theoretical paradoxes. Advocates of Set Theory should demand a very good reason to give up this secure position.

According to [Hintikka, 1967], the problem of semantic omniscience is due to the standard definitions of propositional meaning in possible-worlds semantics. In fact, if a proposition denotes the set of possible-worlds where it is valid (as we can see in [Cunha, 1990a]) then the interpretations of sentences expressing propositional attitudes will suffer from omniscience. Abandoning standard notions is then the solution proposed for the problem. I do not agree entirely with this solution, because I believe there is a better solution. The standard and intuitive notion of *set* remains, but we add to it the notion of *computability*. This can be done using the notion of *domain* and a rich and well-known theory developed by Scott ([Scott, 1976]). This theory is usually associated with the language development methodology of "Denotational Semantics" ([Schmidt, 1986]) which is well-known amongst the Computer Science community.

3.1   Domains and Computability

The first application of Domain Theory to Linguistics was the treatment of nominalization in [Turner, 1983]. Turner used Scott's domains instead of sets to provide models for complex embedding of expressions. The main advantage of his treatment was that while using sets the model equations did not have any solution, but there were non-trivial solutions using domains.

We believe that there is an extremely important aspect of Turner's approach which has never been given quite the importance it deserves. In fact, through the use of Domain Theory and its well established relationship with recursion theory, natural language interpretations are being given *computable denotations*.

Domain Theory has also been used ([Visser, 1988]) to give elegant and clear treatments for some paradoxes in natural language including the famous "Liar Paradox"[5].

One of the particularities of Domain Theory is its definition of an *undefined element* in the structure of domains. This element is used to characterize the meaning of expressions in programming languages which refer for instance to the top of an empty stack or to the front of an empty queue[6]. This element plays an important role in the precise definition of the formal semantics of languages. It is usually used to give total definitions for partial functions, and is associated with lack of 'information'.

One of the main problems with Turner's analysis has to do with the use of this element in the definition of quantification. Either we have an intuitively simple treatment which seems to be insufficient or we must have very complex definitions which are not intuitively obvious.

3.2   Schools of Thought and Notations

The distinction between the different schools that provide mathematical and logical treatments of natural language is, I believe, mostly syntactic. For instance it would not be a surprise if notions of *hypersets*, *types* and *domains* were all being used in the same way.

As was proposed in section 2.5 we isolate three main semantic schools, which obviously share many features.

- Property Theoretic Semantics (see [Turner, 1988]): Among others, Aczel, Feferman, Turner, Thomason, Moennich and Bealer work on this school. Its main characteristic is that the notion of *proposition* is taken as primitive and "is not

---

[5]Previous treatments of this paradox can be found for instance in [Tarski, 1931] and [Barwise and Etchemendy, 1987]. Gödel's famous proof is as well a form of this paradox and [Popper, 1945] (vol.2, pp.355) uses another form of it to argue that Wittgenstein's theories in the 'Tratactus' are not valid.

[6]Type Theoretic Semantics (see section 3.2) is very critical of the use of this element in value-based interpretations, i.e. model theoretic semantics. Type Theoretic Semantics argues that if model theoretic semantics needs such undefined element than something is wrong with it ([de Queiroz, 1990], pp 180-185).

unpacked in terms of possible-worlds and classical set theory" (id.). It mainly differs from Situation Semantics because it is usually presented with both model and proof theoretic descriptions, but has been converging with it on for instance the criticism of possible-worlds.

- Situation Semantics: Among others, Hintikka, Barwise, Aczel, Perry and Cooper ([Cooper, 1990]) have been closely associated with this school. Many of its early results originated in research work at Stanford's *CSLI*. Its main distinction is the importance given to model theoretic semantics, and to the notion of *situation* which replaces the standard set-theoretic notion of *possible-world*. The meaning of a proposition is not a set of possible worlds, but a constraint on situations. In its early days Situation Semantics was based on Hintikka's Game Theoretical semantics, but it has been moving towards Aczel' hyperset semantics and converging with property semantics.

- Type Theoretic Semantics: Its main proponents have been working on Gentzen, Prawitz and Bishop's ideas. Martin-Löf is the leading researcher in this school. It originates from constructivist analysis of mathematics and uses systems of natural deduction. Although its framework has not yet been applied explicitly to natural language modelling, its basic principle of "propositions as types" and its primitive notion of *type*, which replaces the notion of set, seems to offer an interesting alternative semantic foundation. In Martin-Löf's words: "If we take seriously the idea that a proposition is defined by laying down how its canonical proofs are formed and accept that a set is defined by prescribing how its canonical elements are formed, then it is clear that it would only lead to unnecessary duplication to keep the notions of proposition and set (and the associated notions of proof of a proposition and element of a set) apart. Instead, we simply identify them, that is treat them as one and the same notion. This is the formulae-as-types (propositions-as-sets) interpretation on which intuitionistic type theory is based." (quoted in [de Queiroz, 1990], pp. 183).

Most of the results of these theoretical semantics are still being studied mostly in research situations[7], although many of its results are starting to have important consequences in applications which involve the logics of practical reasoning, i.e., when formal systems try to simulate reasoning from individuals' beliefs or knowledge.

This overview would be incomplete without a reference to the work of Quine (see for instance [Quine, 1970]). According to him, Property Theoretic Semantics and Situation Semantics suffer from a fundamental problem. Quine objects to the use of *propositions* or of *statements* at least in the way they are used in the tradition of Russell. "If there were propositions, they would induce a certain relation of synonymy or equivalence between sentences themselves: those sentences would be equivalent that expressed the same

---

[7]On the other hand Denotational Semantics (see section 3) is being thought in many undergraduate Computer Science courses.

proposition. Now my objection is going to be that the appropriate equivalence relation makes no objective sense at the level of sentences" (id.). We do not know if Quine's argument applies as well to Type Theoretic Semantics.

In some respects Quine is criticizing an uncritical use of logical analysis in the treatment of natural language. While being a respected logician, he asserts that analogies between natural language with logic are, at best, unhelpful.

4 Conclusions

We have introduced the major semantic modelling frameworks for natural language, and made reference to the main theoretical schools which use mathematical logic to capture our intuitions of how natural language is or should be used.

Our main conclusion is that the Mathematical Logic being used throughout seems to be a modal logic with different modalities and with simple first order quantification, based on a constructive set theory usually named *First-Order Intensional Logic*.

References

[Abney, 1987] S. Abney. *The English Noun Phrase in Its Sentential Aspect*. PhD thesis, MIT, 1987.

[Aczel, 1980] Peter Aczel. Frege structures and the notions of proposition, truth and set. In J. Barwise, H. J. Keisler, and K. Kunen, editors, *The Kleene Symposium*, pages 31–59. North-Holland, 1980.

[Altmann, 1987] Gerry Altmann. Modularity and interaction in sentence processing. In J. L. Garfield, editor, *Modularity in Knowledge Representation and Natural-Language Understanding*, pages 249–257. MIT Press, Cambridge, MA, 1987.

[Aoun and Sportiche, 1982] J. Aoun and D. Sportiche. On the formal theory of government. *The Linguistic Review*, (2):221–236, 1982.

[Baker, 1988] M. Baker. *Incorporation*. The University of Chicago Press, Chicago, 1988.

[Balari et al., 1990] Sergio Balari, Luís Damas, Nelma Moreira, and Giovanni B. Varile. CLG: constraint logic grammars. In *Proceedings of the 13th International Conference on Computational Linguistics*, Helsinki, 1990.

[Baltin, 1982] Mark Baltin. A landing site theory of movement rules. *Linguistic Inquiry*, (13):1–38, 1982.

[Baltin and Kroch, 1989] Mark R. Baltin and Anthony S. Kroch, editors. *Alternative Conceptions of Phrase Structure*. University of Chicago Press, Chicago, IL, 1989.

[Barss and Lasnik, 1986] A. Barss and H. Lasnik. A note on anaphora and double objects. *Linguistic Inquiry*, (17):347–354, 1986.

[Barwise, 1981] Jon Barwise. Scenes and other situations. *The Journal of Philosophy*, 78(7):369–397, July 1981.

[Barwise, 1985] Jon Barwise. A Model for the Treatment of Anaphora in Situation Semantics. Informal Notes IN-CSLI-85-1, Center for the Study of Language and Information, May 1985.

[Barwise, 1989] Jon Barwise. *The Situation in Logic*. Number 17 in CSLI Lectures Notes. Center for the Study of Language and Information, Stanford, CA, 1989.

[Barwise and Cooper, 1981] Jon Barwise and Robin Cooper. Generalized quantifiers and natural language. *Linguistics and Philosophy*, (4):159–219, 1981.

[Barwise and Etchemendy, 1987] Jon Barwise and John Etchemendy. *The Liar. An Essay in Truth and Circularity*. Oxford University Press, 1987.

[Barwise and Etchemendy, 1990] Jon Barwise and John Etchemendy. Infons and inference. In [Cooper *et al.*, 1990].

[Barwise and Perry, 1983] Jon Barwise and John Perry. *Situations and Attitudes*. MIT Press, Cambridge, MA, 1983.

[Bäuerle *et al.*, 1979] Rainer Bäuerle, Urs Egli and Arnim von Stechow, editors. *Semantics from Different Points of View*. Springer Verlag, Berlin, 1979.

[Bäuerle *et al.*, 1983] Rainer Bäuerle, Schwarze and Arnim von Stechow, editors. *Meaning, Use and Interpretation of Language*. de Gruyter, Berlin, 1983.

[Belletti and Rizzi, 1981] A. Belletti and L. Rizzi. The syntax of ne: some theoretical implications. *The Linguistic Review*, (1):117–154, 1981.

[Bennett, 1974] M. Bennett. *Some Extensions of a Montague Fragment of English*. PhD thesis, UCLA, Indiana University Linguistics Club, 1974.

[Bindi and Calzolari] R. Bindi and N. Calzolari. Statistical analysis of large textual Italian corpus in search of lexical information. Presented in *EUROLEX 1990*, Malaga. forthcoming.

[Boguraev and Briscoe, 1989] B. Boguraev and E. J. Briscoe, editors. *Computational Lexicography for Natural Language Processing*. Longman, London, 1989.

[Boguraev *et al.*, 1989] B. Boguraev, R. Byrd, J. Klavans, and M. Neff. From structural analysis of lexical resources to semantics in a lexical knowledge base. In *Proceedings of the First International Lexical Acquisition Workshop*, Detroit, Michigan, 1989.

[Borsley, 1987] Robert D. Borsley. Subjects and Complements in HPSG. Report CSLI-87-107, Center for the Study of Language and Information, Stanford, CA, 1987.

[Bowers, 1987] John Bowers. Extended X-bar theory, the ECP and the left branch condition. In *Proceedings of the 6th West Coast Conference on Formal Linguistics*, Stanford Linguistics Association, University of Arizona, Tucson, AZ, 1987.

[Bresnan, 1982] Joan Bresnan, editor. *The Mental Representation of Grammatical Relations*. MIT Press, Cambridge, MA, 1982.

[Bruce, 1972] Bertram Bruce. A model for temporal references and its application in a question answering program. *Artificial Intelligence*, (3):1–25, 1972.

[Byrd, 1989] R. J. Byrd. Discovering relationships among word senses. In *Dictionaries in the Electronic Age: Fifth Annual Conference of the University of Waterloo Centre for the New Oxford English Dictionary*, Oxford, 1989.

[Byrd *et al.*, 1987] R. J. Byrd, N. Calzolari, M. Chodorow, J. Klavans, M. Neff, and O. Rizk. Tools and methods for computational lexicology. *Computational Linguistics*, 13(3-4):219–240, 1987.

[Calzolari, 1982] N. Calzolari. Towards the organization of lexical definitions on a data base structure. In E. Hajicova, editor, *COLING'82*, pages 61–64. Charles University, Prague, 1982.

[Calzolari, 1984] N. Calzolari. Detecting patterns in a lexical database. In *Proceedings of the 10th International Conference on Computational Linguistics*, pages 170–173. Stanford, California, 1984.

[Calzolari, 1988] N. Calzolari. The dictionary and the thesaurus can be combined. In M. Evens, editor, *Relational Models of the Lexicon*, pages 75–96. Cambridge University Press, Cambridge, MA, 1988.

[Calzolari, 1989a] N. Calzolari. Computer-aided lexicography: dictionaries and word databases. In I. S. Batori, W. Lenders, and W. Putschke, editors, *Computational Linguistics*, pages 510–519. Walter de Gruyter, Berlin, 1989.

[Calzolari, 1989b] N. Calzolari. Lexical databases and text corpora: perspectives of integration for a lexical knowledge base. In *Proceedings of the First International Lexical Acquisition Workshop*, pages 170–173, Detroit, Michigan, 1989.

[Calzolari] N. Calzolari. Structure and access in an automated lexicon and related issues. In [Walker *et al.*]. Forthcoming.

[Calzolari and Picchi, 1986] N. Calzolari and E. Picchi. A project for a bilingual lexical database system. In *Advances in Lexicology, Second Annual Conference of the UW Centre for the New Oxford English Dictionary*, pages 79–92, Waterloo, Ontario, 1986.

[Calzolari and Picchi, 1988] N. Calzolari and E. Picchi. Acquisition of semantic information from an on-line dictionary. In *Proceedings of the 12th International Conference on Computational Linguistics*, pages 87–92, Budapest, 1988.

[Calzolari *et al.*, 1987] N. Calzolari, E. Picchi, and A. Zampolli. The use of computers in lexicography and lexicology. In A. Cowie, editor, *The Dictionary and the Language Learner*, number 17 in Lexicographica Series Maior, pages 55–77. Niemeyer, Tübingen, 1987.

[Carlson, 1977a] G. N. Carlson. *Reference to Kinds in English*. PhD thesis, University of Massachusetts, Amherst, 1977. Reprinted in Garland Publishing, New York, 1980.

[Carlson, 1977b] G. N. Carlson. A unified analysis of the English bare plural. *Linguistics and Philosophy*, (1):413–457, 1977.

[Carlson, 1989] G. N. Carlson. On the semantic composition of English generic sentences. In [Chierchia et al.,1989], volume II of *Semantic Issues*.

[Carnap, 1946] Rudolf Carnap. *Introduction to Semantics*. 1946.

[Chierchia et al.,1989] Gennaro Chierchia and Barbara Partee and Ray Turner, editors. *Properties, Types and Meaning*. Volumes I and II, Kluwer, Dordrecht, 1989.

[Chodorow *et al.*, 1985] M. S. Chodorow, R. J. Byrd, and G. E. Heidorn. Extracting semantic hierarchies from a large on-line dictionary. In *Proceedings of the Association for Computational Linguistics*, pages 299–304, Chicago, IL, 1985.

[Chomsky, 1965] Noam Chomsky. *Aspects of The Theory of Syntax*. MIT Press, Cambridge, MA, 1965.

[Chomsky, 1970] Noam Chomsky. Remarks on nominalization. In R. A. Jacobs and P. S. Rosenbaum, editors, *Readings in English Transformational Grammar*. Ginn and Co., Waltham, MA, 1970. Reprinted in [Chomsky, 1972] pages 11-61.

[Chomsky, 1972] Noam Chomsky. *Studies on Semantics in Generative Grammar*. Mouton, The Hague, 1972.

[Chomsky, 1973] Noam Chomsky. Conditions on transformations. In Anderson and Kiparsky, editors, *A Festschrift for Morris Halle*. Holt, Rinehart & Winston, New York, NY, 1973.

[Chomsky, 1981] Noam Chomsky. *Lectures on Government and Binding*. Foris, Dordrecht, 1981.

[Chomsky, 1982] Noam Chomsky. *Some Concepts and Consequences of The Theory of Government and Binding*. MIT Press, Cambridge, MA, 1982.

[Chomsky, 1986a] Noam Chomsky. *Barriers*. MIT Press, Cambridge, MA, 1986.

[Chomsky, 1986b] Noam Chomsky. *Knowledge of Language. Its Nature, Origin, and Use*. Praeger, New York, NY, 1986.

[Chomsky, 1988] Noam Chomsky. *Language and Problems of Knowledge*. MIT Press, Cambridge, MA, 1988.

[Chomsky and Halle, 1968] Noam Chomsky and Morris Halle. *The Sound Pattern of English*. Harper and Row, New York, NY, 1968.

[Chomsky and Lasnik, 1977] Noam Chomsky and Howard Lasnik. Filters and control. *Linguistic Inquiry*, (8):425–504, 1977.

[Clements, 1985] George N. Clements. The geometry of phonological features. In *Phonology Yearbook 2*, pages 225–252, 1985.

[Comrie, 1976] Bernard Comrie. *Aspect*. Cambridge University Press, Cambridge, 1976.

[Comrie, 1985] Bernard Comrie. *Tense*. Cambridge University Press, Cambridge, 1985.

[Richard Cooper, 1990] Richard Cooper. *Classification-based Phrase Structure Grammar: an Extended Revised Version of HPSG*. PhD thesis, Centre for Cognitive Science, University of Edinburgh, 1990.

[Cooper, ms.] Robin Cooper. Structural parameters. Centre for Cognitive Science, University of Edinburgh, manuscript.

[Cooper, 1987] Robin Cooper. *Introduction to Situation Semantics*. Draft of Chapters 1, 2 and 3. University of Edinburgh, 1987.

[Cooper, 1989] Robin Cooper. Information and grammar. Technical report, Department of AI, University of Edinburgh, 1989.

[Cooper, 1990] Robin Cooper. Information in the early stages of language acquisition. In [Cooper *et al.*, 1990].

[Cooper and Kamp, forth.] Robin Cooper and Hans Kamp. Negation in Situation Semantics and Discourse Representation Theory. Paper presented at the Second Conference on Situation Theory and Its Applications, 13th-16th September, 1990, Loch Rannoch, Scotland.

[Cooper *et al.*, 1990] Robin Cooper, Kuniaki Mukai, and John Perry, editors. *Situation Theory and Its Applications*. volume 1. CSLI, 1990.

[Cunha, 1989] João Falcão e Cunha. *Denotational Semantics in the Definition of Natural Language Uses*. PhD thesis, Department of Computing, Imperial College, University of London, 1989.

[Cunha, 1990a] João Falcão e Cunha. Compositionality and omniscience in Situation Semantics. This volume, 1990.

[Cunha, 1990b] João Falcão e Cunha. Simplifying and correcting the treatment of intentionality in Montague Semantics. This volume, 1990.

[Cunha and Pitt, 1990] João Falcão e Cunha and Jeremy Pitt. Meaning Postulates as Constraints on Interpretation. Forthcoming.

[Cutland, 1980] Nigel J. Cutland. *Computability. An Introduction to Recursive Function Theory*. Cambridge University Press, Cambridge, 1980.

[Damas and Varile, 1989] Luís Damas and Giovanni B. Varile. CLG: A grammar formalism based on constraint resolution. In [Martins and Morgado, 1989], pages 175–185.

[Devlin, forthcoming] Keith Devlin. *Logic and Information*. Forthcoming.

[Dieu, 1989] Hendrik Dieu. On belief and omniscience. Research report, Dept. of Computing, Imperial College, University of London, 1989.

[Dowty, 1979a] David Dowty. *Word meaning and Montague grammar*. D. Reidel, Dordrecht, 1979.

[Dowty, 1979b] David R. Dowty. *Word Meaning and Montague Grammar. The Semantics of Verbs and Times in Generative Semantics and Montague's PTQ*. D. Reidel, Dordrecht, 1979.

[Dowty, 1982] David Dowty. Grammatical relations and Montague grammar. In [Jacobson and Pullum 1982], pages 79–130.

[Dowty *et al.*, 1981] David R. Dowty, Robert E. Wall, and Stanley Peters. Introduction to Montague Semantics. In *Studies in Linguistics and Philosophy*, volume 11. D. Reidel, Dordrecht, 1981.

[Duarte, this volume] I. Duarte. X-Bar theory: its role in GB theory. This volume.

[Duarte, 1987] I. Duarte. *A Construção de Topicalização na Gramática do Português: Regência, Ligação, e Condições de Movimento*. Doctoral dissertation, Universidade de Lisboa, 1987.

[Duarte, 1989] I. Duarte. La topicalisation en portugais européen. *Revue des Langues Romanes*, XCII, (2):275–304, 1989.

[Emonds, 1978] J. Emonds. The verbal complex V'-V in French. *Linguistic Inquiry*, (9):151–175, 1978.

[Eurotra, 1990] Commission of the European Community, Luxembourg. *The Eurotra Reference Manual*, 1990.

[Evans, 1980] G. Evans. Pronouns. *Linguistic Inquiry*, (11):337–362, 1980.

[Eynde, 1985] Frank Van Eynde. *Betekenis, Vertaalbaarheid en Automatische Vertaling*. PhD thesis, University of Leuven, Belgium, 1985.

[Eynde, 1988] Frank Van Eynde. The analysis of tense and aspect in Eurotra. In Denes Vargha, editor, *Proceedings of the 12th Coling Conference*, John von Neumann Society, Budapest, 1988.

[Eynde, 1989] Frank Van Eynde. A discourse representation model for the semantic analysis of temporal expressions. In Frans Heyvaert and Frieda Steurs, editors, *Worlds behind words*. Leuven University Press, Leuven, 1989.

[Fagin and Halpern, 1985] R. Fagin and J. Y. Halpern. Belief, awareness, and limited reasoning. In *Proceedings of the Nineth International Joint Conference on Artificial Intelligence*, pages 491–501, Los Angeles, August 1985.

[Fenstad *et al.*, 1987] Jens Erik Fenstad, Per-Kristian Halvorsen, Tore Langholm, and Johan van Benthem. *Situations, Language and Logic*. D. Reidel, Dordrecht, 1987.

[Fitting, 1989a] Melvin Fitting. First-order logic and automated theorem proving. August 1989, (to appear).

[Fitting, 1989b] Melvin Fitting. Modal logic should say more than it does. March 1989, (to appear).

[Flickinger et al., 1985] Daniel Flickinger, Carl J. Pollard, and Thomas Wasow. Structure-sharing in lexical representation. In *Proceedings of the 23rd Annual Meeting*. Association for Computational Linguistics, Chicago, IL, 1985.

[Fukui and Speas, 1986] Naoki Fukui and Margaret Speas. Specifiers and projection. In N. Fukui, T. Rappoport, and E. Sagey, editors, *Papers in Theoretical Linguistics*, number 8, pages 128–172, in MIT Working Papers in Linguistics. MIT Press, Cambridge, MA, 1986.

[Gabbay, 1985] Dov M. Gabbay. *Temporal Logic and Computer Science*. Lecture Notes for the FAIT. Dept. of Computing, Imperial College, University of London, 1985.

[Gallin, 1975] Daniel Gallin. *Intensional and Higher-Order Modal Logic*. North-Holland, 1975.

[Gärdenfors,1987] Peter Gärdenfors, editor. *Generalized Quantifiers: Linguistic and Logical Approaches*. D. Reidel, Dordrecht, 1987

[Gawron and Peters, 1990a] Mark Gawron and Stanley Peters. *Anaphora and Quantification in Situation Semantics*, Center for the Study of Language and Information, Stanford, 1990.

[Gawron and Peters, 1990b] Mark Gawron and Stanley Peters. Some puzzles about pronouns. In [Cooper et al., 1990]

[Gazdar, 1981] Gerald Gazdar. Unbounded dependencies and coordinate structure. *Linguistic Inquiry*, (12):155–184, 1981.

[Gazdar, 1987] Gerald Gazdar. Linguistic applications of default inheritance mechanisms. In P. Whitelock, M. M. Wood, H. L. Sommers, R. Johnson, and P. Bennett, editors, *Linguistic Theory & Computer Applications*, pages 37–67. Academic Press, London, 1987.

[Gazdar and Pullum, 1987] Gerald Gazdar and Geoffrey K. Pullum. A logic for category definition. Cognitive Science Research Paper CSRP 072, Cognitive Studies Programme, The University of Sussex, Brighton, 1987.

[Gazdar et al., 1985] Gerald Gazdar, Ewan Klein, Geoffrey K. Pullum, and Ivan A. Sag. *Generalized Phrase Structure Grammar*. Basil Blackwell, Oxford, 1985.

[Gazdar *et al.*, 1986] Gerald Gazdar, Geoffrey K. Pullum, Robert Carpenter, Ewan Klein, Thomas Hukari, and Robert Levine. Category structures. Cognitive Science Research Paper CSRP 071, Cognitive Studies Programme, The University of Sussex, Brighton, 1986.

[Glasbey, 1990] Sheila Glasbey. *Tense and Aspect in Natural Language Processing: a Situation Semantics Approah.* MSc dissertation, Department of AI, Edinburgh University, 1990.

[Glasbey, forth.] Sheila Glasbey. Incorporating tense and aspect into a situation theory approach to natural language processing. Paper presented at the Second Conference on Situation Theory and Its Applications, Sept. 13-16th, 1990, Loch Rannoch, Scotland.

[Grimshaw, 1981] Jane Grimshaw. Form, function, and the language acquisition device. In C. L. Baker and J. J. McCarthy, editors, *The Logical Problem of Language Acquisition*, pages 165–182. MIT Press, Cambridge, MA, 1981.

[Groenendijk *et al.*, 1981] Jeroen Groenendijk, Theo Janssen and Martin Stokhof, editors. *Formal Methods in the Study of Language. Proceedings of the Third Amsterdam Colloquium*, Mathematical Centre Tracts 135, Amsterdam, 1981.

[Groenendijk *et al.*, 1984] Jeroen Groenendijk, Theo Janssen and Martin Stokhof, editors. *Truth, Interpretation and Information*, Foris, Dordrecht, 1984.

[Groenendijk *et al.*, 1987] Jeroen Groenendijk, D. de Jongh and Martin Stokhof, editors. *Studies in Discourse Representation Theory and the Theory of Generalized Quantifiers*, 1987.

[Gunji, 1987] Takao Gunji. *Japanese Phrase Structure Grammar.* D. Reidel, Dordrecht, 1987.

[Hamm, 1989] F. Hamm. Natürlich-sprachliche Quantoren, Modelltheoretische Untersuchungen zu universellen semantischen Beschränkungen. Niemeyer, Tübingen, 1989.

[Harris, 1951] Z. Harris. *Methods in Structural Linguistics.* University of Chicago Press, Chicago, 1951.

[Heim, 1982] I. Heim. *The Semantics of Definite and Indefinite Noun Phrases.* PhD thesis, University of Massachusetts, 1982.

[Hindle, 1988] D. Hindle. Acquiring disambiguation rules from text. In *Proceedings of the 27th Annual Meeting of the Association for Computational Linguistics*, pages 118–125. Morristown, NJ, 1988.

[Hintikka, 1967] Jaakko Hintikka. Individuals, possible-worlds and epistemic logic. In *Noûs*, pages 33–62. 1967.

[Hintikka, 1975] Jaakko Hintikka. Impossible possible worlds vindicated. In E. Saarinen, editor, *Game-Theoretical Semantics*, pages 367–379. D. Reidel, Dordrecht, 1975.

[Hobbs and Shieber, 1987] Jerry Hobbs and Stuart Shieber. An algorithm for generating quantifier scopings. *Computational Linguistics*, (13):47-63, 1987.

[Hodges, 1977] Wilfrid Hodges. *Logic*. Penguin Books, 1977.

[Hoeksema, 1983] J. Hoeksema. Plurality and conjunction. In A. Ter Meulen, editor, *Studies in Modeltheoretic Semantics*. Foris, 1983.

[Hudson, 1987] Richard A. Hudson. Zwicky on heads. *Journal of Linguistics*, (23):109–132, 1987.

[Hughes and Cresswell, 1968] G. E. Hughes and M. J. Cresswell. *An Introduction to Modal Logic*. Methuen, London, 1974 edition, 1968.

[Hukari and Levine, 1987] Thomas E. Hukari and Robert D. Levine. Rethinking connectivity in unbounded dependency constructions. In *Proceedings of the 6th West Coast Conference on Formal Linguistics*. Stanford Linguistics Association, University of Arizona, Tucson, AZ, 1987.

[Jacobson and Pullum 1982] P. Jacobson and G. K. Pullum, editors. *The Nature of Syntactic Representation*, D. Reidel, Dordrecht, 1982.

[Johnson, 1981] Marion Johnson. A unified temporal theory of tense and aspect. In Tedeschi and A. Zaenen, editors, *Tense and aspect*. Academic Press, New York, 1981.

[Johnson, 1987] Mark Johnson. Grammatical relations in attribute-value grammars. In *Proceedings of the 6th West Coast Conference on Formal Linguistics,*. Stanford Linguistics Association, University of Arizona, Tucson, AZ, 1987.

[Johnson, 1988] Mark Johnson. *Attribute-Value Logic and the Theory of Grammar*. Number 16 in CSLI Lectures Notes. Center for the Study of Language and Information, Stanford, CA, 1988.

[Kamp, 1981] H. Kamp. A theory of truth and semantic representation. In [Groenendijk *et al.*, 1981]. Reprinted in [Groenendijk *et al.*, 1984], pages 1-41.

[Kamp and Christian, 1983] Hans Kamp and Rohrer Christian. Tense in texts. In [Bäuerle *et al.*, 1983].

[Kant, 1800] Immanuel Kant. *Introduction to Logic*. Vision Press Limited, London, 1963 edition, 1800. Translated by T. K. Abbott from the introduction in Kant's *Logik*.

[Kaplan and Bresnan, 1982] Ronald M. Kaplan and Joan Bresnan. Lexical-Functional Grammar: a formal system for grammatical representation. In J. Bresnan, editor, *The Mental Representation of Grammatical Relations*, pages 173–281. MIT Press, Cambridge, MA, 1982.

[Kaplan *et al.*, 1989] Ron Kaplan and Klaus Netter and Jürgen Wedekind and Annie Zaenen. Translation by structural correspondences. In *Proceedings of the European Association of Computational Linguistics*, pages 272-281, 1989.

[Karttunen, 1984] Lauri Karttunen. Features and values. In *Proceedings of the 10th International Conference on Computational Linguistics*, Stanford, CA, 1984. Also in [Shieber *et al.*, 1986] pages 17–36; and [Shieber *et al.*, 1984] pages 17–36.

[Karttunen, 1989] Lauri Karttunen. Radical lexicalism. In [Baltin and Kroch, 1989], pages 43–65. Also manuscript, 1986, Artificial Intelligence Center, SRI International, Menlo Park, CA.

[Kasper and Rounds, 1986] Robert T. Kasper and William C. Rounds. A logical semantics for feature structures. In *Proceedings of the 24th Annual Meeting of Association for Computational Linguistics*. Columbia University, New York, NY, 1986.

[Kasper and Rounds, 1990] Robert T. Kasper and William C. Rounds. The logic of unification in grammar. *Linguistics and Philosophy*, (13):35–58, 1990.

[Kay, 1985] Martin Kay. Parsing in Functional Unification Grammar. In D. R. Dowty, L. Karttunen, and A. M. Zwicky, editors, *Natural Language Parsing*, pages 251–278. Cambridge University Press, Cambridge, 1985.

[Kayne, 1981] R. Kayne. On certain differences between French and English. *Linguistic Inquiry*, (12):349–371, 1981.

[Kayne, 1983] R. Kayne. Unambiguous paths. In *Connectedness and Binary Branching*, pages 129–163, Foris, Dordrecht, 1984.

[Keenan and Stavi, 1986] E. Keenan and J. Stavi. A semantic characterization of natural language determiners. *Linguistics and Philosophy*, (9):253–326, 1986.

[Keenan, 1987] E. Keenan. Unreducible n-ary quantifiers in natural language. In [Gärdenfors,1987].

[Konolige, 1986] Kurt Konolige. *Deduction Model for Belief*. Pitman, London and Morgan Kaufmann, CA, 1986.

[Koopman and Sportiche, 1988] H. Koopman and D. Sportiche. *Subjects*. Manuscript, UCLA, 1988.

[Larson, 1988] R. Larson. On the double object construction. *Linguistic Inquiry*, (19):335–391, 1988.

[Lasnik and Saito, 1984] H. Lasnik and M. Saito. On the nature of proper government. *Linguistic Inquiry*, (15):235–289, 1984.

[Lear, 1980] Jonathan Lear. *Aristotle and Logical Theory*. Cambridge University Press, Cambridge, 1985 edition, 1980.

[Levesque, 1984] Hector J. Levesque. A logic of implicit and explicit belief. In *Proceedings of the National Conference on Artificial Intelligence*, pages 198–202, 1984.

[Lewin, 1990] Ian Lewin. A quantifier scoping algorithm without a free variable constraint. In Proceedings of *COLING'90*, pages 190–194, 1990.

[Lewis, 1979] David Lewis. Scorekeeping in a language game. In [Bäuerle *et al.*, 1979].

[Lindström, 1966] P. Lindström. First order predicate logic with Generalized Quantifiers. *Theoria*, (35):1–11, 1966.

[Link, 1983] G. Link. The logical analysis of plurals and mass terms: a lattice-theoretical approach. In [Bäuerle *et al.*, 1983].

[Link, 1984] G. Link. Hydras, on the logic of relative constructions with multiple heads. In F. Landman and F.Veltman, editors, *Varieties of Formal Semantics*. Foris, Dordrecht, 1984.

[Link, 1987] G. Link. Generalized Quantifiers and plurals. In [Gärdenfors,1987].

[Loebner, 1987a] S. Loebner. Natural language and Generalized Quantifier Theory. In [Gärdenfors,1987].

[Loebner, 1987b] S. Loebner. Quantification as a major module of natural language. In [Groenendijk *et al.*, 1987].

[Maling and Zaenen, 1982] Joan Maling and Annie Zaenen. A phrase structure account of Scandinavian extraction phenomena. In [Jacobson and Pullum 1982], pages 229–282.

[Malmgren, 1971] Helge Malmgren. *Intentionality and Knowledge. Studies in the Philosophy of G. E. Moore and Ludwig Wittgenstein*. Goteborgs Universitet, Sweden, 1971.

[Martin-Löf, 1983] Per Martin-Löf. On the Meaning of the Logical Constants and the Justification of the Logical Laws. University of Stockholm, Sweden, 1983. Lecture notes to the meeting Teoria della Dimostrazione e Filosofia della Logica, Siena (1983).

[Martins and Morgado, 1989] J.P. Martins and E.M. Morgado, editors. *Proceedings of the 4th Portuguese Conference on Artificial Intelligence (EPIA 89)*, number 390 in Lecture Notes in Artificial Intelligence. Springer-Verlag, Berlin, 1989.

[May, 1977] R. May. *The Grammar of Quantification*. PhD thesis, MIT, 1977.

[May, 1985] R. May. *Logical Structure: Its Structure and Derivation* MIT Press, Cambridge, MA, 1985.

[Moennich and Bealer, 1988] Uwe Moennich and George Bealer. Property theories. In Dov Gabbay and F. Guenthner, editors, *Handbook of Philosophical Logic*, volume 4, pages 133–252. D. Reidel, Dordrecht, edition 1989, 1988.

[Montague, 1970] Richard Montague. Universal grammar. In Richmond H. Thomason, editor, *Formal Philosophy. Selected Papers of Richard Montague*, pages 222–246. Yale University Press, New Haven and London, edition 1974, 1970.

[Montague, 1970] Richard Montague. The proper treatment of quantification in ordinary English. In J. Hintikka, J. Moravcsik and P. Suppes, editors, *Approaches to Natural Language: Proceedings of the 1970 Stanford Workshop on Grammar and Semantics*. D. Reidel, Dordrecht,1973. Reprinted in *Formal Philosophy. Selected Papers of Richard Montague*, Yale Univ. Press 1974.

[Moreira, 1989] Nelma Moreira. Semantic analysis of time and tense in natural language: an implementation. In [Martins and Morgado, 1989], pages 198–209.

[Moshier and Rounds, 1986] M. Drew Moshier and William C. Rounds. A Logic for Partially Specified Data Structures. Manuscript, Electrical Engineering and Computer Science Department, University of Michigan, Ann Arbor, MI, 1986.

[Mostowski, 1957] A. Mostowski. On a generalization of quantifiers. *Fundamenta Mathematicæ*, (44):12–36, 1957.

[Nagao, 1989] M. Nagao. *Machine Translation - How far can it go?* Oxford University Press, 1989.

[Nagao and Nakamura, 1988] M. Nagao and J. Nakamura. Extraction of semantic information from an ordinary English dictionary and its evaluation. In *Proceedings of the 12th International Conference on Computational Linguistics*, Budapest, 1988.

[Oehrle 1976] R. T. Oehrle. *The Grammatical Status of the English Dative Alternation*. PhD thesis, MIT, 1976.

[Partee, 1987] B. Partee. Noun phrase interpretation and type-shifting principles. In [Groenendijk *et al.*, 1987].

[Partee *et al.*, 1990] B. Partee, R. Wall and A. ter Meulen. *Mathematical Methods in Linguistics*. Kluwer, Dordrecht, 1990.

[Pereira, 1987] Fernando C. N. Pereira. Grammars and Logics of Partial Information. Technical Note 420, SRI International, Menlo Park, CA, 1987.

[Pereira and Shieber, 1984] Fernando C. N. Pereira and Stuart M. Shieber. The semantics of grammar formalisms seen as computer languages. In *Proceedings of the 10th International Conference on Computational Linguistics*, Stanford, CA, 1984. Also in [Shieber *et al.*, 1986] pages 37–54 and [Shieber *et al.*, 1984] pages 37–54.

[Pereira and Warren, 1978] Fernando Pereira and David H. D. Warren. Definite Clause Grammars Compared with Augmented Transition Networks. Research report, Department of AI, University of Edinburgh, 1978. Also in *Artificial Intelligence*, (13):231-278, 1980.

[Peres, 1987] João Peres. *Para uma Semântica Formal da Quantificação Nominal Não-Massiva* Doctoral dissertation, Universidade de Lisboa, Lisboa, 1987.

[Peres, 1989] João Peres. A semantic argument for an NP-S'analysis of relative structures. In W. Bahner et al., editor, *Proceedings of the 14th International Congress of Linguists, Berlin, August 1987*, 1989.

[Peres, this volume] João Peres. Basic aspects of the Theory of Generalized Quantifiers. This volume.

[Perlmutter, 1983] David M. Perlmutter, editor. *Studies in Relational Grammar 1*. University of Chicago Press, Chicago, IL, 1983.

[Picchi and Calzolari, 1986] E. Picchi and N. Calzolari. Textual perspectives through an automatized lexicon. In *Methodes quantitatives et informatiques dans l'etude des textes*, pages 705–715. Slatkine, Geneva,1986.

[Picchi et al., forthcoming] E. Picchi, C. Peters, and N. Calzolari. A tool for the second language learner: organizing bilingual dictionary data in an interactive workstation. In *Proceedings of the XX ALLC Conference*, Jerusalem, 1988.

[Pitt, 1990] Jeremy V. Pitt. *Compositional Grammars and Natural Language Processing*. PhD thesis, Department of Computing, Imperial College, University of London, 1990. Forthcoming.

[Pollard, 1984] Carl J. Pollard. *Generalized Phrase Structure Grammars, Head Grammars, and Natural Language*. PhD thesis, Stanford University, Stanford, CA, 1984.

[Pollard, 1985] Carl J. Pollard. Phrase structure grammar without metarules. In *Proceedings of the 4th West Coast Conference on Formal Linguistics*. Stanford Linguistics Association, UCLA, CA, 1985.

[Pollard, 1988] Carl J. Pollard. Categorial grammar and phrase structure grammar: an excursion on the syntax-semantics frontier. In R. T. Oehrle, E. Bach, and D. Wheeler, editors, *Categorial Grammars and Natural Language Structures*, pages 391–415. D. Reidel, Dordrecht, 1988.

[Pollard, 1989] Carl J. Pollard. The syntax-semantics interface in a unification-based phrase structure grammar. In S. Busemann, C. Hauenschild, and C. Umbach, editors, *Views of the Syntax/Semantics Interface, KIT - Report 74*. Technische Universität Berlin, Berlin, 1989.

[Pollard, 1990] Carl J. Pollard. On head non-movement, 1990. Paper read at the Symposium on Discontinuous Constituency, Tilburg University, Tilburg.

[Pollard and Sag, 1987] Carl J. Pollard and Ivan A. Sag. *Information-Based Syntax and Semantics 1: Fundamentals.* Center for the Study of Language and Information, Stanford, CA, 1987.

[Pollard and Sag, 1988a] Carl J. Pollard and Ivan A. Sag. Argument structure and binding in English. Carnegie Mellon University, Pittsburgh, PA & Stanford University, Stanford, CA, 1988.

[Pollard and Sag, 1988b] Carl J. Pollard and Ivan A. Sag. An information-based theory of agreement. Carnegie Mellon University, Pittsburgh, PA & Stanford University, Stanford, CA, 1988.

[Pollard and Sag, in prep.] Carl J. Pollard and Ivan A. Sag. *Information-Based Syntax and Semantics 2: Topics in Binding and Control.* Center for the Study of Language and Information, Stanford, CA, in preparation.

[Pollock, 1989] J.-Y Pollock. Verb movement, UG and the structure of IP. *Linguistic Inquiry*, (20):365–424, 1989.

[Popper, 1935] Karl Raimund Popper. *Logik der Forschung.* Hutchinson, London, 1968 edition, 1935. Translated under the title *The Logic of Scientific Discovery.*

[Popper, 1945] Karl Raimund Popper. *The Open Society and its Enemies.* Routledge & Kegan Paul, London, 1966 edition, 1945.

[Popper, 1974] Karl Raimund Popper. *Unended Quest. An Intellectual Autobiography.* Fontana Paperbacks. Collins Publishing Group, 1974. First published as Autobiography of Karl Popper in *The Philosophy of Karl Popper*, in *The Library of Living Philosophers*, Paul Arthur Schlipp (ed.), Open Copurt Publishing Co., IL, 1974. Flamingo revised edition, with Postscript and updated bibliography, 1986.

[Proudian and Pollard, 1985] Derek Proudian and Carl J. Pollard. Parsing head-driven phrase structure grammar. In *Proceedings of the 23rd Annual Meeting of the Association for Computational Linguistics.* Association for Computational Linguistics, Chicago, IL, 1985.

[de Queiroz, 1990] Ruy José Guerra Barreto de Queiroz. *Meaning As Use, Not Content: An Alternative View on The Proof-Theoretic Account of Meaning.* PhD thesis, Department of Computing, Imperial College, University of London, 1990.

[Quine, 1970] W. V. Quine. *Philosophy of Logic.* 1986 edition, 1970.

[Raposo, 1987] E. Raposo. Case-theory and Infl-to-Comp: the inflected infinitive in European Portuguese. *Linguistic Inquiry*, (18):85–109, 1987.

[Rantala, 1982] V. Rantala. Impossible worlds semantics and logical omniscience. *Acta Philosophica Fennica*, (35):106–115, 1982.

[Reape, 1989] Mike Reape. Untitled lecture notes on feature structures and feature logics. Summer School on Natural Language Processing, Logic and Knowledge Representation, Groningen, 1989.

[Reichenbach, 1947] Hans Reichenbach. *Elements of Symbolic Logic*. University of California Press, Berkeley, CA, 1947.

[Reyle and Rohrer, 1988] Uwe Reyle and Christian Rohrer, editors. *Natural Language Parsing and Linguistic Theories*. D. Reidel, Dordrecht, 1988.

[Rizzi, 1982] Luigi Rizzi. Violations of the Wh island constraint and the subjacency condition. In L. Rizzi, editor, *Issues in Italian Syntax*. Foris, Dordrecht, 1982. Also in Journal of Italian Linguistics (5), 1980.

[Rizzi, 1986] L. Rizzi. Null objects in Italian and the theory of *pro*. *Linguistic Inquiry*, (17):501–557, 1986.

[Rohrer, 1985] Christian Rohrer. Indirect discourse and *consecutio temporum*. In Vincenzo Lo Cascio and Co Vet, editors, *Temporal structure in sentence and discourse*. Foris, Dordrecht, 1985.

[Rounds and Kasper, 1986] William C. Rounds and Robert T. Kasper. A Complete Logical Calculus for Record Structures Representing Linguistic Information. Electrical Engineering and Computer Science Department, University of Michigan, Ann Arbor, MI, 1986.

[Rudin, 1988] Catherine Rudin. On multiple questions and multiple Wh fronting. *Natural Language and Linguistic Theory*, (6):445–501, 1988.

[Sag, 1986] Ivan A. Sag. Grammatical Hierarchy and Linear Precedence. Report CSLI-86-60, Center for the Study of Language and Information, Stanford, CA, 1986.

[Sag and Pollard, 1987] Ivan Sag and Carl J. Pollard. Head-Driven Phrase Structure Grammar: An Informal Synopsis. Report CSLI-87-79, Center for the Study of Language and Information, Stanford, CA, 1987.

[Sag and Pollard, 1988] Ivan A. Sag and Carl J. Pollard. A Semantic Theory of Obligatory Control. Stanford University, Stanford, CA & Carnegie Mellon University, Pittsburgh, PA, 1988.

[Sag and Pollard, 1989] Ivan A. Sag and Carl J. Pollard. Subcategorization and head-driven phrase structure. In [Baltin and Kroch, 1989], pages 139–181.

[Scha, 1984] R. Scha. Distributive, collective and cumulative quantification. In [Groenendijk *et al.*, 1984].

[Schmidt, 1986] David A. Schmidt. *Denotational Semantics - A Methodology for Language Development*. Allyn & Bacon Inc., Boston, 1986.

[Schrödinger, 1967] Erwin Schrödinger. *What is Life ? & Mind and Matter*. Cambridge University Press, Cambridge, 1967.

[Scott, 1976] Dana S. Scott. Data types as lattices. *SIAM Journal on Computing*, 5(3):522–587, September 1976.

[Shieber, 1984] Stuart M. Shieber. The design of a computer language for linguistic information. In *Proceedings of the 10th International Conference on Computational Linguistics*, Stanford, CA, 1984. Also in [Shieber *et al.*, 1986], pages 4–16 and [Shieber *et al.*, 1984], pages 4-16.

[Shieber, 1986] Stuart M. Shieber. *An Introduction to Unification-Based Approaches to Grammar*. Center for the Study of Language and Information, Stanford, CA, 1986.

[Shieber, 1987] Stuart M. Shieber. Separating linguistic analyses from linguistic theories. Technical Note 422, SRI International, Menlo Park, CA, 1987. Also in [Reyle and Rohrer, 1988], pages 33–68.

[Shieber *et al.*, 1983] Stuart M. Shieber, Hans Uszkoreit, Jane J. Robinson, Fernando C. N. Pereira, and Mabry Tyson. The formalism and implementation of PATR-II. In B. J. Grosz and M. E. Stickel, editors, *Research on Interactive Acquisition and Use of Knowledge, Final Report*, pages 39–79. SRI International, Menlo Park, CA, 1983.

[Shieber *et al.*, 1984] Stuart M. Shieber, Lauri Karttunen, and Fernando C. N. Pereira. Notes from the Unification Underground: A Compilation of Papers on Unification-based Grammar Formalisms. Technical Note 327, Artificial Intelligence Center, SRI International, Menlo Park, CA, 1984.

[Shieber *et al.*, 1986] Stuart M. Shieber, Fernando C. N. Pereira, Lauri Karttunen, and Martin Kay. A Compilation of Papers on Unification-based Grammar Formalisms. Report CSLI-86-48, Center for the Study of Language and Information, Stanford, CA, 1986.

[Smith, 1980] Carlota Smith. Temporal structure in discourse. In Christian Rohrer, editor, *Time, Tense and Quantifiers*. Niemeyer, Tübingen, 1980.

[Stowell, 1981] Tim Stowell. *Origins of Phrase Structure*. PhD thesis, MIT, 1981.

[Stowell, 1989] Tim Stowell. Subjects, specifiers, and X-bar theory. In [Baltin and Kroch, 1989], pages 232–262.

[Sportiche, 1988] D. Sportiche. A theory of floating quantifiers and its corollaries for constituent structure. *Linguistic Inquiry*, (19):425–449, 1988.

[Tarski, 1931] Alfred Tarski. The concept of truth in formalized languages. In *Logic, Semantics, Metamathematics*, pages 152–278. Oxford University Press, 1956 edition, 1931.

[Travis, 1984] L. Travis. *Parameters and Effects of Word Order Variation*. PhD thesis, MIT, 1984.

[Travis, 1989] L. Travis. Parameters of phrase structure. In [Baltin and Kroch, 1989], pages 263–279.

[Turner, 1983] Raymond Turner. Montague semantics, nominalization and Scott's domains. *Linguistics and Philosophy*, (6):259–288, 1983.

[Turner, 1988] Raymond Turner. Properties, propositions and semantic theory. Presented at the *Workshop on Computational Linguistics and Formal Semantics*, Lugano, 1988.

[Uszkoreit, 1986] Hans Uszkoreit. Categorial Unification Grammars. Report CSLI-86-66, Center for the Study of Language and Information, Stanford, CA, 1986. Published in COLING'86, Bonn, pages 187–194.

[van Benthem, 1986] J. van Benthem. *Essays in Logical Semantics*. D. Reidel, Dordrecht, 1986.

[van Benthem, 1989] J. van Benthem. Polyadic quantifiers. *Linguistics and Philosophy*, (12):437–464, 1989.

[van der Hulst and Smith, 1982] Harry van der Hulst and Norval Smith. An overview of autosegmental and metrical phonology. In H. van der Hulst and N. Smith, editors, *The Structure of Phonological Representations I*, pages 1–45. Foris, Dordrecht, 1982.

[van der Hulst and Smith, 1985] Harry van der Hulst and Norval Smith. The framework of nonlinear generative phonology. In H. van der Hulst and N. Smith, editors, *Advances in Nonlinear Phonology*, pages 3–55. Foris, Dordrecht, 1985.

[van Noord et al., 1990] Gertjan van Noord, Joke Dorrepaal, Pim van der Eijk, María Florenza, and Louis des Tombe. The MiMo2 research system. Technical report, Research Institute for Language and Speech, State University of Utrecht, Utrecht, 1990.

[Visser, 1988] Albert Visser. Semantics and the liar paradox. In Dov Gabbay and F. Guenthner, editors, *Handbook of Philosophical Logic*, volume 4, pages 617–706. D. Reidel, Dordrecht, 1989 edition, 1988.

[Walker and Zampolli, 1989] D. Walker and A. Zampolli. Foreword. In [Boguraev and Briscoe, 1989].

[Walker *et al.*] D. Walker, A. Zampolli, and N. Calzolari, editors. *Automating the Lexicon: Research and Practice in a Multilingual Environment*. Oxford University Press. Forthcoming.

[Walker *et al.*, 1987] D. Walker, A. Zampolli, and N. Calzolari, editors. *Towards A Polytheoretical Lexical Database*. ILC, Pisa, 1987.

[Warner, 1989] Anthony R. Warner. Multiple heads and minor categories in Generalized Phrase–Structure Grammar. *Linguistics*, (27):179–205, 1989.

[Webster and Marcus, 1989] M. Webster and M. Marcus. Automatic acquisition of the lexical semantics of verbs from sentence frames. In *Proceedings of the 27th Annual Meeting of the Association for Computational Linguistics*, pages 177–184, Vancouver, British Columbia, 1989.

[Westerståhl, 1986] D. Westerståhl. Quantifiers in Formal and Natural Languages. Report CSLI-86-55, Center for the Study of Language and Information, Stanford, CA, 1986.

[Westerståhl, 1990] Dag Westerståhl. Parametric types and propositions in first-order situation theory. In [Cooper *et al.*, 1990].

[Whitelock *et al.*, 1987] P. Whitelock, M. Wood, H. Somers, R. Johnson, and P. Bennett, editors. *Linguistic Theory and Computer Applications*. Academic Press, New York, 1987.

[Wilks *et al.*, 1989] Y. Wilks, D. Fass, C.-M. Guo, J. McDonald, T. Plate, and B. Slator. A tractable machine dictionary as a resource for computational semantics. In [Boguraev and Briscoe, 1989], pages 193–228.

[Zampolli, 1983] A. Zampolli. Lexicological and lexicographical activities at the Istituto di Linguistica Computazionale. In [Zampolli and Cappelli, 1983], pages 237–278.

[Zampolli, 1986] A. Zampolli. Multifunctional lexical databases. *Encrages*, (16):56–65, 1986.

[Zampolli, 1987] A. Zampolli. Progetto strategico: Metodi e strumenti per l'industria delle lingue nella cooperazione internazionale. Pisa, 1987.

[Zampolli, 1989] A. Zampolli. Progetto speciale: Aquisizione di una base di conoscenze lessicali per il trattamento automatico dell'italiano: obiettivi nazionali e cooperazione internazionale. Pisa, 1989.

[Zampolli and Calzolari, 1977] A. Zampolli and N. Calzolari, editors. *Computational and Mathematical Linguistics, Proceedings of the International Conference on Computational Linguistics 1973*, Firenze, 1977.

[Zampolli and Calzolari, 1985] A. Zampolli and N. Calzolari. Computational lexicography and lexicology. *AILA Bulletin*, pages 59–78, 1985.

[Zampolli and Cappelli, 1983] A. Zampolli and A. Cappelli, editors. *The Possibilities and Limits of the Computer in Producing and Publishing Dictionaries*. Linguistica Computazionale. Academic Press, 1983.

[Zampolli et al., 1985] A. Zampolli, L. Cignoni, and S. Rossi. Problems of textual corpora. ILC-9-2, Pisa, 1985.

[Zeevat et al., 1987] Henk Zeevat, Ewan Klein, and Jonathan Calder. Unification Categorial Grammar. In N. Haddock, E. Klein, and G. Morril, editors, *Categorial Grammar, Unification Grammar and Parsing*, number 1 in Edinburgh Working Papers in Cognitive Science. Centre for Cognitive Science, University of Edinburgh, Edinburgh, 1987.

[Zwarts, 1983] F. Zwarts. Determiners: a relational perspective. In A. Ter Meulen editor, *Studies in Model-theoretic Semantics*. Foris, Dordrecht, 1983.

[Zwicky, 1985] Arnold M. Zwicky. Heads. *Journal of Linguistics*, (21):1–29, 1985.

Lecture Notes in Computer Science

This subseries of the Lecture Notes in Computer Science reports new developments in Artificial Intelligence research and teaching – quickly, informally and at a high level. The type of material considered for publication includes preliminary drafts of original papers and monographs, technical reports of high quality and broad interest, advanced level lectures, reports of meetings, provided they are of exceptional interest and focused on a single topic. The timeliness of a manuscript is more important than its form which may be unfinished or tentative. If possible, a subject index should be included. Publication of Lecture Notes is intended as a service to the international computer science community, in that a commercial publisher, Springer-Verlag, can offer a wide distribution of documents which would otherwise have a restricted readership. Once published and copyrighted, they can be referred to in the scientific literature.

Manuscripts

Manuscripts should be no less than 100 and preferably no more than 500 pages in length.
They are reproduced by a photographic process and therefore must be prepared with extreme care according to the instructions available from the publisher. Proceedings' editors and authors of monographs receive 75 free copies. Authors of contributions to proceedings are free to use the material in other publications upon notification to the publisher. The typescript is reduced slightly in size during reproduction; best results will not be obtained unless the text on any one page is kept within the overall limit of $18 \times 26,5$ cm ($7 \times 10\frac{1}{2}$ inches). On request, the publisher will supply special paper with the typing area outlined.

Manuscripts should be sent to Prof. J. Siekmann, Institut für Informatik, Universität Kaiserslautern, Postfach 30 49, D-6750 Kaiserslautern, FRG, or directly to Springer-Verlag Heidelberg.

Springer-Verlag, Heidelberger Platz 3, D-1000 Berlin 33
Springer-Verlag, Tiergartenstraße 17, D-6900 Heidelberg 1
Springer-Verlag, 175 Fifth Avenue, New York, NY 10010/USA
Springer-Verlag, 37-3, Hongo 3-chome, Bunkyo-ku, Tokyo 113, Japan

ISBN 3-540-53678-7
ISBN 0-387-53678-7